Letters to a
YOUNG
SISTER

ALSO BY HILL HARPER

Letters to a Young Brother: MANifest Your Density

HILL HARPER

Letters to a YOUNG SISTER

DeFINE Your Destiny

GOTHAM BOOKS

GOTHAM BOOKS
Published by Penguin Group (USA) Inc.
375 Hudson Street, New York, New York 10014, U.S.A.

Penguin Group (Canada), 90 Eglinton Avenue East, Suite 700, Toronto, Ontario M4P 2Y3, Canada (a division of Pearson Penguin Canada Inc.); Penguin Books Ltd, 80 Strand, London WC2R 0RL, England; Penguin Ireland, 25 St Stephen's Green, Dublin 2, Ireland (a division of Penguin Books Ltd); Penguin Group (Australia), 250 Camberwell Road, Camberwell, Victoria 3124, Australia (a division of Pearson Australia Group Pty Ltd); Penguin Books India Pvt Ltd, 11 Community Centre, Panchsheel Park, New Delhi–110 017, India; Penguin Group (NZ), 67 Apollo Drive, Rosedale, North Shore 0632, New Zealand (a division of Pearson New Zealand Ltd); Penguin Books (South Africa) (Pty) Ltd, 24 Sturdee Avenue, Rosebank, Johannesburg 2196, South Africa

Penguin Books Ltd, Registered Offices: 80 Strand, London WC2R 0RL, England

Published by Gotham Books, a member of Penguin Group (USA) Inc.

First printing, June 2008
10 9 8 7 6 5 4 3 2

"Ego Tripping" © 1970 by Nikki Giovanni. Reprinted with kind permission of the author.

Gotham Books and the skyscraper logo are trademarks of Penguin Group (USA) Inc.

LIBRARY OF CONGRESS CATALOGING-IN-PUBLICATION DATA
Harper, Hill, 1966–
    Letters to a young sister: define your destiny / Hill Harper.
      p. cm.
    ISBN 978-1-592-40351-6
    1. Young women—Conduct of life.   2. Teenage girls—Conduct of life.   3. Teenagers, Black—Conduct of life.   I. Title.
    BJ1681.H37 2008
    170.84'22—dc22   2008007113 vxpt

Printed in the United States of America
Set in Dante MT with Liteweit • Designed by Sabrina Bowers

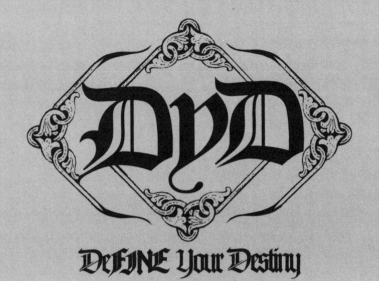

DeFINE Your Destiny

Contents

Foreword by Gabrielle Union   XI

Introduction   XIX

Part One
Empowerment 3.0

"EgoTripping (there may be a reason why)" by Nikki Giovanni   3

1. Young Sistah: Your FINE Destiny   5
   E-mail: Teased for Being Outstanding—MICHELLE OBAMA   II

2. Designing Your Destiny in This New-School World   13
   E-mail: Divine Purpose—TAVIS SMILEY   21

3. Sistahs: As Unique as Snowflakes and Fingerprints   23
   E-mail: It's a Hard-Knock Life for Us—EVE   30

4. The J.J.: Journaling & Journeying Through Life:
   The Power of One   32
   E-mail: No R-E-S-P-E-C-T—ALFRE WOODARD   42

5. The Difference Between Need and Purpose   44
   E-mail: My Morals for Success?—CIARA   52
   E-mail: Too Much Pressure!!—SANAA LATHAN   54

Part Two
Relationships: Family, Friends, and Boys

6. Ain't Nothin' but a "G" Thang: GOSSIP   59
   E-mail: Gossip Girls—JASMINE GUY   70

7. The Parent Trap: You Can Choose Your Friends,
   but You Can't Choose Your Family   72
   E-mail: OOOOHH BABY!!—SHAR JACKSON   78
   E-mail: Make Me Beautiful!—CHANEL IMAN   79

8. R.E.S.P.E.C.T.: How a Boy Should Treat You   81
   E-mail: Boys, Boys, Boys . . .—NIA LONG   90
   E-mail: Dating My BGF—KIM PORTER   91

9. The Taboo Topic: SEX   93
   E-mail: No Hook-Up/Hurt Feelings—BLAIR UNDERWOOD   98
   E-mail: The Dating Game—LAUREN LONDON and EVAN ROSS   100

10. Sex, Lies, and Texting: The Lies Boys Tell   102
    E-mail: Cheating and Lying!?!—BLAIR UNDERWOOD
    and TERRI J. VAUGHN   109
    E-mail: Love, Sex, and STDs—SHAHDAE JANELLE HOLLAND   111

11. Daddy's Little Girl: How Shadows Can Loom Large   113
    E-mail: Quality Man—RUBY DEE   121

Part Three
Overcoming Obstacles

12. Breakup, No Makeup   125
    E-mail: Heartache—NIECY NASH   129
    E-mail: I Don't Wanna Look Like a Clown—KENYA MOORE   131

13. Words Have Power: The *B*, *H*, and *T* Words   133
    E-mail: Nappy-Headed, Well, You Know!—DEVYNITY   139

14. Double Jeopardy: Racism and Sexism as Obstacles
    to Success   142
    E-mail: Million-Dollar Baby—CATHY HUGHES   149

15. Food for Thought   151
    E-mail: Is My Fat Phat?—DR. S. ELIZABETH FORD   156
    E-mail: The Not-So-Celebrity Fit Club—CHARIESSE GRIFFIN   158

16. Hillified Hugs: Dealing with the Blues   160

17. "It Really Hurts": Dealing with More Than Just the Blues   165
    E-mail: Lonely and Depressed—BISHOP NOEL JONES   171

Part Four
Your Future

18. Educatin' Excellence   175
E-mail: Do I Really Need to Go to School??
—DR. MELISSA NOBLES   183

19. The New Cool Money Rule   185
E-mail: Own Business/Own Boss—MARVET BRITTO   190

20. The Deadliest Trap: Staying Out of the Debt Pit   193
E-mail: Unhappy and Unorganized—CHRISTINA M. GOMES   199

21. The Linked *S*'s: Savings and Self-Empowerment   202
E-mail: Jane of All Trades, Master of None?
—ANGELA BASSETT and NICOLE LOFTUS   212

22. Careering and Steering   215
E-mail: Career Choices—CANDACE BOND MCKEEVER   222
E-mail: When I Grow Up, I Wanna Be . . . ?—SHARLA CROW   224

Part Five
The Wonderment of Life

23. Chocolate Cake and Four-Letter Words   229
E-mail: A Dream Deferred—CONGRESSWOMAN
CAROLYN CHEEKS KILPATRICK and MALINDA WILLIAMS   234

24. Your Heart: Always Follow It (Except with Boys)   236
E-mail: Me and My Boyfriend—TATYANA ALI   241

25. Throwing Off Limitations   243
E-mail: ¡Ayúdeme!—ZOE SALDANA   248

26. Seeing Rainbows: Wonderment of the Everyday   250
E-mail: Dreaming Big???—TAVIS SMILEY   256

27. Keys to REAL Happiness: Faith and Service   258
E-mail: Voting and Politics—MICHELLE OBAMA   266

Final Letter: Time to Make History   268
E-mail: The Secret of How to Be Happy (Growing to
Be Me)—NIKKI GIOVANNI   275

Acknowledgments   277

Definitions belong to the *definer*—
not the defined.

—Toni Morrison

Foreword

BY GABRIELLE UNION

WHEN HILL FIRST TOLD ME about *Letters to a Young Sister*, my first thought was how badly I could have used a book like this growing up. Reflecting on my teens and early twenties, I see all the mistakes I made and how so many of them could have been avoided had I been given the right advice (from someone I would be willing to listen to). Truth be told, I was hardheaded growing up, meaning it took a lot for anyone or anything to get through to me. It was "my way" no matter what the outcome. In fact, I rarely stopped to think about what consequences my actions would have. I never had an older brother looking out for me or stepping in to be my protector from some of the craziness we all experience growing up. Through the years, as my friendship with Hill has grown, his presence in my life has become invaluable. We talk about what's going on in our lives, give advice, support each other in making decisions, and, most importantly, challenge each other to be the best version of ourselves at all times. He is unconditional in his love and support. Hill is always there not only to toast my success but to lend a helping hand if I falter. After years of that kind of friendship, I am happy and honored to write the foreword for *Letters to a Young Sister*. I am excited to begin this fantastic collection of stories, letters, and pieces of love and inspiration.

I'm a lifelong charter member of the "sisterhood," and if there is one thing I know about my sister-girlfriends, it's that we need straight-up advice and none of that cookie-cutter nonsense. We are all uniquely different. As Black women, we are even more diverse when you take into account the differences in our skin tones, hair textures, booty sizes, and other features. I even stood out from the other girls in my own family. They were always described as "pretty, dainty, feminine, and beautiful." When it was my turn, I got "You have such a good crossover, Gab" or "Gab, you are such an excellent student." Much to my disappointment, my physical appearance was never complimented. On the one hand, when I was younger, I can proudly say I focused on more important things, such as being a great athlete and an excellent student. At the time, I didn't care about being pretty or having lighter skin or longer hair. But then I reached puberty and with hormones going crazy and emotions on a roller coaster, I was left feeling immensely insecure. I could have used a big brother to give me some wisdom and advice, especially since I also started liking boys and they didn't like girls who looked like me. I'd always been a tomboy. As an athlete, I couldn't worry about my hair and primping. I wasn't even in a training bra and I had this hair that was unruly. Simply put, I was a bit of a hot mess.

The other day my friend's ten-year-old daughter, Zoë, was watching *High School Musical*, and when the song "Popular" came on, which is basically an anthem for teenage popularity, all I could do was groan. This adorable fifth grader told me how badly she wanted to be popular. I explained to Zoë that the last thing she needed was to peak in elementary school, and popularity now really isn't important in the scheme of things. She gave me that look that only a kid can issue to an adult, which means, "This isn't the Stone Age anymore and things are different." As often as I had given that same look to my parents, no one had ever done it to me and all I could do was laugh. If there is one thing I've learned, it's that people don't change that much and we never really graduate school. Till the end of time, little girls and boys will clamor to become popular.

Ironically I was popular, but not for all the reasons you might think. I was good at making people laugh and, as I mentioned, I was a good athlete and student. I had always been confident until suddenly the things that had defined me—sports and good grades—were not enough, and I began to lose my self-confidence. I started developing crushes on guys, but they'd wind up liking my friends over me. So I started questioning why nobody liked me: "Maybe it's my hair, maybe it's the size of my nose, maybe it's my skin color?" These were thoughts that hadn't ever occurred to me until it came to guys. I started begging my mom to get me a relaxer. Hair was so important that I really believed if I had the right hairstyle, my life would magically improve. I just wanted to look like my friends. I would put pillowcases on my head, or T-shirts, and prance around in front of the mirror imagining that it was my hair and that I was finally beautiful. I would make my mom leave the relaxer on until it would burn because I knew the longer she left it on, the straighter my hair would become. I'd wind up with lesions on my scalp, trying to fit into this idea of what I thought was pretty. Then came the seventh grade and New Wave, when I dyed my hair to resemble Duran Duran and Depeche Mode. I got a bowl of hydrogen peroxide, stuck my bangs in the bowl, and sat out in the sun so I could get that perfect punk New Wave look everyone had. Unfortunately, it turned my hair Ronald McDonald red and it stayed like that for years—and all of that because I wanted to fit in so badly. I was basically trying to become everything I wasn't and, in doing so, only became more insecure and less happy.

But like all growing pains, it had to get worse before it could get better. One summer I went away to basketball camp and had a whole other crew of girls to compare myself to. I went from having low self-esteem, from never being considered as "pretty" as the white girls at my school, to competing against other African American girls who physically covered the whole spectrum from biracial to jet-black, from flat-chested to having body and booty. I wish I could say this made me a happier person and improved my self-image, but it didn't. My first boyfriend cheated on me with a light-skinned girl, and then a second boyfriend did the same thing. Instead of realizing that these guys were not worthy of my attention, I blamed the light-skinned girls and believed that if my skin were lighter, then I would be happy. It got to the point where any time a light-skinned girl came into a room, I immediately felt ugly; my nose was too big, my hair was too nappy. I thought that no one was ever going to pay attention to me if those types of girls were around. Instead of finding value in my talents, my accomplishments, and my particular brand of beauty, I became this insecure person who was mean toward light-skinned women. In my mind they were the only thing stopping me from being happy.

In their presence I felt I was invisible. I look back now and realize how much time I wasted and how all the hair products, padded bras, and makeup weren't going to fix what I was feeling inside. Changes had to be made, and they had to be made from the inside out.

Through the bulk of my adolescent insecurity, I didn't have anyone telling me to just be myself and things would eventually work out— that change would inevitably come and it would be the growing kind, the maturing kind, the kind that makes you see how it's your inward beauty that reflects who you are and what you look like to the outside world.

It's painful to remember being that unhappy and insecure, but one of the things I have learned is that "it's important to be human." Being human is having all the emotions, which includes feelings of sadness, insecurity, and at times inadequacy, yet realizing that, though we may have these feelings from time to time, we are *NEVER* inadequate. We are every bit the person we are supposed to be and always everything we need. Hill has been instrumental in reminding me of this.

Live long enough and you will have more than one unpleasant or painful experience. It's just the way life is. However, you must understand that it's not what happens to you in life that defines who you are. People too often say that people are a summation of their experiences, but I do not believe that to be true. I believe that it's what we do with our experiences, how we react, how we grow from them that makes us who we are.

When I was nineteen I experienced a brutal rape by a man who held a gun to my head and threatened to kill me. Though I could go into detail about what happened and how it happened, and try and figure out why, all of that is irrelevant to me now. My experience and what became my ultimate healing is how I chose to deal with it and how I defined myself afterward. You don't always get handed the best cards in life, but you can create victory through any adversity. It's your choice. So when people say to me, "I don't have money to go to college" or "I can't do this because I don't know how," I'm not always the most patient person. There is too much federal money that goes unused to have excuses not to get an education. It's a matter of finding out and informing yourself and putting yourself in a place to receive. And anyone can do it. It's a matter of making the choice to not be defined by anyone else's limitations of you and your life. There is too much information in the world to allow ignorance to be an excuse. According to rape statistics, I was supposed to be incapable of forming healthy relationships afterward, and ultimately to commit suicide. In other words, my life was supposed to have ended because I was raped. What those statistics don't tell you is that you have a choice. You can choose to be a victim and become another statistic or you can make the choice to triumph over whatever adversity you experience.

One of the best gifts my parents ever gave me was a sense of independence, but you might say it came in a bit of a backward way. My mom is a scholar and she loves learning, so I learned early that college was not optional. I got my first library card when I was five years old and she made my sisters and me understand that it was a privilege to check out books. But she never wanted to limit our learning to the classroom: She'd take us on adventures to Chinatown to celebrate Chinese New Year and into Latin communities to have the full experience of Cinco de Mayo. We saw Nikki Giovanni at the Museum of Children's Art in Oakland, the Alvin Ailey dancers, and Shakespeare in the Park in the summer. That was the experience my mother wanted us to have. My father was equally supportive of this kind of cultural education, and he was especially supportive when it came to money. As long as I followed his rules, he would financially support me. That worked until I turned eighteen, went to college, and figured "Hey, I'm an adult now, I can make my own rules." Again, he was very supportive of my quest for independence, but a change of rules would not include his money to support this newfound independence.

So at nineteen I stopped taking money from my parents and I've never taken a dime from them since. Don't get me wrong—I missed the perks of having them pay my bills, being free to hang out and have a charmed college life. I just didn't want to listen to anybody telling me how to live my life. I think that's a big lesson to learn. Lots of people approach me and ask, "How do your parents feel about you being an actor?" because let's face it, there is not a lot of job security in the arts. My answer is always the same: "My parents don't care what career I choose as long as I'm not hitting them up for cash." Technically, after you graduate from high school, your parents are not obligated to financially support you. It's their choice to contribute to your education, career path, and lifestyle. In other words, you need to prepare for adulthood.

Nowadays, kids have credit cards, phones, Internet, and all those things that come with bills that need to be paid. If you don't want to hear your mom complain about how much you're talking on the phone or how many songs you are downloading from iTunes, then you have to take responsibility and start paying for these luxuries yourself. Remember these are wants, not things you need, and in order to buy these things of "want," you need money. In other words, you better get a job. And if you're thinking you'll just be with someone who has lots of money, one of the best things I ever heard as a young person was, "If you marry or get into a relationship for money, you will earn each and every penny." When I was in high school I dated one of the biggest basketball players in the country and I got a charge out of being his girlfriend until I realized nobody cared about my successes because I was living in the shadow of being "Such-and-such's" girlfriend. Eventually I realized that I wanted to have my own identity and I wanted to enter a relationship of two wholes. I didn't want to latch on to somebody else's rising star; I wanted to be a star on my own. All of this is possible. It's simply a matter of controlling your destiny. And a huge part of that is controlling your own finances.

Financial independence and good credit are important. Taking care of your credit is like taking care of a baby, and you would never let anything bad happen to your baby, right? So if you're in a position where you want to make impulse purchases that you know you can't afford, stop and ask yourself, "Am I really taking care of my future credit?" It's like getting grades in school: Lenders keep a record of the way you pay your bills and how late you are making payments, and based on your performance record, they give you a score. You want to always keep your credit score above 700; that way when you're in the position to buy a home or lease a car, you're the customer banks are seeking out. Remember that number. Good credit is better than a good man. You can go anywhere with good credit, but you can't always go anywhere with a dude. This is another reason why I'm so excited you're getting to read this book, because Hill talks about these things in a different way than my parents ever did and makes it much easier to understand!

Part of the reason I love having a friend like Hill is because during a time when my goals and dreams are constantly changing, he helps me find clarity. When I was sixteen, my goal was to graduate college and perhaps become a lawyer. In my midtwenties, my goal was to get a callback for an audition. In my late twenties, my goal was to get married. And now at thirty-five and recently divorced, my goal is simple: to be a little bit better today than I was yesterday.

In *Letters to a Young Sister*, Hill has covered all the important issues. As a woman, I can't agree more with how important it is to focus on becoming your best self, a point that Hill makes several times in this book. That means focusing on individual accomplishments and doing the things that help you become a whole person. In a romantic relationship the concept of "you complete me" is BS. I don't want to complete someone. I want him to be pretty close to complete when we meet. I'm not trying to fix people. We all need to do our individual work and ask ourselves better questions: Am I as smart as I want to be? Have I learned everything I want to know? Have I traveled everywhere I want to go? Hill constantly reminds me that there is no rush because there is no trophy at the end of our lives. As Hill writes in the book, "The journey is the destination." Because it is so true that the journey to happiness starts with being happy with yourself.

Hill is one of those people who refuses to settle in any area of his life, and he doesn't put a time limit on anything. He never responds with my old inner dialogue, "I'm such-and-such age so this should be happening." He helps me remember that my journey is to find my own personal happiness based on those things I am passionate about. He wants to make sure I always do my best and challenge myself. He constantly reminds me that I am worthy and deserving of the best. There truly are good "brothas" out there, and Hill is one of the best. I hope you enjoy the book.

Introduction

THE FIRST TIME IT HAPPENED was in Atlanta, during one of my initial stops on the tour for my newly published book, *Letters to a Young Brother: MANifest Your Destiny*. It was standing room only, nearly 300 people, yet during the reading and discussion portion of my appearance, I kept catching the eye of the same person, a young lady in the audience. She was tall and graceful, with a stare that both questioned and captivated. I was expecting her to ask a question during the Q&A time, but she didn't. She remained silent and waited till the time came to form a line for those who wished to have me sign their books. It was a long line, but she stood, and waited patiently, for her turn.

"LaTonya," she announced as I flipped open her book to find the page on which I usually sign my name. I smiled and repeated it to myself: LaTonya. For some reason, I hesitated and held the pen over the page a few seconds longer, and looked up at LaTonya. I suppose I was waiting for her to say something; she seemed poised to do so. But after a few seconds, when she still hadn't, I signed the book, gently closed the cover, and handed it back to her. LaTonya began to step away, then she stopped, turned to me, and said, "Can I ask you a question?" Of course she could ask me a question, but she knew that already. I had been answering all kinds of questions since I arrived at the bookstore. The uncertainty that I heard in her voice spoke of her fears about *her* ability to ask, rather than of her fears about *my* willingness to answer. She seemed to be seeking permission from herself to ask me the question. "Sure," I said. But she thought it was too late. The next person in line, a young brother, was already standing square in front of me, his arm reaching out, handing me a book to sign. I looked up at him and the dozens of people standing behind him, all waiting. "Don't leave," I told her. "I'll talk to you as soon as I'm done." LaTonya nodded her head, then walked away; and I got back to the business of signing books, meeting and greeting the rest of the young brothers and sisters who were in the line.

When the event was over and the last book had been bought and signed, I looked around for LaTonya. I wanted to make good on my promise, and I was also really curious about the question she wanted to ask me. But she was nowhere to be found. I didn't know whether she'd waited until she absolutely had to leave or she'd changed her mind about asking the question.

As I was gathering my belongings, the bookstore owner came over and handed me a note. "A young lady left this for you," he said. Right away, I knew that it could only be from LaTonya. Her handwriting was at an upward angle and it definitely seemed as if she had written the words in a hurry. I pictured her in the bookstore, standing at the counter, near the cash register, rushing to write the question that she had dared, despite all her apprehensions, to ask:

> *In your book, you talk about young men being the "newest perfect model" and being "unreasonably happy." Please tell us sisters what is good about us. Do you think that we are also capable of being unreasonably happy? If so, what can we do to get there because I haven't been truly happy in so long I can't even remember when the last time was.*

LaTonya wanted encouragement that was directed specifically to her, specifically to sisters. But why ask me? Because I was a man? From that moment I started searching the bookshelves for books that addressed the issues affecting young women like LaTonya, but all I kept coming across were books by women or psychologists. While these books were helpful, most came from the same vantage point, of women talking to women. I even found a few books written by fathers to address the needs of their daughters, but it made me wonder about young girls who didn't have fathers. Where did they get their advice? I even started to learn things I had never thought about, such as the fact that many young women derive elements of their self-esteem from their fathers. In a time when nearly two-thirds of ethnic girls are raised in fatherless households, where do those girls get their self-esteem? How do they develop healthy, platonic relationships with men? When do they get to hear a loving, supportive male voice? As often happens in life, by asking myself these questions I opened myself up to more. Much to my surprise, questions like LaTonya's were questions that I would find myself being asked again and again throughout my book tour.

Meeting and speaking with groups of young brothers was not a new experience for me. I'd been doing it for years already. Stepping into a role as mentor to the young men whom I met during my tours, press junkets, and speaking engagements was a choice that I had made long ago, quite consciously and happily. My grandfather Harry Harper was a doctor who made sure that if any young man or woman desired an education, he helped them get into college. I was raised in an environment where passing the proverbial baton of experience and wisdom was not an option but an expectation, a privilege, an honor that meant something—to the people at both ends of the stick, so to speak. It was our way of saying, and of showing, that we matter. To each other first and foremost, and to the world ultimately and defiantly—We matter.

What I had not prepared myself for was the sight, in event after event and city after city, of so many women, of all ages, in my audience, holding the book, so aptly subtitled *MANifest Your Destiny*. Young sisters, some barely into their teens, others not yet out of high school, but already wearing the disappointment and disillusionment that people often ascribe to adulthood. There were twentysomethings, thirtysomethings, older professional sisters who had surrendered an hour or two of their evening—sacred time—to listen to a brother speak. These women had interest and empathy for the young men in their lives, their brothers, nephews, sons, friends, but they also had questions. They wanted to know why I had written a book only for men and not for women. Until those women started to ask their questions, that thought hadn't occurred to me. When Oprah opened a school, it happened to be a school for girls and it made sense. After all, she had once been a young girl and knew firsthand what they needed at that age because it was many of the things she had once needed.

I knew everything about the mirror that I was holding up for young Black men. Yet what mirror could I hold for Black women? What images would they find rippling underneath? Would or could I have any understanding of all the complexities of identity that go along with being a Black woman? Would I understand and be sensitive to all the limitations and lies that our society places on Black women and girls? Would I, as a man, be able to "get it"?

To be fair, inasmuch as I have been nurtured and supported by a strong circle of men, my life has been equally shaped by the hands of women. My mother spent her life defying stereotypes, statistics, and any other type of crippling categorization. She has been a trailblazer. As a Black female anesthesiologist, my mother had to grow accustomed to standing alone, to breaking new ground. She made many personal sacrifices in order to be relevant and successful. At a time when most women, especially African American women, were afterthoughts when it came to higher education and career ambitions, my mother chose to walk her own path into the white male–dominated world of medicine and surgery. She chose never to stand in another person's shadow and didn't care that society expected her to be at home baking bread instead of bringing home the bacon. I have been informed by so much of my mother's journey. Even the painful memories, like listening from my cracked bedroom door to the ugly fights she and my father would have before and after their divorce. For my mother the choices she made proved fulfilling. The lessons that I learned from watching her were innumerable. My mother's experiences gave me insight into the various negotiations Black women must make to claim the professional and personal landscapes of their lives.

My aunt Ercelle, my mother's sister, chose to be a mother, wife, and homemaker. She loved everything about being the strong, nurturing, feminine presence in her household. Her days were spent shuttling kids to piano lessons, being in the PTA, cooking three meals a day for her family, and being a faithful wife. She made it seem effortless and without sacrifice because it was exactly the life she chose for herself. I asked her one day if she wished she had had a successful career and she smiled at me and said, "I did." To my aunt, there was nothing more important than providing a stable, loving environment for her husband and children, and she taught me so much about the value of selflessness.

My paternal grandmother was another Black woman who left a tremendous impression on me. She had an amazing ability to create both home and community for everyone around her. Every morning that I awoke in her home, I was greeted with a huge homemade breakfast. That was important to her, for us to begin the day with a meal she had prepared—scrambled eggs, little Vienna sausages, grits, and toast. It was her way of showing that she cared, her way of sending us off into a new day, into the world, with sustenance that was more than just physical. It was a habit that she passed on to my father. Those mandatory morning breakfasts defined every single day that I spent under his roof as well.

And there are also the women in my life whom I call my "surrogate sisters." Women who have become my best friends in this world. These women are part sister, part mother, part best friend, part healer, and part life coach. With them I can be honest and open. If I'm having a problem in a friendship or relationship, I always feel comfortable going to them for advice and help—and it's not because they always agree with me, because a lot of times they don't. They offer a different point of view from my guy friends. I often see things in black and white ("He didn't repay the loan in the time he said he would so he doesn't respect my friendship"), but these wise women help me see the gray area (being unable to make good on a promise might leave a brother feeling uncomfortable and vulnerable). We all need somebody who allows us to be ourselves and who helps us to become more. Just witnessing the way they walk through their lives leaves me in awe. Not only do we have an amazing friendship, they know that I have their back and they mine in everything we do. All of the work in this book is aided by them directly or indirectly. I am a living testament that deep, amazing platonic friendships can and do exist between men and women, and my life is the better for all of my surrogate sisters.

The more I thought about the enriching impact the women in my family as well as my female friends have had on my life, the more I realized that I did possess a mirror to hold up for young women—a mirror uniquely filtered through my perspective as a Black man. I did know the images they would see—or, at least, the images that I would attempt to imprint, with pen and paper, in their consciousness, in their vision of themselves as people who could and would make a difference, as people who profoundly matter.

During that first bookstore event in Atlanta, when LaTonya said, "Can I ask you a question?" she was offering me permission. Permission to begin an honest dialogue, Black man to Black woman. This dialogue began with LaTonya's question and continues with all the other questions I have been asked, in person and via e-mail, by the countless women who have read *Letters to a Young Brother* and decided to reach out to me. Too often in our society, men try to brush off or redirect women's questions and concerns, not because they don't think they matter but because they think they aren't qualified to answer them. But segregating women's concerns as "none of men's business" doesn't do men or women any favors. Reaching out to young brothers while ignoring the invitation to have a dialogue with sisters is not only a refusal to engage with sisters but does a disservice to our larger community.

As my tour wore on and I saw sisters standing there, I realized that they were there to hear what I had to say, not in spite of the fact that I am a Black man but rather *because* of the fact that I am a Black man. Certainly, they, like the brothers, were there to hear me say to them that their lives, goals, and dreams *do* matter. But also many of the sisters showed up to offer support and encouragement for what I was doing for young brothers. This book, in turn, is my effort to lift up women as so many women have lifted me.

To be clear, praise is not the sole focus of *Letters to a Young Sister*, though the letters definitely speak to the possibilities and the potential for progress that sisters have in themselves and in their lives. The "Young Sistah" and I explore the ways young women sometimes sabotage their own ascension and how to avoid these pitfalls. Additionally, the letters address misconceptions that sisters have of brothers and that brothers have of sisters, and how to avoid falling prey to them in friendships, business relationships, and romantic relationships.

Many of the questions I am asked by women have to do with the lies they have been told by men. The thing about lies is that they hold just enough truth, warped and misrepresented though it may be, to invoke fear. That's what makes them so dangerous, so poisonous to the spirit. When we start to believe them, we allow them to influence and eventually impair our vision—our vision of others and, perhaps most damaging, our vision of ourselves. Sometimes the messages we take in are subtle, yet they make us believe our goals are not achievable, our lives are without value. Sometimes they creep in so slowly that we are unaware of the intrusion. My hope is that this book will educate, uplift, and inspire. As young women read it, they will hear the voice of a man—a Black man—encouraging them and explaining to them how and why they truly are queens, constantly reminding them that they are beautiful, magnificent, brilliant, and deserving of unreasonable happiness.

Just as I told people about my first book, there's most likely nothing in this book that you haven't in some way heard before. But hopefully, as you read it, you may receive and understand it in a new way. In other words, all of the issues that the "Young Sistah" and I discuss are not new, but perhaps the way they are read and understood will be. I truly believe there are no coincidences, and it's not a coincidence that you are reading these words right now in the place where you are. That means that you, right now, are ready for a shift. A shift that will close the gap between the you that you are right now and the you that you truly want to become, a change that allows you to move in emphatic and powerful ways to *DeFINE Your Destiny*.

PART ONE

Empowerment 3.0

DeFINE Your Destiny

Ego Tripping
(there may be a reason why)

NIKKI GIOVANNI

I was born in the congo
I walked to the fertile crescent and built
   the sphinx
I designed a pyramid so tough that a star
   that only glows every one hundred years
      falls
   into the center giving divine perfect light
I'm bad

I sat on the throne
   drinking nectar with allah
I got hot and sent an ice age to europe
   to cool my thirst
My oldest daughter is nefertiti
   the tears from my birth pains
   created the nile
I'm a beautiful woman

I gazed on the forest and burned
   out the sahara desert
   with a packet of goat's meat
   and a change of clothes
I crossed it in two hours
I'm a gazelle so swift
   so swift you can't catch me

For a birthday present when he was
      three
I gave my son hannibal an elephant
   He gave me rome for mother's day
My strength flows ever on

My son noah built new/ark and
I stood proudly at the helm
   as we sailed on a soft summer day
I turned myself into myself and was
   jesus
   men intone my loving name
   All praises All praises
I am the one who would save

I sowed diamonds in my back yard
My bowels deliver uranium
   the filings from my fingernails are
   semi-precious jewels
   On a trip north
I caught a cold and blew
My nose giving oil to the arab world
I am so hip even my errors are correct
I sailed west to reach east and had to round
      off
   the earth as I went
   The hair from my head thinned and gold
      was laid
   across three continents

I am so perfect so divine so ethereal so
      surreal
I cannot be comprehended except by my
      permission

I mean . . . I . . . can fly
   like a bird in the sky . . .

LETTER 1

Young Sistah:
Your FINE Destiny

People often say that "beauty is in the eye of the beholder," and I say that the most liberating thing about beauty is realizing that you are the beholder. This empowers us to find beauty in places where others have not dared to look, including inside ourselves.

Salma Hayek

June 27, 2006
Los Angeles

Dear Young Sistah,

WOW.

Okay. First, let me say that I'm sorry. Yes, I got your letter, then your e-mail asking me if I received your letter, and a few weeks later, I also got your follow-up letter telling me that I was a complete jerk for not responding. Honestly, I took your letter with me to Atlanta last weekend. I thought I would answer when I was there. I went to Spelman (a very prestigious all-female historically African American college) to talk to their seniors. I figured that would be the perfect setting to respond to the questions in your letter. As I waited in the "green room" (not sure why they call it that) before my speech, I pulled your letter out and looked at it, and I started to write you back . . . but then I paused, put the pen down, and stopped myself. And I'm sorry for that.

But before you write me off as yet another man who has disappointed you, let me explain why I didn't respond. It wasn't that I didn't care about the questions you asked me and it wasn't that I was uncomfortable with the personal things you shared about yourself in your letter. (Okay, maybe a little uncomfortable, but not in the way you think.) The real reason I didn't respond was because I doubted myself. I wasn't sure of what to say. I questioned whether I had something of value that I could offer you.

I didn't want to be another man who disappointed you. Yeah, I could talk a tough game about not being stopped by fear, but I was falling victim to my own. I shared some of my doubts with my friend Meri, and after listening to me ramble on and on about my concerns and my worries, and basically my drama over your letter, she looked at me and said, "Well, I'm sure you saying nothin' will *really* help that Young Sistah out." Wow. Kind of cut to the heart of the matter there, didn't she? Then she reminded me that if we only did things we knew we could do perfectly, we'd never do anything new. And since I'm always encouraging all of the young brothers **and** sisters that I meet out there on the road to dream big, shine, take risks, and be their best selves, even if it means failing a couple of times to get there, I couldn't really ask less of myself, could I? So Meri sent my butt home to write you back.

When I got home, I took out your letter, where you told me how so many men in your life have let you down (especially your father) and that you wanted to have a big brother—someone you could talk to honestly, openly, and without judgment. So that's what I'll try to be. And as we embark on the journey of building a friendship through these letters, I will make you this promise: Unlike some other men you've had in your life, I commit to you to *always* be honest. I may not always know what to say, or how to respond to some of the issues you raise. I can't promise that I'll always be helpful. But I will do my best to answer your questions. And if I'm really stuck? Well, instead of sitting around doing nothing, I'll recruit help from some of my surrogate sister-friends to lend their wisdom.

(And maybe a couple of really smart brothers I know, too.) So do we have a deal? Do you forgive me? I'm gonna be on the ball from now on, I promise. Okay. So now that we've got that out of the way, let's jump into the questions you had in your letter.

You hit me with so many questions on so many different subjects, and I truly understood how you have been waiting "forever" (your word, not mine) to ask these questions. I want you to know that I totally hear the confusion and frustration you expressed in your letter to me. You wrote about how in one sense people are always saying how much better girls are doing than boys (more girls attending college for the first time ever, boys getting involved in crime, etc.), but at the same time, you don't necessarily *feel* like you are doing all that great. You said that you look around at your friends and you all are contending with so many serious issues. And it sounds like a lot of them relate to self-esteem. Like when you said that you and some of your girlfriends don't feel like you're "pretty enough" or "thin enough." And dang! You are so much smarter than you give yourself credit for because you have clarity about what answers you need to find. I was so much older than you before I recognized that I actually needed answers to all of the questions I had about things that just didn't make sense. I thought I had to be cool and to just pretend I had all the answers, which did nothing to decrease my ignorance or increase my self-esteem. Instead, acting like I knew it all just made me unhappy. But thankfully, I eventually learned better.

So I'll not only share with you what my experiences have taught me, but even more importantly, I'll try to point out when you say something that subconsciously means you're saying something else. I say this to you because in your letter when you were talking about boys and whom you choose to date, you never tied it into the self-esteem concerns you talked about earlier in the letter. Like when you said that you have met boys and have seen your friends date boys who treat them without dignity, pride, or the respect they deserve. You said that you often see boys talk down to girls. You mention that you've seen them cheat, and although you didn't say it directly, you hinted at the way boys mentally and physically abuse some girls. We'll talk about this in much more depth later on. But what I want to remind you of (no matter how many times you've heard it before) is that we all must love ourselves first . . . and that means *all* of our selves, before anyone else will. You then ran down all sorts of other issues to me, ranging from materialism, sex, pregnancy, and children out of wedlock, to respecting your body, attending college, and money and credit. All of these things are huge issues, and things that you as a "young sistah" are dealing with, but I'll tell you what: "Older folk" are dealing with the exact same things. Do I think I have all the answers to all of those problems? No. But let's take a look at them and maybe we will be able to help each other grow and to ultimately live our best lives—smiling and laughing all the way.

So, I may not know all the answers to your questions, but I do know one thing. And that is that you are F.I.N.E. And by *FINE*, I mean not just the limited way most of us use the word. I want us to take the word *FINE* and break it down so that the next time you hear the word or say the word, you'll be absolutely certain that it pertains to you. First of all you are Fantastic. You are so special, so unique, that the word *fantastic* doesn't even capture how wonderful I think you are. Next, you are Interesting. All of the different things that are going on in your life . . . the questions you have, the concerns, even the goals that you are too afraid to express to me or to anybody else, make you uniquely interesting. And I'm so excited God has put us in each other's paths. None of us are in this life to grow and succeed alone. We are all a Necessary part of the way the world is happening. Why? Because this world would not be the same without the contributions *you* are going to make to it over the course of your life. Just having read one of your letters, I can already tell the impact you are going to have. And finally, you are Exceptional. And that means you are without exception, and no one can "write you off."

> You truly are as unique as a fingerprint.

You truly are as unique as a fingerprint. You've got to believe me that there is power in the simple fact that there is no one in the world exactly like you. There never has been and there never will be again. For that, I celebrate you, I love you, and I am in awe of you.

You are:

F – Fantastic

I – Interesting

N – Necessary

E – Exceptional

Your destiny is already written, and I'm glad to say I am a small part of helping you deFINE yours . . . which means you are also a part of defining mine.

And that leads me to what I really, really want to tell you, and I didn't say this starting out in the letter because I didn't want to scare you, but here's the deal: *The time for you to take on your life and to turn all of your dreams into reality is NOW.* Today, this second, this moment as you're reading this, a shift is happening in your life. You and I have connected for a reason, and it really doesn't matter to me what went on yesterday, last year, or two generations ago in your family. I know that greatness is your destiny. And the time is now for that shift to occur. Granted, all significant change is gradual; just like when we are little kids and we grow taller, we can't necessarily see it day to day because we are too close to ourselves. But think about the person who hasn't seen us in three years. Immediately, they'll notice that we have gotten taller. That's how this will work for us: Change will come—and it will be in stages—and one day, everywhere you go people will notice different, positive shifts in who you are. No more sitting on the sidelines.

You are the star of this show.

Step out of the chorus line. You are the star of this show, and I need you to take your place at center stage. You deserve *top billing* from now on for the rest of your life! So I will say it again. The time is now, and the fact that you reached out to me means that you are ready.

All of this reminds me of a great quote from Albert Einstein: "We cannot solve our problems with the same thinking we used when we created them . . . but, when the solution is simple, God is answering." Through this newfound friendship, we will help reveal simple solutions for each other. Have a beautiful and blessed night, and I look forward to hearing from you soon.

Much Love,
Hill

P.S. Oh, and remember you are FINE. So begin to think of yourself that way. In everything you do. Let that calm confidence and love of self breathe through every action you take, whether it's with a teacher, your mother, father, friend, or that boy at school, you are FINE. And I'm excited to get to know you.

P.P.S. Oh, oh, oh! And one last, last thing. I'm going to check out that Chris Brown song you said you like. I'll let you know what I think the next time we talk. Good night [for real this time]. ☺

Date: July 8, 2006 7:45 PM
From: Young_Sistah@home.net
To: Hill@manifestyourdestiny.org
Subject: Teased for Being Outstanding

Hill, I have always been teased because of my intelligence and I sometimes feel bad in making good grades. What should I do?

Date: July 11, 2006 2:12 PM
From: Hill@manifestyourdestiny.org
To: Young_Sistah@home.net
Subject: Re: Teased for Being Outstanding

You know what's funny? I was asked a very similar question by a young brother (see page 17, *Letters to a Young Brother*), but rather than repeat what I said to him, I figured I would forward your question to one of the most intelligent women I know, Michelle Obama.

She is not only an incredibly successful Harvard-trained lawyer; she is also the mother of two wonderful daughters. She is intelligent, dynamic, independent, and fierce. And oh, by the way, she just happens to be married to my former Harvard Law School classmate Senator Barack Obama. Let's see if she has any insight on your question.

HH

----------Begin Forwarded Message----------

Dear Young Sister,

I hear you. I was once in your shoes. I used to get up very early before school to get a handle on my studying when the small house I grew up in was quiet, and I would give myself the time and space to learn and think and dream.

Neither of my parents went to college, and I never knew colleges or Ivy League universities were an option for me until my big brother Craig (he's a very big brother—he's 6'6") was encouraged to apply to Princeton because he was smart and a good basketball player. And when he went there I thought, well, shoot! I'm smarter than him! So I applied, and I got in.

And because of how hard I worked and the grades I made, I was ready for anything—ready for Princeton, and next Harvard Law—ready to move home to Chicago to give back to my community, to work in corporate law and community service and health care. Ready to be a strong woman and raise two strong daughters. And ready to be the next First Lady of the United States, if that's what the future holds for me.

So I encourage you, young sister, to stay smart and thoughtful and creative. And encourage your girlfriends to do the same. Keep reading and learning and sharing your thoughts and ideas. Own who you are and be proud of you. I am.

Michelle Obama

LETTER 2

Designing Your Destiny in This New-School World

Every people should be originators of their own destiny.
Martin R. Delany, abolitionist (1812—1885)

August 31, 2006
New York City

Dear Young Sistah,

Today I'm filming a scene for *CSI: NY* in Central Park. What's crazy is that in this huge concrete jungle of a city you can find this lush tropical oasis in the middle. There is even a small lake in the park where you can feed the ducks and watch people in rowboats. It's strange that in one of the most fast-paced cities in the world, there is this old-fashioned park. I have to say, after reading your letter my head was spinning. Do you realize how many "new-school" things you mentioned? How much shorthand and IM speak that just flows out of you? How fast-moving and technology-charged your life is right now? It's clear to me that you have gotten on the information super-highway and taken off. Text-ing, Blog-ing, Facebook-ing, Xbox 360-ing, MySpace-ing, AIM-ing, Google-ing, Wikipedia-ing, MP3-ing, PS3-ing, iTune-ing, E-mail-ing, DVR-ing, Wi-Fi-ing, Cell-ing, Flickr-ing,

CDR-ing, Wii-ing, iPod-ing, Twitter-ing, Ringtone-ing, YouTube-ing, Yahoo-ing . . . I mean, that's what's up!

Not to age myself, but when I was young, we had a pen and paper, a rotary-dial telephone that plugged into the wall at home, and a typewriter. There was no medium to get information out any faster than dialing the phone. But your generation has many diverse ways to get things out into the world in a matter of seconds. No matter how many "new" communicating and technological tools are out there, there are some fundamental principles that still apply for creating an amazing life and making our life look the way we want it to look. And you know what? It is perhaps even more important to look at these fundamental principles today when we are constantly being bombarded with technology, advertisements, texts, e-mails, and on and on. All of that stuff can cause sensory overload, no doubt. Did you know that as a young person in this country, you are bombarded by 500–600 product advertisements a day? I mean, everywhere you look, you're getting sold something. They're trying to push you to take an action, to buy their product. Trying to convince you that your self-esteem is attached to whether or not you have what they are selling. Will boys really like you better if you're wearing Roca-wear jeans as opposed to Apple Bottoms jeans? Or if you wear Nike vs. Converse vs. Vans vs. Ugg vs. Puma vs. Crocs? (Okay, not them, Crocs are ugly, don't wear those—ha-ha). But the reason I even bring this up is because I'm worried that for me to get through to you, I've got to bombard you just as hard. But there's no way that I can. So instead of trying to compete with this new media for your undivided attention, I need you to do me a favor. When you read my letters, allow yourself to do it in a quiet space, away from the computer, cell, or texting, so that you can really understand, think about, and connect with what I'm writing to you. The information that I'm hoping to impart will come to you quietly. I can't compete with the loudness of the pop-ups, and the commercials, and the billboards that are invading your life. But I promise you that this "old-school" letter writing is just as powerful as any of those "new-school" tech tools, and it will never go out of style.

My first question to you is a very simple one. What do you want your life to look like? What do you want your life, right now, to look like? And your life next week, next month, next year, and next decade? What if you could take a pencil and a piece of paper and sketch out your life, and whatever you sketched, it would be *guaranteed* to be your life one day? Huh? What if you could do that? Would that be cool? Or would having that much power over your life scare you?

Hmm . . . Okay. So what was your answer? Don't tell me yet. I want you to start thinking about that. And dream about that. I want you to start seeing yourself in a way that will allow you to know you have these magical powers—that you can literally sketch your dreams into reality. So that would lead us to the next question: What are your goals and dreams? What do you dream about? Huh? I want you to start dream-

> I want you to dream big.

ing more. Yeah. I want you to dream big; then I want you to dream bigger; and *then* whatever dream you come up with, then make it even bigger. Then I want you to dream double that, times ten.

There is no dream that you could ever have that you do not have the ability to sketch into reality. But you have to believe that you can sketch out your life, that you can create any life you choose. Because you know what the funny thing is? You are already sketching out your life, whether you know it or not. Think about the last test you took at school. Did you plan for it and then get a good grade? Or did you prepare for it, expect to get a low score, and then get a low score? Or did you forget to study and fail it totally? Is this making any kinda sense? Do you understand what I am trying to get you to see? Everything "good" in your life, you've been involved in creating. And the same holds true for the negative things that have happened to you. You have been involved in creating those as well. Now, I know that's kind of hard to hear and understand, but I think as we go down this journey of building a friendship, you'll come to understand that your words and actions have a certain power and you will begin to make that power work for you. One of the first things you have to understand on the road to creating your life is that you have to believe that your dreams are possible. So first, let's talk about this whole idea of believing.

The power of belief is the single most powerful tool that we have. And I want you to start using that power. I remember when I was seven years old I wrote a poem, and the last line in the poem was, "Goals and dreams are one in the same/Just say you believe and both you will attain." So I've known about this whole "power of belief" thing for a long time. But there have been situations in my life where I have forgotten that I create my own destiny and because of it I was led off track.

Like when I first moved from New York to Hollywood. I went because that's where everyone said I had to be if I wanted to "make it" in show business. I had gotten my first taste of success in the theater in New York, so I felt I was ready. But a year later the only part I had gotten in Hollywood involved me saying, "Hello, may I take your order?" waiting tables at this twenty-four-hour diner. I went on auditions, but all I got was a steady stream of rejection. I was too young, too old, too inexperienced, too short, too tall, too good-looking, not good-looking enough, too Black, not Black enough, and perhaps the worst one of all, "He's just not right." Rejection after rejection after rejection after rejection. All that rejection can really start to wear on your self-esteem! I'm telling you, if there was an excuse for why I couldn't have the job, I had gotten it, and no matter how nice the casting director had been, it all came down to one thing: rejection. Around this time, my uncle Frank came to town. He had always been my biggest fan, but he had chosen a very different path for his life, and so he didn't quite "get" what I was doing with mine. Uncle Frank was a doctor, practicing family medicine, and he couldn't understand why I would choose a career that guaranteed uncertainty and rejection, particularly since I had earned a law degree, from Harvard no less. I thought he'd come out to see me and be supportive, but it turns out the real reason Uncle Frank had come to Los Angeles was to have a good old-fashioned "come to Jesus" talk with me. "Hill, you have to give up this pipe dream and become a man," he said. "Dreams are for children." And truthfully, in that moment he said everything I had been thinking but not wanting to admit, even to myself. Maybe I wasn't cut out for this life. Maybe I just wasn't talented enough to make it in L.A. Maybe my intuition was wrong, and I was way off the right path.

Uncle Frank arranged for me to meet with a friend of his who owned a successful law firm in town. On the day of the interview at the law firm, my agent called, excited about a callback (that's when you go to an audition a second time, when they think they might seriously want you for the part) for the show *Married with Children*. I called Uncle Frank to see if he could reschedule the appointment for me, but he wasn't having any of that. He wanted me to be more "practical" and rethink my dreams. I got off the phone, and I sat there, scared and confused. I asked myself: Is giving up on this dream going to make me a man? In the end, I decided that sticking to my goals and dreams and taking total responsibility for the choices I made were what would define me as a man. Even though I had never disappointed my uncle Frank before, I knew that this time I had to stand up and do what I knew was right for my life, and not try to fit into a mold somebody else had set for me. As hard as it was to make that choice, I went to that audition, and for the first time I was no longer playing at being an actor. I was one. I had made a choice, trusted my intuition, and I was willing to stand behind that choice no matter what. And guess what? I didn't get that job either! But . . . the producers of the show were impressed with me and a few months later hired me for an even better role.

There is an old Latin proverb that reads, "A wise [wo]man learns by the mistakes of others, a fool by [her] own." So I want you to learn from my mistakes, so you don't have to repeat them in your life. I want you to start using the power of belief because if you learn to truly believe that the dreams you sketch out will manifest in your life, then I promise you, they will happen. It will happen for you, and the reason I am so certain is because it has already happened for me, and it is still happening every day.

No belief is right or wrong, it is just either moving you toward your dreams or away from them. You are believing something all the time. The question is whether what you are believing is empowering you or limiting you. And from some of the words you've used in your letters to me when speaking about yourself and others, it seems to me as if you have some limiting beliefs that we're going to have to get rid of and replace with empowering beliefs. One of the best ways to reinforce your power of belief is by visualization: creating a vision in your head and holding on to it until it becomes a reality. You probably see people doing the negative version of this all the time. How many times have you heard someone say out loud, "I don't want X anymore!" talking about bad grades, bad guys, bad luck, etc. . . . but all that passion and focus they put on what they *don't* want to happen winds up making it happen again and again. Now try this. When you go out today, envision something positive happening to you as you go through your day. Nothing earth-shaking, just something small. Get excited about how that will make for a good day, and see

> You can define and design your future.

how that energy creates positive opportunities moving toward you. Now, tomorrow, concentrate on something you're worried about, and notice how that not only draws those negative things and people toward you, but it drags you down and affects your whole mood.

So right now, I want you to write out, as best you can, at this very second, a definition for how you want your life to be. And since putting desires down on paper helps them manifest (come true), I want you to be as detailed as possible with what you "sketch." Put in as much information as possible about what you want your life to look like in every area. How do you want your life to look in school? What kind of grades would you like to have in school? After school? How do you want your relationship with your mom to look? With friends? With boys? How do you want your job and career to look? How do you want the room you live in now to look? How do you want your house in the future to look? How happy do you want to be? How do you want your future family to look? Think about and then define on paper what you want out of every possible area of your life. Now, when you write out these answers, I don't want you to use a computer. I want you to be super-detailed and, using a pencil, write out these answers as if you are writing definitions for your life. And be totally, totally honest. Don't let those false voices of fear and doubt stop you from writing down something that you really want. You're truly defining your life with these details. The one cool thing about definitions is that they are always really specific, and I want you to be just as specific about how you want your life to look. Grab any dictionary, or go to dictionary.com, and look at how the words are defined. Under each word there are multiple, very specific, definitions. Definitions break down the meaning of a word. With your answers, I want you to break down the meaning of your life. I want you take control and define your destiny. Don't just be like, "I want to be rich." That's not a blueprint. Think about what "rich" means and in what way you might want to be "rich." Own your own home rich? Own two homes rich? Own Bill Gates's home rich? Be able to send two hundred needy kids to college rich? Maybe you just want to be rich enough to go to the grocery store and shop for whatever you feel like eating without having to cut coupons. Any of those are fine definitions of "rich." Figure out what yours is; then write it down.

You see, I want you to be an active architect of your own life. By creating a mental picture, then writing down and defining all aspects of what you want your life to look like, you will have created a blueprint for the rest of your life. When architects set out to build their goals, their dreams, their structures, a blueprint is always the first step. Frequently it changes along the way. Yours will, too, but you always need a place to start. So go ahead and take that first step today. Is this confusing? Let me break it down a different way.

You know how you can go online now and design your own sneakers? You can make the exact color combo you want. The style and color of the laces. The logo color and everything. Well, I want you to think of your life that way. You have the power to design your life and customize it and make it look exactly the way you want it to look. Do you believe me? Whether you do or not, give it a try, okay? What harm can be done with trying? Sketch out exactly what you want your life to look like—and don't worry, you don't have to show it to me, or anyone else—so make it as personal as you want. Got your paper yet?

Well, I'm gonna go and let you get to that. I hope in your next letter you will tell me that you created a little blueprint sketch of your future life—and I hope that true *belief* in how magnificent your life is gonna be is starting to seep in a little bit.

And since you used so much IM speak to me in your last letter, I'm gonna leave you with a li'l somethin' somethin'; let's see if you can keep up with me! I want you to BRB w/a letter to me so I can TTYL 'cause I want us to become BFFLS and OMG write something that gets me ROTFLMAO and BTDubs PLZK I TYVM for the AMZ YS you are. So TTYL and IDK if you know and I ain't ashamed to say that ILYVM and trust I will BBL with another letter!

XOXO! Ha-ha!

Okay. Good night.

Much Love,
Hill

P.S. As I was walking to the post office to put this letter in the mail to you, an elderly woman with a church hat on handed me a flyer, and just as I was about to throw it away, I turned it over and on the back it said: "Believe that you have it, and you have it." Wow—isn't life amazing! No coincidences! Hit me back soon!!

Date: September 2, 2006 4:40 PM
From: Young_Sistah@home.net
To: Hill@manifestyourdestiny.org
Subject: Divine Purpose

Hill, what can I do to truly understand my divine purpose
in life?

Date: September 9, 2006 1:32 PM
From: Hill@manifestyourdestiny.org
To: Young_Sistah@home.net
Subject: Re: Divine Purpose

Wow, that's a big question. But I am so happy you are even asking
me. Because that means you are already starting down the road to
discover what your divine purpose is. I believe your intuition will
always tell you if you're on the right track toward your purpose.
And there is one person who immediately came to mind when you
asked me that question who I knew could lend perfect insight into
its answer.

Tavis Smiley is a man of character, intelligence, and honor. He is
someone who I believe has an incredibly strong sense of his
purpose and is executing his mission flawlessly. He is a bestselling
author and one of the country's most respected television and
radio hosts. He has built an incredibly successful for-profit
company as well as a foundation that is changing lives across the
country. I humbly consider him a hero, mentor, and friend. I know
of no better person to answer your question, so I forwarded your
e-mail to him.

HH

----------Begin Forwarded Message----------

Easy to answer: a challenge to fulfill. What is the one thing you
enjoy doing so much that—if you had to—you'd do it for free?
Beyoncé would still sing . . . Tiger would still play golf . . . I'd still be

running my mouth . . . even if we weren't being paid. Your calling, your vocation, your purpose is your life.

How do you live a life of purpose? By purposely deciding that you will do your work so well that the dead, the living, or even the unborn will not do it better than you.

Tavis Smiley

LETTER 3

Sistahs: As Unique as Snowflakes and Fingerprints

> Like snowflakes, the human pattern is never cast twice. We are uncommonly and marvelously intricate in thought and action.
>
> **Alice Childress, writer (1920–1994)**

October 12, 2006
Los Angeles

Dear Young Sistah,

Very cool. I got your letter. I'm glad you went ahead and sketched a life "blueprint," even if you did feel "kind of goofy" doing it. It probably feels a little weird right now because you're not necessarily used to dreaming that big for yourself. But stick with me, little sistah, and we'll have you dreaming IMAX-size in no time! And thanks for thinking to send a picture, too. You're right, it is nice to have a visual image to keep in my head as I read your letters, especially since we've never met face-to-face.

What do you think about that Alice Childress quote at the top of the letter? Have you ever heard of Alice Childress before? She's a great writer and wrote this cool book called *A Hero Ain't Nothin' but a Sandwich*. If you've never read it, you should check it out sometime.

When I read Alice's quote, I immediately thought of you. Because in the picture you sent, I couldn't help but notice that big electric smile of yours. The first thing it made me think was, is this the same person who sounded so sad in her letter? You mentioned that sometimes you feel like you go through life pretending to be something and someone you're not. Well, I don't know if the beautiful young sistah staring back at me in the photograph is the same someone you feel like you're pretending to be, but I can tell you this: Who you are is and will always be enough. We spend so much time being seduced by advertisers, peers, and "frenemies," we wind up believing that we need to be someone else in order to be happy. In order to be accepted and popular. You said that you feel one way at home and another way when you are in school or with your friends. I can tell you this for a fact:

> Who you are will always be enough.

You are not alone. Hear me when I say that most of us don't go out into the world the same way we are when we wake up in the comfort and safety of our home. Or you might feel safer and more accepted out in the world with your friends than at home with your family, where people have certain expectations of how you should be or who you should be.

You are just beginning to define yourself, and in the next few years you will grow, and change, and become different in so many ways. That process of evolving never stops for any of us. We are all continuously on a journey of changing, hopefully for the "better." So just because you act one way, but feel a different way, doesn't necessarily make you dishonest. For instance, if you're miserable because you've been fighting with your mom or your sister, and once you get to school you paste on a happy face and pretend to be all right, that's okay sometimes. It's simply a way for you to mentally distance yourself from some negative energy. If you could be a fly on the wall in your friends' homes, you would probably discover that many of them do the same thing. I know I do.

You see, growing up, I moved around a lot, so much so that by the time I went off to college, I had already attended eight different schools. Eight! But as much as I longed for us to just settle down someplace once and for all as a kid, I eventually came to see that there was some benefit to the constant change. At every new school, although at times it was difficult to make new friends, I had the potential to be a completely new person. I wasn't burdened by people's idea of who I was and how I should behave. Because the reality was that these people knew nothing about me. People I met in my new school in fourth grade had no idea about all the embarrassing things that had happened to me in kindergarten. Or that I was kicked out of the third grade because they said I "acted up" too much. They didn't know that my parents had gotten a divorce or that I now lived with my dad. To them, I had always been this person I was introduced as at age eight.

As much as I missed my old friends I had history with, I was able to constantly redefine myself in each new environment as I grew and learned more about who I was becoming. For instance, I was really quiet and shy in elementary school. By the time I got to junior high, I made the decision to work on my shyness and to be more outgoing. On day one of the seventh grade, the kids at my new school met the outgoing, funny person I had decided to be. And they never had a clue that I had ever been a mousy, shy kid. This constant transitioning went on through the remaining schools I attended until I went to college on a football scholarship. (And, yeah, to this day I can surprise people on set when I tell them I used to be a football player.) From all my moving around, I learned to not be afraid of change. I also stopped worrying about what other people thought of me. Learning how to do that, to change how I thought of myself and then how I presented myself to the world, is probably one of the reasons I became an actor. "Pretending" is exploration, it's trying something new, it's visioning, and those are the ways we create the blueprint that eventually becomes our life. Sometimes it feels like "pretend" when we take risks. But we have to take risks to move forward.

Let me tell you about Taylor, one of the girls I used to hang out with in college. She told me one time that all a guy has to do to make friends and be popular is pick up a book or pick up a ball. "It doesn't matter if you're ugly, your clothes don't match, or your friends are all nerds. When you're a guy, if you're smart in school or if you're good in sports, people give you mad props. Everybody likes you. It's not the same with girls," Taylor said. "If you're a girl, it doesn't matter how smart you are. You've got to either be pretty, be in with the right folks, wear the right clothes and hairstyle, or you'll be a total outcast."

Ironically, while we were in college, Taylor got great pleasure from being an outcast. She was so determined to be herself and to honor that self, with all its quirks and idiosyncrasies, that she became popular for it. She was known as "the nonconformist," and people respected her for her courage. While the other girls were sporting designer labels on their clothes and purses, Taylor would tell anybody who asked that she rummaged through bins at the thrift store for her outfits. And that was way before vintage clothing was cool.

But Taylor didn't arrive at the point of determination by accident. She'd apparently spent her high school years playing the role of the prettiest, meanest, and most popular girl in school. She'd been a cheerleader, and had even been voted homecoming queen. She was the girl that all the other girls wanted to be and all the boys wanted to date. "And I hated it," Taylor told me. During junior high school, she had a strong circle of friends and was liked well enough by the other kids, but she envied that circle of girls who seemed to get all the attention, the girls whose names seemed to be on everybody's lips and at the top of everybody's invitation list, the ones that crowds in the hallway parted for. During the summer between junior high and high school, Taylor promised herself that she'd find a way to fit in with that popular crowd. And she did just that. Ever hear the saying "Be careful what you wish for . . . you just might get it"? Taylor changed her clothes, she changed her hairstyle, her interests, and she even changed her friends. She changed everything about herself and she got exactly what she thought she wanted—only to find out that she didn't like it. And she especially didn't like the person she was pretending to be in order to fit in with that group of girls.

"I'd made this decision," Taylor said, "and then suddenly I realized I was trapped in it. I didn't know how to get out. I'd turned my back on all my real friends. Sure, I was popular, but I was lonely." When the time came to apply to colleges, Taylor chose schools that were as far away from her hometown as possible because she wanted to escape that false reality she'd created for herself. She wanted to go back to being herself. And her problem wasn't that she tried to reinvent herself. It was that she reinvented herself into what she *thought* would make her happy, what the kids around her defined as what a girl was supposed to be. And that wasn't who she really was.

Mariah Carey, who, I'm willing to bet, has probably faced a lot of pressure to live up to the expectations of others, once said, "You really have to look inside yourself and find your own inner strength, and then say, 'I'm proud of what I am and who I am, and I'm just going to be myself.'"

Maybe that sounds simple and trite to you. Maybe you're saying, "Yeah, right, Hill," and rolling your eyes at my letter right now. But sometimes, the best way to get through the most difficult situations is just to take a deep breath, put one foot in front of the other, and do what comes naturally—and what could come more naturally than being yourself?

And don't think I didn't notice that even though you said you wanted me to have your picture so that I could have an image of you in my mind, you also used up a whole lot of ink apologizing for different things about it. You said you thought you looked better without your glasses but that you didn't take them off because the lenses leave these marks on your skin that, you thought, would have made you look like you had huge bags under your eyes. And your hair, you said, looked "worse than usual," because when the picture was taken, you hadn't been to the hairdresser in weeks. And the braces, and on and on.

But you wanna know something? I wouldn't have thought twice about any of that stuff if you hadn't brought it up. Your hair doesn't look bad; in fact it looks great, and I think your glasses suit your face just fine. They don't hide your features at all. Your braces are there because you want to straighten your teeth, which just might lead you to smile more, and there's nothing wrong with that. In fact, I think your braces are a really positive thing because your having them means that you are consciously or subconsciously thinking about your *future.* Anyway, I think it's a wonderful photograph. It makes you look like a fun, interesting person, somebody who is engaging. Somebody I'd want to get to know. And after reading and rereading your letter, I have to say that everything I believed that picture suggested turned out to be true. So don't be so harsh on yourself. Would you ever look at a picture of someone else and immediately start telling them how bad they looked? Then why would you treat yourself with any less respect? Don't ever apologize for the you that you are. Remember you are a special and unique human being and no one else in the entire world is like you. Nobody looks like you, sounds like you, walks like you, talks like you, dreams your dreams, or came into this world to accomplish the things you came into this world to do.

I've become even more aware of this in the last few years because the show I work on, *CSI: NY*, is all about identity. Yeah, you thought it was all about crime, didn't you? But think, what is my character trying to do every week? Find out which specific person, out of the billions of people on the planet, committed one specific crime. Of course, that's not how *you* want to distinguish yourself, but discovering the myriad ways in which crimes can be investigated and suspects can be identified has really made me see how unique each of us is. There is nobody else in this world like you. There may be people who resemble you in looks or voice or behavior, but that's where the similarities end. Nobody has the same fingerprints as you. Nobody has the same DNA as you (well, unless you have an identical twin you haven't told me about). Alice Childress was right; our patterns are never cast twice. You are as rare and exotic as any flower or plant or animal on an endangered species list. Your presence and your contributions are vital to the future of this world.

> There is nobody else
> in this world like you.

Zora Neale Hurston, a folk historian and one of the leading figures in twentieth-century African American literature said, "I love myself when I am laughing . . . and then again, when I am looking mean and impressive." She was not only aware of her various emotions and personas, she also accepted and loved the way they came together to form the *real* her. And let me tell you, she was as unique and extraordinary as they come. Zora Neale Hurston was a true original, just as Taylor is a true original—and you are a true original.

We so often spend our time trying to figure out the things about ourselves that we believe we could or should change that we forget to stop and take inventory of the things about ourselves that define us, make us who we are. Usually, it is those traits we eventually discover that we love the most about ourselves.

So, tell me, young sistah, what are the things you love most about yourself, the things that set you apart from everybody else? They don't have to be huge, complex, or earth-shattering. What are the little things, the small traits and characteristics that make you, well, you? I already have an idea of what some of those things probably are, but I'm interested to see how *you* see *yourself*. So will you do me a favor and write those things down? And write them out with a pencil and paper. Yeah, it's the pencil and paper thing again, I know. No one uses pencil and paper anymore. But that's just it. I find that when I'm typing stuff, I don't always allow myself to really think, and go to the place of quiet contemplation I need to ask and answer the most personal questions about myself. That's why I want you to go all "old school" and use a pencil and paper. And remember what I told you in my last letter: It's no coincidence that when architects first set out to design their dream structure, they use a pencil and paper. Fashion designers do the same thing when they're planning their latest couture creation. So that's what I want you to do. Put pencil to paper and write out all of the magnificent things that make you the amazing young woman I am getting to know.

I gotta go now, but I can't wait to hear back from you. Oh, and I meant to tell you I am about to do a little traveling to a cool place. I will tell you all about it soon! Have a great day, my friend.

Much love,
Hill

Date: October 26, 2006 6:04 PM
From: Young_Sistah@home.net
To: Hill@manifestyourdestiny.org
Subject: It's a Hard-Knock Life for Us

Hill, why does it seem like life is so much harder for girls?

Date: November 1, 2006 7:49 AM
From: Hill@manifestyourdestiny.org
To: Young_Sistah@home.net
Subject: Re: It's a Hard-Knock Life for Us

Life is a long journey where we are often given opportunities to grow and change. Unfortunately, many of those opportunities to grow are painful and can seem relentlessly hard. When you sent me this e-mail, I started to answer but then I reached out to a sistah who I knew had taken hits for being a female. Her earliest successes have been in the male-dominated field of rap music. Eve, the award-winning rapper, hip-hop artist, actress, and clothing designer, has never had an easy road, and that's why I want her to answer your e-mail. This sistah knows all about taking those hard life lessons and turning them into big successes in many different careers. E-mail me after you read her e-mail and let me know what you think.

HH

----------Begin Forwarded Message----------

Young Sistah,

I used to ask myself the same question when I was younger. Even as a woman, that question at some point comes to mind.

Unfortunately, because we are more in tune with our emotions, we are often looked at as the weaker sex. We most definitely are not valued or respected as much as we could or should be!

But I have to say . . . that it is up to us! As women we must remember that we have the power and that we are in control of our minds, bodies, futures, and destinies. With that in mind, things will still be challenging but not as hard.

We give life! How amazing is that! Never give in to the propaganda that just because we are women we are any less than men or can't achieve what a man can.

Is it hard to be a strong, intelligent, independent woman who knows who she is and is in charge of her happiness? Yes, but it's also a beautiful thing! Pray for strength and embrace it!

EVE

LETTER 4

The J.J.:
Journaling & Journeying
Through Life:
The Power of One

Success for me isn't a destination, it's a journey.
Everybody's working to get to the top, but
where is the top? It's all about working harder
and getting better and moving up and up.

Rihanna

November 18, 2006
Accra, Ghana

Dear Young Sistah,

I was thrilled to get your letter, but if it had arrived five minutes later, I would have missed it! I already had left for the airport when I realized I'd forgotten something, so I turned around and went home to get it. When I came back out, there was the mailman, about to drop your letter into my box. Seems like you're always able to find me at just the right time!

I told you I had exciting travel news, and you'll never guess where I am. I'm in Africa, in the country of Ghana, the center of the world.

They call Ghana that because about five miles off the coast is where the equator, which is 0° latitude, intersects with the prime meridian, which is 0° longitude. My friend Jordan was going, and he asked me to tag along. He's a director and one of my best friends. We've already done two movies together, *The Visit* and *Constellation*. He is scouting out different locations for a film he's making about his search for his ancestry. Pretty amazing story. (I told him there better be a part for me in it!)

It's gorgeous here, warm tropical weather, lots of palm trees. Right now, I'm in Accra, the capital, sitting in an outdoor café, using a straw to drink the milk straight out of a coconut. A few minutes ago, a car drove by blasting one of the songs you told me was one of your top ten favorites. I looked up when I heard the music and behind the wheel was this young sistah who couldn't have been more than a couple years older than you. She looked a little like you, too, at least in profile, with that same warm complexion and beautiful skin like "fresh brown rolls right out of the oven" as my gram used to say. Oh, and she was feelin' that song, too. I could hear her voice over Lil Mama's, singing, "What you know about me, what you, what you know? They say my lip gloss is cool, my lip gloss is poppin' . . ." I bet you sing along that loudly, too, don't you? Yeah, you do . . . don't lie.

Let me start by answering the question you ended your last letter with. Yes, I do keep a journal. I've kept a journal for most of my life, definitely since high school. It's kind of like my catchall, a combination journal and mini-scrapbook. I write down my thoughts, wishes, plans, and ideas in it, but I also jot down quotes and lyrics that move me. I sometimes write poetry in it, and I might tape ticket stubs and programs from events that I want to remember. I even taped my first pay stub from the first paid "acting" job I ever did. I made sixty dollars for being an extra in Spike Lee's *Malcolm X*. We shot the scene in Brooklyn, and I dressed up in 1940s clothes. I have the pay stub taped in my journal to this day. I was so proud to earn that sixty dollars; I felt like I was on my way. And you know what's funny? Just a few years later I was starring in back-to-back movies with Spike Lee, *Get on the Bus* and *He Got Game*. So it really is true that if you believe and you imagine it, it will happen. Just from the short exchanges we've had already, I know that infinite blessings, good times, health, happiness, love, and more are headed your way. I hope you are beginning to believe it as well. So why a journal? Let me tell you.

For me, keeping a journal is an important exercise because it gives me a place to "say" things that I don't necessarily want to tell anybody else, things that I want to release but, at the same time, keep to myself. It's a way for me to check in with myself, and sometimes I wind up writing down thoughts I didn't even know I had. I think it's wonderful that you're so committed to writing in your journal, and that you've found a way and a place in which you can fully express yourself. Some of the most powerful and poignant lessons about humanity I've learned I got from reading the journals that people have kept. A lot of what you wrote to me about your relationship with your journal mirrored something Anne Frank wrote about her relationship with her journal, which she treasured so much that she even named Kitty.

"I have my own views, plans, and ideas, although I can't put them into words yet," Anne Frank wrote in her journal. "Oh, so many things bubble up inside me as I lie in bed, having to put up with people I'm fed up with, who always misinterpret my intentions. That's why in the end I always come back to my diary. That's where I start and finish, because Kitty is always patient." Sounds familiar, doesn't it? If you haven't already read *Anne Frank: The Diary of a Young Girl*, you should consider doing just that.

Like you, Anne Frank used her diary to capture her internal life, one that she wasn't able to display or share with the outside world. In her case, a large part of her inability to share her emotions and personal awakenings was that she was in hiding with her family from the Nazis. But that was only a part. Another part of it was that these thoughts and feelings she was having were still in formation. She was still in the process of discovering herself, of naming her fears and claiming her strength.

I get what you're saying about the "you" that is revealed in the pages of your journal, and the "you" that is revealed to people. Of course they're different and separate. I would be surprised if you, or anyone else, were to tell me that they weren't. One is public; the other is private and intimate. Though I'm glad you clarified what you meant in your letter about pretending, I still don't agree that it's the most fitting word to use in this context.

You said that the reason you "pretend" to be someone else is that you're afraid people won't accept you for who you are and for what you want to be. What is it that you want to be? You didn't say, and I gotta confess, it's made me very curious. So much so that I'm really looking forward to learning all about the ways you're dreaming your future into being, all of your possibilities. I've learned that possibilities are a lot like fruit growing on the vine. They ripen in their own time. And that's the time when it's best to share them because that's when they can be fully appreciated. Trust me; you'll know when that is.

Your future is limitless, and I completely understand why that can be intimidating. Your vision of yourself is probably so dynamic and your dreams of your future are probably so daring, you're wondering whether they will ever be fulfilled. How do I know all this? It's simple: If that weren't the case, you wouldn't be worried about people accepting you. When we try to please others, we usually end up hiding our talents and shrinking our vision of ourselves so that others don't feel threatened or uncomfortable around us. We do our best to fade into the background by becoming unnoticeable. There is a quote I love about this. Herbert Bayard Swope, who was the first journalist to win the Pulitzer Prize for Reporting, wrote, "I cannot give you the formula for success, but I can give you the formula for *failure*—which is: Trying to please everybody all the time."

As we grow to realize and fulfill our highest vision of ourselves, it forces those around us to look at themselves and gauge their own growth. The people who want you to be anything less than your biggest and best self are the people who are very likely frustrated and frightened because, for whatever reason, they're not rising up to meet their own potential.

I'm not going to lie to you, there will be people who may not accept you for who you are, but that doesn't mean you should change or confine the person you are becoming to the pages of your journal. As a matter of fact, the truer you are to yourself and the tighter you hold on to your dreams of your future, the more likely it is that your example will lead them—even beyond the point of being able to accept you. It will lead them to a place where they will be able to accept themselves.

It's true! We can get so focused on how other people are affecting us that it blinds us to the effect our behavior can have on them. And we do have an effect, whether we're trying to or not. That's one thing I do know for sure, that one individual can make a difference in this world. I'm talking about those individuals who see you every day, the young sistahs and brothas who sit in math class with you and take PE with you and eat lunch in the same cafeteria as you. Though it seems as though only a small group's opinions, fashions, and comments have an impact on the whole population, it's not true. Each and every one of us affects each other. Even the shiest, the quietest, and the most antisocial of that group will potentially offer something positive to your life and to the lives of your friends and the other kids in school. You may be aware of that influence as soon as it happens, or you may not realize it until years later, but it's true. One person can make a difference.

Author and spiritual leader Marianne Williamson has written about this phenomenon. She said, "Our deepest fear is not that we are inadequate. Our deepest fear is that we are powerful beyond measure. It is our light, not our darkness, that most frightens us. We ask ourselves, 'Who am I to be brilliant, gorgeous, talented, and fabulous?' Actually, who are you not to be? . . . And as we let our own light shine, we unconsciously give other people permission to do the same. As we are liberated from our own fear, our presence automatically liberates others."

When we first started our letter exchange, I said that I wanted to know all the ways you're dreaming your future into being. I know that being questioned in this way can sometimes feel intimidating because we're not always able to translate our dreams into words. I don't want you to feel like you're being pressured to do that, by me or anybody else. That's not my intent. What I want you to know is that no matter how strange or silly you may think your dreams might seem to others, there will always be someone who will listen and who will take you, and those dreams, very seriously. I bet that by the time each of those fruits turns ripe on the vine, you'll find there will be many "someones" in your life to share them with. Just make sure you don't forget to count me as one of them.

In the meantime, it's good to allow yourself to go through the process of self-discovery by claiming those dreams, no matter how unbelievable they may seem today. Exercising and encouraging your own imagination can only bring you that much closer to turning those aspirations into a reality. This world offers itself to your imagination. And know that it is vast enough to handle anything you dare to dream.

You know, some of the greatest and most successful people in history were able to carve out careers that nobody had even dared to define by simply being who they were, and by claiming the highest vision they had of themselves. What do I mean by "the highest vision of yourself"? I mean seeing your own greatness. We all have moments when we catch a glimpse of ourselves in some other reality, doing or accomplishing something amazing. Maybe we see ourselves delivering an acceptance speech at the Academy Awards; or we see ourselves winning at Wimbledon; or sitting at a beautiful mahogany table in the dining room of a home that we own, eating Sunday dinner with our loving spouse and wonderful children.

Far too many people dismiss these images. They write them off as pie-in-the-sky fantasies, but they're not. They are a flash forward, a look at all that is possible in our lives, all that is probable if only we are daring enough to say *yes*. Do you get where I'm going with this? Maybe it'll be easier to understand after I tell you this story that I recently read about Oprah Winfrey.

She spent the first six years of her life living in rural poverty with her grandmother, Hattie Mae. I'm sure that if she had told anybody that one day, she was going to become a self-made billionaire (and that's with a *B*) and one of the most powerful and influential people in the world, they would have laughed her all the way to Britney Spears's psychiatrist. I'm sure, given all the perceived lack and limitation surrounding her life, even she could not have articulated a dream of that magnitude.

Still, she had a vision of herself and how she wanted to live in the world. During her teen years, which were filled with enormous obstacles and disappointments, she had a chance encounter with Aretha Franklin. Oprah spotted the Queen of Soul as she was getting out of a car. Oprah went over to Aretha Franklin and convinced her that she was an orphan from Ohio who was trying to raise enough money to get back home. Aretha Franklin was so touched by the story that she gave Oprah $100. Oprah used that money to rent a nice hotel room and order room service. She stayed there and lived that reality for three whole days which, I'll bet, felt like a lifetime.

When she lived with her grandmother, Oprah lived in a home that didn't even have an indoor toilet. Despite all that, she was able to envision a future in which she could pamper herself by staying in a fancy hotel and ordering whatever she wanted off the room service menu. She filled her heart with that desire. And when she saw her chance to taste that dream, she took it. Of course, the story she told Aretha Franklin so that she could get a small taste of the life she'd dared to dream of was not the whole truth. And I'm not saying that's the right way to go about things. It's not. But, in the end, that's not how Oprah manifested the highest vision she had of herself. She did it through determination and hard work and a commitment to excellence. Now not only does Oprah have the means to rent a room in any hotel she chooses (or to buy the entire hotel), she also has a platform that she can use to honor Aretha Franklin, the woman who unknowingly encouraged Oprah to continue her process of self-discovery.

There are many people who, like Oprah, are living a reality that could only have come about because they said *yes* to that glimpse they had of all that was possible for their future. People like Mary J. Blige, Maya Angelou, Jennifer Hudson, Condoleezza Rice, Madonna, Tyra Banks, Venus and Serena Williams, Beyoncé, Michelle Obama, bell hooks, Nikki Giovanni, and now you. By saying *yes*, they made it more than possible. They made it probable.

That's what my mother, Marilyn Hill Harper, did. At a time when African American women could barely give themselves permission to consider a career in nursing, Marilyn Hill Harper saw a future for herself in the medical field as a doctor. She went on to become one of the first Black female anesthesiologists in the country. My mom is not the only person in my life whose courage to conceive of and drive to achieve her goals has liberated me and given me the strength to soar. There are lots of others. If you stop and think about it, I know you'll be able to come up with the names of people like that in your life as well. Maybe a teacher, or a relative, or a neighbor?

What I want you to do is make a list of these people. If you want, you can begin with the names of celebrities, historical figures, authors, or other well-known people, but I also want to you to include the names of people in your life, people from inside your community. You'll probably be surprised by the number of people you'll come up with. Write all of the names in your journal and add to them as you think of more.

And remember, whenever you're afraid that you won't be accepted or you start to feel like you're pretending to be something or somebody other than yourself, look at your list, and let these people be a source of inspiration to you. The routine of our daily lives can sometimes narrow the scope of our vision, if only momentarily. Doing the same thing day in and day out, seeing the same people, it can fake us out, make us lose sight of the fact that there's a larger world out there to explore and to invite into our thoughts. That list can be your way of remembering, and of confronting whatever doubts you may have. Each time you look at your list, you can say to yourself, "Not only were they able to let their light shine, they're helping others—by simply being who they are." They are helping others by living their life fully. And I want you to live *your* life

> I want you to live your life fully.

fully, and surround yourself only with people who hold as great a vision of you as you have for yourself. I count my buddy Jordan as a friend I have in my life who helps me hold a great vision for myself. We need others in our lives, and bringing the right people in and letting the "wrong" ones go are crucial for us to live our lives fully. You know how in every building, architects put in doors to let some people walk in and let some others walk out. That's how we have to look at the "doors" in our own lives.

To achieve our goals and dreams it is essential to let certain people into our lives, because we cannot get there from here by ourselves. Tiger Woods, the greatest golfer in history, has a coach! Why does he need a coach if he's better than anybody who's ever played? Because you can't do it alone no matter how good you are. He needs someone to help him to see what he can do differently and where he can make improvements. Meryl Streep, one of the best actresses in the history of film, always has a director, and Beyoncé has a choreographer to teach her the right moves.

To ensure that you have good solid "doors" often means developing and creating relationships where you can meet new people by being of service. When you volunteer to read to the elderly, or tutor kids in math, or raise money for a worthwhile cause, it allows you to be with like-minded individuals. Our "doors" also serve the purpose of letting us choose who will gain entrance into our lives. We all have people we need to let out of our lives, family members who have gotten toxic, someone from our Facebook, MySpace, or Friendster page whom we need to let go of. It takes courage to let people out and to lock the door after they're gone, but that is also how we remain healthy. There are people in each and every one of our lives right now who we have to let out of our lives in order to get to a healthy place. If we allow them to stay around, they will inhibit us in reaching our goals and dreams.

And remember, by your unapologetically achieving your goals and dreams, you are leaving your imprint, your legacy on the world. The same way our ancestors have. I've been thinking about that a lot while I've been here in Ghana. It's one of the countries to which many African Americans trace their ancestry. For that reason, Jordan decided to film here. Ghana has more slave forts and castles than any other country that participated in the Transatlantic Slave Trade. Yesterday, Jordan and I traveled a couple of hours outside of Accra to a city called Cape Coast, where there are two huge slave castles. We took a guided tour of one of them, called Cape Coast Castle.

Inside, there were two slave dungeons, one for the men who were held captive, and the other for the women. These dungeons were relatively small, like an average-size living room in an American home. There were no bathrooms, and of course there was no electric light. It was just four stone walls and a concrete floor. Once the door to the dungeon was closed, the only source of light and air was a tiny window, about as big as the screen of a laptop, with metal jailhouse-style bars on it. The window was much too high for anybody to look out of, not that there'd have been anything for them to see if they could.

Jordan and I walked into the male slave dungeon. It was completely quiet in there, just the sound of our own breathing. We stood there for a while, looking and thinking. And I swear, the longer I listened, the more convinced I became that I could feel the power of each and every prayer that had been whispered in there. I could feel it inside of myself, with every inhale and exhale. Talk about intense.

Jordan felt it, too. He even told me that he'd experienced something like that before, when he was in Poland, at Birkenau. He and his girlfriend traveled there together after they graduated from college. Birkenau was the largest death camp inside Auschwitz, the Nazi concentration camp. Millions of Jewish people were killed there during World War II. Jordan said he'd always wanted to be a filmmaker, but that trip to Poland filled him with a sense of purpose he'd never really had before. It was a reminder to him, just as being in the slave dungeon was a reminder to me, that we are part of a legacy.

We are the answer to our ancestors' prayers. We carry them inside of us, just like they carried the vision of us inside of them, at the height of their joys and in the depth of their sorrows. Thich Nhat Hanh, a Vietnamese Buddhist monk, wrote, "If you look deeply into the palm of your hand, you will see your parents and all generations of your ancestors. All of them are alive in this moment. Each is present in your body. You are the continuation of each of these people."

So look at your palm now. See all those lines? That's how many dreams I want you to have. That's how many journeys that have been taken for you to be able to dream and do anything. And by the same token, the best way to figure out new goals and dreams is to have new experiences. And how do you do that? By journeying, of course (*grin*). So on that note, I'm gonna take a walk. Traveling, journeying, and discovering—that's what I want you to do. Will you put coming to Ghana someday on your "to do" list?

> Discover—that's what I want you to do.

Oh, all this talk about walking reminds me, I learned how to say a couple of words in Twi, one of the local languages. *Nante yie* is used in the same way we use *good-bye*, when two people are parting company. But when it's translated literally, *nante yie* means "walk well." So I'm gonna walk on out of this café, and after I've journeyed a bit I'm going to walk right back to the hotel and take a nice, long shower. It is seriously hot in this country! I hope things are cooler where you are. And remember, if you ever feel lonely, isolated, or alone—just write in your journal. And if you don't feel like doing that, shoot me an e-mail or write a letter. I love hearing from you, and now that you've just read this one, you owe me one. So gets to writin'! Can't wait to get your letter.

Nante yie—
Hill

Date: November 20, 2006 3:22 PM
From: Young_Sistah@home.net
To: Hill@manifestyourdestiny.org
Subject: No R-E-S-P-E-C-T

Hill, people are always telling me as a girl that I "need to respect myself." I always just nod my head, but what does that really mean anyway? It sounds stupid to me. How do you "respect" yourself? What is your advice to a girl who does not have much respect for herself?

Date: December 1, 2006 7:18 AM
From: Hill@manifestyourdestiny.org
To: Young_Sistah@home.net
Subject: Re: No R-E-S-P-E-C-T

Well, to answer your question, I figured I would forward your e-mail to two women who I think have amazing amounts of self-respect and not coincidentally the rest of the world has amazing respect for both of them. Alfre Woodard has been nominated for fourteen Emmy Awards and has won four times; she has won a Golden Globe and been nominated for an Oscar. She is one of the most "respected" actors in the world. I also forwarded your e-mail to congresswoman Carolyn Cheeks Kilpatrick.

----------Begin Forwarded Message----------

My dearest young sister,

As you navigate your way through adolescence you are increasingly in charge of your own choices. You are becoming a young woman, but the little girl you once were will remain a part of who you are, even when you are ninety! When you respect yourself you are giving that Precious-Little-Girl-Self the encouragement and protection she deserves.

Say you were put in absolute charge of a real little girl. How would you treat her? I know you would make sure she was well fed with nutritious foods to sustain her body. No dumping of sugar and grease and drugs; no cutting or abusing that perfect body into which she was born. I'm sure you would rise up like a tigress to defend her from men, young and old, who would seek to exploit, demean, or devalue baby-girl's body or mind. You would certainly steer her away from other girls who would belittle her dreams because theirs are drowning in booze and casual sex. (All they really want is something to fill their hearts.) You would be there to reinforce that little girl's image of herself, by reminding her of how powerful she is when she follows her intuition (the quiet voice inside) for doing the right thing. You would speak to her of how beautiful she is, when she swings her unique body in the rhythm of grace. You, my sister, would teach that little girl entrusted to you that she is descended from women who have built and suckled civilizations, that it is her heritage to stride boldly through this world, living her dreams, and that you will be there to comfort her, to inspire her, to laugh and dance with her. I know you would do all that, and even more. You would be guiding the little girl on her journey into womanhood.

My sweet sister, that little girl lives inside of you. She always will. Her well-being and sense of self blossoms or withers on your watch. The world has a history of not looking out for little brown girls. So, you are her/your last line of defense. I trust you to take care of her. To respect yourself.

Always joy,

Alfre Woodard

LETTER 5

The Difference Between Need and Purpose

Anything that you do in life, make sure it is something you truly want and sincerely love to do. . . . And make sure whatever you pursue, it's something you can be the best that you can be at, because you don't want to sell yourself short.

Ciara

December 28, 2006
Los Angeles

Dear Young Sistah,

In your last letter to me, there was a word that you used several times that stuck out like a sore thumb. It's a word that's overused and mis-used all the time, and in your last letter to me you used the word seven times. At one point in your letter you wrote you "needed" to lose weight. And later on you said you "needed" to finish your home-work. And at another point you said you "needed" a pair of Apple Bottoms jeans because everybody's wearing them. Now, you could probably say I'm being nitpicky, but I do think it's interesting that you use the word *need* a lot. You're probably like, "Come on, Hill, it's just a word. . . ." But words aren't just words, and you're gonna hear me say this a million times, in a million different ways—*words have power.*

Let's be clear. I don't mind you wanting things, even nice things. I like nice things. I have nice things. In fact, I have some jeans that I love, too. But, every time you think you "need" something, I want you to replace that "need" with the idea of

> I want you to be "purpose-driven."

"purpose." I never want you to be "need-driven." I want you to be "purpose-driven."

So what would it mean to live a life of purpose? What would it mean if all of the choices you made in life were driven by what you think is purposeful, which means being full of *purpose*? One definition for purpose is "an anticipated outcome that is intended or that guides your planned actions." But that's just a highfalutin way of saying: An action that you take is purpose-driven if that action fits into the overall goals you've set out for your life. For instance, in your last letter, you said you "needed" to get those Miss Sixty Halle jeans. I looked up how much those jeans cost and my question to you is: Would spending $275 on those jeans fit with the blueprint that you've already sketched out to achieve your life's goals? Would spending $275 on those jeans fit with your purpose?

Now, to answer that question, let's compare another way of using that $275. One way, spend it on the jeans. Purpose-driven? Well, maybe. You said they would make you feel better, like yourself better. But really? For how long? As an alternative, you could put the $275 in a mutual fund investment account. Now, over the next twenty years, assuming a conservative 8-percent growth rate, that $275 *alone* will be worth $1,281.76. Not impressed? How long would those jeans last you? A year? What if you put the $275 that would have gone toward replacing those jeans every year for the next twenty years into that mutual fund? All of a sudden that $275 a year has become $14,873.07!

So, with the overall goals and purposes that we've articulated, would having jeans that are going to be out of style in less than a year fit with your purpose more than having $14,873.07 to do whatever you want with twenty years from now? I don't think so! Now, I know it's super-hard to think about things that far in the future, but being able to think about our future is why purpose- versus need-driven thinking is essential. If you're thinking about where you want to be twenty years from now, when your friends who have been drinking say, "Get in the car!" you'll have the courage to say, "I'll find my own way home." Because you know the totality of your life is just like the interest that you'd be making on that $275 every year. Each and every year you are getting stronger, smarter, wiser, and more spirit-filled. So you don't want to risk injuring the amazing future of the magnificent woman you and I both know you are becoming. I already know how amazing, talented, smart, and wonderful you are. And unless you keep living healthily and happily, the rest of the world won't be able to meet this young woman that I'm having the pleasure of getting to know.

And there's one more thing I wanted to address that you hinted at in your letter. You spoke of feeling "lonely." A lot of times people confuse being alone with being lonely. I'm not trying to say that's what's going on with you, but I know it's something that took me a while to figure out. I mean, you can be surrounded by people and still feel lonely. More than a few of my loneliest moments ever have been spent in the company of other people. It was almost as if the loneliness was inside of me. You get what I'm saying? It didn't have anything to do with who I was with or whether I was by myself. For me, loneliness is sometimes like a hunger, or a craving for something. It's kinda like when you want a certain type of food. You can eat and eat and eat and be as full as you wanna be, but until you get that exact thing you're craving, a part of you will continue to feel empty and dissatisfied.

Unfortunately, we're not always able to name our emotional hungers as specifically as we do our physical hungers. This doesn't mean we don't know what they are. We do, and if we trust our intuition, it will usually guide us straight to the very thing, or person, we're missing in our lives.

I once read a quote about this by David Foster Wallace that really hit home. He's the guy who wrote the novel *Infinite Jest*, which, by the way, is one of the longest books I've ever read. It's over a thousand pages (!!!), but it's really interesting.

Anyway, the quote is, "We're all lonely for something we don't know we're lonely for. How else to explain the curious feeling that goes around feeling like missing somebody we've never even met?" Isn't that deep?

You know what else is deep? For the last few weeks, I've been feeling some pangs of loneliness myself. Then I got your first letter, and I knew it was what I'd been craving. I can't say it came as a surprise, though. I knew it was coming. I'm serious. I'd been walking around with this strong feeling that someone special was about to come into my life. And there you were, in black and white, ink on paper, introducing yourself to me in print and in a picture. My new friend!

So tell me this: What would it take to get you to walk deeper into your life? To walk deeper into loving *yourself* more with every step you take. And when I say "loving yourself," I really mean loving yourself unconditionally. That means being able to look at all the aspects of your life, even the ones that you'd like to change, and still loving them. For instance, as I've gotten older, I've noticed that I have the same love handles that my dad had. Now, do I like those? Absolutely not. Do I think they're cute or sexy? No, no, no, I don't. But I can still love them from the standpoint that they are a part of me and they've been handed to me.

However, I want to change them. So I'm going to watch what I eat and exercise more, and do some more sit-ups and leg lifts. When I say "loving yourself," I don't mean that you have to be happy about everything that is you. There's no doubt that you can still seek to change, alter, and improve yourself, but we want to do that from a place of self-compassion and self-love.

It is my hope that you will learn to love yourself unconditionally and that the way you speak about yourself and the words you choose will reflect that. I want you to learn to love and celebrate your beautiful eyes, your smile, your spirit, your history, and even the parts of yourself that you aren't entirely happy with. Now, this may sound totally weird to you, but what about the idea of loving those zits that you complained about in your last letter? Right now you're probably like, "Eww, that's gross!" But I'm serious. It's all about your perspective. What's wrong with having the perspective of, "Yeah, I want to get rid of my zits, but while I have 'em, I'll just give them some nicknames. That one's Doris, this other one's Pookey, and this one that pops up on my chin? I'm going to call him Fred." That is a great example of self-compassion and self-forgiveness. We don't have to take things in our lives too seriously, because remember, this world has been around for fifteen billion years. That's fifteen thousand million years. And even if you and I are lucky, we'll only be in this flesh body on this earth for about one hundred years. Which, compared to fifteen billion, is shorter than a snap. So why not celebrate the whole snap we got? Whether it's zits, or the boy you like doesn't like you as much, or the grade that wasn't as good as you wanted. I'm not saying accept the things that you don't like and not try to improve. I'm just saying, love all aspects of yourself, as my boy the poet David Whyte says, "Love even the fading moon part of yourself." He talks about how great of a world it would be if we as individuals learned to love the part of ourselves that says the wrong thing at the wrong time. If we were able to laugh and enjoy the part of ourselves that trips and stumbles, or the part of ourselves that didn't have the courage to talk to the boy we liked. It's all okay. It's all okay.

I hope you understand all of the wonderful things that I see in you, and if you could see yourself the way I see you, there is no doubt that you would love and celebrate all aspects of yourself. To me, you are already perfect. You are the perfect product of fifteen billion years of this majestical God-created evolution, so how can you not be anything but perfect? It's impossible. And moreover, so many women who were your ancestors chose to forsake and subordinate their dreams in hopes that the future generations would have more opportunity. They sacrificed so much so that you could dream as big as you want, and attain any of those dreams. It was not too long ago that women and African Americans in this country couldn't even vote. And many of your ancestors worked very hard to change that. Now *you* can be president, if that's what you choose. So with that foundation to stand upon, and that legacy from which you come, I'm so proud that you are beginning to see yourself in the magnificent way that I see you.

Historically, many women have made the choice to sacrifice their dreams in support of the dreams of others, primarily their children and their spouses. I do not want you ever to think that subordinating your dreams is a good thing. The best thing you can do for yourself and your future family is to embrace your dreams completely and fully.

Now, I know if we don't have examples around us of people exhibiting the behavior that we want to model, it can be tough to find our own way. But it's not impossible. We just have to seek out other examples. Where? How about books? I see Paul Robeson as a mentor. Since he has passed on, I'll never meet him, but I can still learn from him. Instead of asking him for advice directly, I read his autobiography, and biographies that other people have written about him, and try to model the choices I make for my life around the choices he made. You can do the same vis-à-vis people you respect, and seek out resources and tools to stay in that self-compassionate, self-forgiveness space.

Now embracing this idea of self-compassion and self-forgiveness is one of the most difficult things there is to do. And oftentimes when things are difficult to do, we need help and resources and we have to practice it, to reinforce it. So I have a little assignment for you. I want you to go online and just listen to any India.Arie song. Her music is so full of self-compassion, it's amazing. As I've told you before, sometimes it's necessary to take quiet moments, write in your journal, pray, or listen to music that can help fill your heart and spirit. That's what I love about India's music. It's all about what self-compassion and self-forgiveness looks and feels like. Sit by yourself and download her song "Not the Average Girl." It's truly beautiful, and every time you're feeling you can't forgive yourself for something, or you don't love yourself that day, you can listen to that song. That's why she wrote it. For you to be able to use it as a tool.

Using tools like meditation, prayer, or listening to music is the same as using different ingredients to create an amazing meal. Each one is important to make the whole. I want you to learn to cook an entrée that warms your heart, spirit, and soul.

I can't help but wonder whether writing to me is your way of easing your loneliness, of filling a hunger. What I said earlier about one person being able to make a difference in your life doesn't apply just to people outside of yourself. You can also be that person who ushers in change. Times of real loneliness can also give way to deep creativity. I'm sure you've probably written some of your most honest and heartfelt journal entries during the moments when you felt the loneliest. Maybe it was even during one of those times that you decided to write to me.

Your first few letters to me have been great, and I am loving having the opportunity to get to know you better and better. But come on, let's cut through it! Can I ask you something? How come you are being so dang polite? For the first couple letters I figured maybe it was because you were shy, and since you really don't know me very well, you figured you'd put on this polite "face." But just as you ask me to be real with you, I need you to have the courage to be really "real" with me. I need you to be really honest and open, so I need you to talk *your* talk.

There is nothing you can tell me about what you have done, want to do, have seen, said, heard, or thought that will scare me off. I won't judge you because, Lord knows, I am no one to judge anyone. I certainly have made many, many, many mistakes in my life and have done things that I'm not proud of. You can be certain that there is no person you will ever meet in your life who has not made mistakes. There is no person you will ever meet who has never done something she later regretted. And there is no one you will ever meet who hasn't hurt someone else's feelings and had their own feelings hurt. So can you and I stop being so dang polite in our letters to each other, and start getting to some of the real stuff that is going on in your life? Let's dive in below the surface 'cause it seems today with all the texting and e-mailing in our lives that we have gotten used to shorthand surface communication. But that shorthand stuff is not real communication. It's what I call "surface contact."

I want you and me to start exercising our muscle of going beneath the surface and really communicating. And like anything else, I know it's a two-way street. So if I'm asking you to go below the surface, I have to be willing to go there, too. And I am willing if you are. I'm not gonna to be a hypocrite and ask you to be vulnerable if I'm not willing to be vulnerable as well. So, in your next letter, you can ask me *anything* you want to ask me about. Anything! It could be about me, life, family, goals, dreams, self-esteem, dating, sports, video games, politics, school, even my secret family gumbo recipe! I promise, I will answer any question completely honestly. Except for my gram's secret recipes—knowing her, she might come back from heaven with that same switch she used to use and whup me if I gave those up.

Well, it's late here in L.A., and I'm tempted to take a late-night dip in the pool, but I think I'm just going to crash. So as I finish this letter and get down on my knees to say my night's prayer, I'm going to include you in it. And I'm going to pray that God gives you the strength to make all of your decisions, at least the most important ones, filled with purpose. And you know what? I know you will, 'cause you got it like that. Good night. And as my surrogate sister Tracey says whenever we talk before bed, "Sweetest dreams." So, sweetest dreams, you, sweet dreams.

XO
Hill

P.S. The next time you write, tell me more about this "special" friendship between you and Nasir.

Date: January 10, 2007 4:25 PM
From: Young_Sistah@home.net
To: Hill@manifestyourdestiny.org
Subject: My Morals for Success?

Hill, do I have to compromise my morals and values to make it in
the entertainment business?

Date: January 12, 2007 11:05 AM
From: Hill@manifestyourdestiny.org
To: Young_Sistah@home.net
Subject: Re: My Morals for Success?

Absolutely not! You should never feel as if you have to compromise
your morals and values to succeed in the entertainment industry
(or any industry for that matter). If someone proposes that you
should compromise your beliefs and morals for an entry into an
industry—then that is not the job for you. Never devalue yourself
for anyone or anything!

But don't listen to me; take a lesson from a beautiful young woman
who is at the top of the entertainment industry. Yes, Ciara, the
multiplatinum singer and actress and my co-star in *Mama, I Want
to Sing!* Ciara has very strong opinions when it comes to this
matter.

HH

----------Begin Forwarded Message----------

Dear, sweet young sister . . .

Do not ever think you have to compromise your morals, values, or
your body for anything or anyone to make it in the entertainment
industry. You are worth more than any job or man can provide.

I made up my mind when I started and I've always said that if
anyone will be the one to bring me down, it will be me. When you
do what others want you to do and you're unsure of it, nine times

out of ten you will end up being unhappy. Don't allow anyone to take your beauty or innocence for granted. You are in control of you and your destiny!

One Love,
Ciara

Date: January 20, 2007 10:00 PM
From: Young_Sistah@home.net
To: Hill@manifestyourdestiny.org
Subject: Too Much Pressure!!

Hill, why is there so much pressure on girls about looks and other stuff?

Date: January 23, 2007 1:05 PM
From: Hill@manifestyourdestiny.org
To: Young_Sistah@home.net
Subject: Re: Too Much Pressure!!

I decided to forward your e-mail to one of my best friends, Yale School of Drama graduate and Tony award–nominated actress Sanaa Lathan. Chances are you've seen her in *Love & Basketball, AVP, Something New,* and the television adaptation of the Lorraine Hansberry play *A Raisin in the Sun.* When it comes to a straight-forward, no-nonsense answer to any of the hard questions in my own life, I can always depend on my surrogate sister Sanaa. Sanaa is a stunning beauty, but it is her inner beauty that radiates beyond anything I have ever seen.

HH

----------Begin Forwarded Message----------

Movies, television, videos, commercials, and magazines place much more value on a woman's looks than who she is on the inside. The people who run these industries are a very small group. And therefore you have a very small group of people, mostly white men, dictating what is beautiful in our world. Their ideal woman is white, super thin, tall, fine-featured, and has straight hair. Very few people look like that. I think we all know beauty comes in all colors shapes and sizes. But sadly that's not the message that we're given as little girls in this country. And so you have all these girls and women trying to fit into this tiny little box of what "they've" told us is beautiful. And of course that will never happen because most of us look nothing like that. The great thing is, we as women don't have to succumb to this pressure. I do know that beauty comes in all shapes sizes and colors. But TRUE beauty comes from the inside. When a woman FEELS beautiful, then she is. Haven't you ever seen a woman who wasn't necessarily the prettiest woman and had all the guys' attention? Or a woman who is "gorgeous" and had trouble keeping a date? That's because the first woman felt beautiful and it radiated from within. When you feel beautiful, other people will see you that way. Start admiring yourself. Take notice of the things you like about yourself and give thanks. I don't believe God makes any mistakes. He wanted you to have the nose you have, the hair you have, the skin color you have. . . . Try this exercise every day before you leave your room: look in the mirror, smile, and say to yourself "I am beautiful." It may seem silly at first, but watch what happens. Do it every day until you start truly believing it. When you start believing it, people will begin to see you that way. . . . And we'll have a lot more beautiful girls in the world. ☺

Sanaa Lathan

PART TWO

Relationships: Family, Friends, and Boys

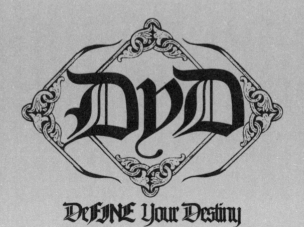

LETTER 6

Ain't Nothin' but a "G" Thang: GOSSIP

To find out a girl's faults, praise her girl-friends.

Benjamin Franklin

February 12, 2007
Los Angeles

Dear Young Sistah,

It's late, that time of night when all the sounds turn into whispers, and then, eventually, turn into silence. I'm just in from work. Depending on how long we shoot, I often don't get back home until right about this time. Sometimes, I'm so tired I go straight to bed. Other times, I'll return e-mails or phone calls from friends and maybe catch up with someone I haven't connected with in a long while. It's a good opportunity to do all the little things I can't get done during the day because I'm running around so much. But it's also the perfect time to do nothing, to just be with myself and to clear all the clutter from my head. You know clutter. All the worries and anxieties and frustrations that pile up as you go through the day, stuff that you just have to get rid of every once in a while. Maybe it was that thing someone said that hurt my feelings, that I was too shocked at the time to respond to, but that

I've been stewing about ever since. Or maybe it's the pain that a family member is going through that I can't change or do anything to help heal. Or the five things that I didn't get around to doing that I swore I was finally going to get to when I got up that morning. These are the kinds of things that weigh on you. And if you hang on to them, they can lead to stress, and stress can lead to more serious issues. It can cause problems with your health, and just wear you down emotionally.

So tonight, I decided the best way to release that clutter was to treat myself to a nice, relaxing night of solitude. Have you ever done that? Treated yourself to a date with yourself, some time, in the company of nobody else but yourself, to do something that is healing? My girlfriends named the act of being alone after that India.Arie song, "Private Party." The lyrics say, "Learning how to love me, celebrating the woman I've become." Now of course, as a guy, that isn't my anthem unless I change the words, but I thought it was a perfect song for you, my Young Sistah, to sing. To have your own private "clutter-cleaning" party . . . and you don't even have to leave your house.

So I've fixed myself a big ole cup of tea and slid a CD into the player. I know, I know, I'm old school, but I haven't made the time yet to download all of my music onto my iPod. I'll get around to it soon enough, but tonight is about clearing *out* the mental clutter, not adding anything new to the to-do list. Tonight, I revel in my disks . . . maybe I'll even put on a record later on. Yep, I, Hill Harper, still own a record player. Don't hate the vinyl, baby!

So now I'm sitting here sippin' on some yerba mate (it's a kind of tea—good, too!), reading your letter. And I gotta tell you—and I mean this in the best way—you make me laugh sometimes. After my eloquent paragraphs in the last letter about "going deeper" I was actually kinda nervous about what you might come back at me with. And I'm crackin' up right now, reading your letter, realizing the first thing you wanna get deep on is some gossip! You know, you just taught me a valuable lesson. Sometimes I can take myself and the world too seriously and think that everything is "life or death." But, come to think of it, I guess in high school, gossip is kinda life or death, huh? It's all about perspective.

So let's dive in. From what I read, it seems, just like me, you've got a whole lot of clutter to clear up, too. Your letter was jumping all around from one thing to the next and then back again, but I can definitely understand why you were so hurt, angry, and confused. Rumors and gossip are never easy to deal with because they're intentionally malicious and mean-spirited. I hope writing it all down helped you blow off some of that steam.

So let me get this straight. This girl Caroline, your friend, your "BFF," started rumors about you at school. Rumors are bad enough, but I feel even worse for you that someone you considered a friend would do something like that to you. I can only imagine how tough it must be for you right now.

Yes, you attempted to "serve others" like I recommended and you decided to tutor someone, and because of that you got hated on and gossiped about. First, let me say I'm sorry this happened to you, but know this: It will not be the last time you're talked about or falsely accused of doing something to or with someone. People who step out to *live* life often get talked about by others. When you choose to take risks in life, you are no longer flying below the radar. Others who are afraid to take risks in their own lives will try to knock you down and throw stones at you. So I think it's actually good that folks are "talkin' 'bout" you. That means you are being a leader. And like I've told you before, I want you to *lead* in all aspects of your life.

When I was in high school, my friend Anisa Tremaine and I unofficially adopted each other as sister and brother. I'll get into the reasons why a little later, but she was the first real female friend I had since elementary school. Through her, and our friendship, I started to become a little familiar with some of the inner workings of young sisterdom. I tell you, I thought it was tough being a young brother, but after hearing the dramas and goings-on that Anisa would tell me about, I realized that it was nowhere near as tough as being a teenage girl. What I remember most was the endless gossip that the sisters would spread about each other, sometimes out of jealousy, and other times out of what looked like just plain cruelty.

It never really made any sense to me, why one group of girls would gang up and tell lies about another group of girls. Or, even worse, why friends, good friends, BFFs, would suddenly turn on each other. I remember one time when Anisa was all upset because her girlfriends had started avoiding her during school and afterward. They'd even gone to the movies, like they always did on Friday nights, without her. When she tried to talk to them, they ignored her and treated her like a complete stranger.

That afternoon when Anisa went to gym class, the word *slut* had been written in huge letters with red lipstick all across her locker. She was so upset, she couldn't participate in the class. She pretended to have cramps so that the teacher would let her go lie down in the nurse's office. In the nurse's office of our high school, there were two cots. When Anisa got there, another girl who ran in a different circle was also there. That's where she found out why her so-called friends were avoiding her like the plague.

Meanwhile, I was hearing about it at football practice, while we were changing in the locker room. One of the guys had come up to me and said, "Yo, Hill, I hear your girl Anisa's been giving up the goods. You think she might pass a li'l Somethin' Somethin' my way?" I was confused and speechless. All I could manage to say in response was, "Yeah, right. You wish."

As it turns out, what Anisa did was something quite innocent and harmless. During that previous week, she'd been called out of one of her classes to pick up an envelope in the office, which she was supposed to deliver to her mother. As a result, she missed a lot of what had gone on in class. Later that morning, she spotted Jeff, a guy who was in her class. She asked him if she could copy his notes. Jeff made a joke about the teacher. They laughed. She took his notes and left.

Anisa copied Jeff's notes during her next class and then returned the notebook to Jeff at his locker before the next period. After she thanked him, Jeff suggested that the two of them exchange numbers so they could "spot" each other if one of them was absent or had a question while studying. Someone saw them exchange numbers and created an entirely different story and relayed that back to Jeff's girlfriend, one of Anisa's best friends.

Within twenty-four hours, Anisa, who was probably the most loyal friend a person could have, became known as the kind of girl who would try to snatch her best friend's guy. Her best friends, a clique of four girls, weren't having it, or her. Once the rumor got started, it became a living, growing thing, feeding off of people's boredom, curiosity, meanness, and envy.

That night when she and I spoke, she asked if I would call Jeff for her so that he could explain things to his girlfriend. I did, and he did.

After Jeff explained to his girl what really went down, Anisa's girl-friends came and sat with her at lunch and started talking to her as if nothing had ever happened between them. They didn't even really say they were sorry. Anisa forgave them, but she found it hard to forget, and even harder to place her faith and trust in those friendships the way she once had.

I wish I could say gossiping stops after high school, but it happened to me not too long ago. Last week I went to a party with one of my closest girlfriends, Gabrielle Union. Gabrielle and I have been friends for years, and I often find myself having to protect her from the large groups of men vying for her attention. She's like my sister in that way. At the end of the event I took her hand and led her out of the party because all these guys were reaching out trying to holler at her.

The next day, this shows up on the Web:

Bossip.com Exclusive: Hill Harper and Gabrielle Union arrived at the Maxim Style Awards Tuesday night in Hollywood. Guess what the new rumor is now? **She is dating Hill Harper.** *First Dwayne, Luda was next and now Hill? I honestly think people are pulling these items out of their ass. Gabby, please set the record straight soon, because these rumors are making you look like a jump off.*

Sources exclusively tell Bossip Gabrielle Union decided to take a break from her usual football player fetish to hook up with CSI: NY

actor Hill Harper. *He must've put that good mack on her because,
they were on each other the entire time at the Maxim Style Awards
last night in Hollyweird. A highly placed source from the party says
the two were tonguing it up all night long before leaving together
hand-in-hand.*

**The new "friends with benefits" situation grew out of a long
friendship says the source.**

All of a sudden my BlackBerry is blowing up. I'm on the set working, so I miss all the calls. When I finally check my phone, my voice
mail is full of people congratulating me for hooking up with Gabrielle. I also have a phone call from my girlfriend, who is pissed off that
I've been caught cheating on her. I finally see the story and then I'm
not just confused and angry, I'm downright worried because there
are so many people who could get hurt by this lie.

Gabrielle's ex-husband, Chris, is a friend of mine, and I supported
both of them while they were married and managed to stay friends
with them after their divorce. Now I had to call Chris and tell him it
was all some spin to sell papers and advertising space on these gossip
Web sites. But the call that concerned me the most was from my girlfriend. One of her frenemies (you know that type) gave her the "I told
you he was no good" speech. By the time I reached her, she had already tried and convicted me. It didn't matter that we'd hung out with
Gabrielle a number of times. Eventually, I talked her down, but the
whole gossip thing reminded me that I have no control over what
people choose to say about me on Web sites, TV shows, and gossip
rags. It wasn't the first time this had happened to me, but this time
I had a fuller life and a lot more to lose.

What do you do next? It's a difficult question to answer. I'm sure
you've already asked yourself that question a hundred times as you
try to come up with an answer that addresses not just the situation
but how it's made you feel about yourself, and about your friendship
with Caroline. Have you considered talking to your mother about
what's going on? Yeah, yeah, you're thinking I must be joking.

I know you've mentioned to me a couple of times in your letters
that you and your mom aren't as close as you used to be when you
were younger, but this might very well be a chance for you guys to
start moving toward a better relationship. Sometimes our parents

can surprise us by being incredibly available to us when we need them most. They can also be unusually understanding about the hurtful situations in which we find ourselves.

This is where communication comes in. We all have the power of words at our disposal. Just because someone's an adult doesn't mean he or she can read minds. Our parents rely on us to communicate with them, to tell them what we're feeling and what we're doing. There are so

> We all have the power of words at our disposal.

many changes going on in our lives every single day, so many things we're getting into or growing out of. Talking is a way of touching base, letting our folks know what's happening with us, and to us.

One of the great things about adults is that they were once your age and have gone through some of the same things. It's easy to forget sometimes that our parents have experienced hurt and betrayal at some point in their lives as well. Sure, they didn't have people blogging rumors about them on Facebook, but they had their version of dealing with gossip, lies, and rumors. So if you think you can trust your mother to hear you, talking to her about what's up might be one of the best things you've ever done.

You said it's hard for you to talk to your mom, but you didn't really go into why. Is it because it's difficult to find time in her schedule to sit down and have a serious one-on-one? Or is it because you think she might not get what you're going through? Or could it be that you think her life is too stressful to add anything else to worry about, meaning you? Either way, you should consider letting her know that there are things on your mind you need to share with her. You might just find that in her own way, your mom's also been trying to figure out how to approach you. She may really need to be closer to you and not know how to bridge the gap. Moreover, any relationship can get locked into ruts, habits, and expectations, so talking to your mom about something new that really matters to you from a really honest place could be good for you and her. Even parents want to feel like they matter. So let your mom matter.

Now, I'm not trying to say that if you and your mom sit down and talk, it's gonna turn out like it does on TV where everybody automatically understands each other and major life problems are solved in the course of a half hour. TV shows are scripted, and a lot of us fail to remember that when we start setting our expectations by them. In real life, people aren't always sure they're doing or saying the right things. But that's not the point. The point is to open up and to let the other person in by having an honest exchange, kinda like what you and I are doing.

Sure, I get why you might be hesitant about telling your mom the terrible lies that Caroline has been spreading. But do you think it's going to change the way your mom sees you, or somehow lessen the faith she has in you? I may not know your mom, but I've got a feeling that she's gonna know the principles and values she raised you with, and they're going to shine through in your words. You'll see. She'll believe you. Besides, she was once a Young Sistah. Your mom's not as out of play as you might think. Who knows, maybe talking to your mom will help, like it helped my friend Anisa. What Anisa's mom told her, when she was feeling rejected by her friends, was that rejection is usually God's protection. And she was right.

Beyond speaking with your mom, I'm wondering how *you* plan to handle the situation with Caroline. Friends can serve as mirrors through their actions as well as through their words. When we support a friend's ambition or we inspire a friend to reach higher, we are being a mirror for them. We also serve as mirrors by leading lives that are exemplary of the values and beliefs that our friends want to abide by.

There are times in life when you're going to really need your friends to come through for you. And when some "friends" show you that they are only able to walk with you in fair weather, they save you the trouble and pain of looking to them for shelter during the stormy seasons of life. Anisa's mom told her that her situation was a blessing in disguise because it would give her the chance to find out who her real friends are.

And it's not just rumors or hard times that can show us who our true friends are, nor does it only happen when you are young. It happens throughout your entire life. This week, a friend of mine made an amazing announcement; you probably heard about it, in fact. On Saturday, one of my law school classmates, Senator Barack Obama, announced he planned to run for president of the United States. We all knew he was considering it, but as soon as he made his final decision and his official announcement occurred, I knew I was going to do everything in my power to help him achieve his dream of being president. Friends help friends manifest their destinies. But I also noticed that a lot of so-called friends and colleagues immediately started to criticize his decision by saying things like "He's not ready" or "He's gotten overconfident since he won the Senate." Or even more ludicrous things like "He's not Black enough." I tell this story because I don't want to sugarcoat the reality to you: True friends do hold up your vision of yourself, but at times there will be folks in your life who act like friends but are actually jealous of you. "Haters" will show their true stripes when things are going well for you. Jealousy is usually bred of someone's own insecurities. Does that make sense?

I'm not saying that that's why Caroline started that rumor about you, but it's certainly possible. No matter what her reason, though, when you consider what you are going to do about it, consider what your actions will say about you . . . just like what Caroline's actions say about her. Mahatma Gandhi once said, "You must be the change you wish to see in the world." I couldn't help but take note of the fact that in your letter, the emotions you expressed as the result of Caroline's actions were sadness and pain. Yes, you expressed anger, too, but even that seemed to be centered mainly around your feelings of disappointment in your friend, for spreading the rumors, than any true rage. That says a lot about who you are. Compassion is an essential part of goodness and greatness. God and this universe have given us permission to be great, and our true friends will always reflect the best vision we have of ourselves like a beautiful mirror. But you have to reflect that vision back on them as well. So I hope you choose to reflect a compassionate vision back onto Caroline.

As much as it might seem that Caroline is in need of a good cussin' out or some other form of payback to put her in her place,

> Consider what your actions will say about you.

that's not what *you're* in need of. Revenge is a form of self-destruction. It sabotages every effort we've ever made toward self-improvement and success in our lives. To quote Dr. King, "That old law about 'an eye for an eye' leaves everybody blind. The time is always right to do the right thing." So I want you to do the right thing with Caroline, whatever that is for you.

So when you hear people hatin' on or gossiping about you or someone else, just remember they're attempting to make you feel small in order to make themselves feel big. Instead of feeling down or angry, try to explore compassion for the "hater." Or just ask yourself, what kind of person do I want to be? Am I cool taking people down in order to prop myself up, or can I be a bigger person and work to make people feel good about themselves?

By tutoring your football player friend, you're being in service to someone, and nobody can take that away from you. Hold your head up high every day no matter what people think they know about you. Young Sistah, you are an amazing new perfect model and don't let anybody let you forget that. You've got huge amazing dreams and huge amazing things in your future, so I don't want you letting someone else stop you from moving toward all of the things you've been writing to me about. And don't forget that old saying, "Whatever don't kill you will make you stronger." Kanye sampled that saying for his song "Stronger," but he didn't write it. It's been around since before you, he, and I were even born. Ha-ha.

> You've got amazing things in your future.

And the next time you're in the supermarket aisle and you think about picking up that magazine and reading about Rihanna, Britney, Lindsay, Beyoncé, Angelina, Whitney, or any of the current media darlings, you might want to think again. Except if you're picking it up just to laugh. If that's it, then go on! 'Cause there is nothing wrong with laughin'. I will admit I look and laugh at the "Who Wore It Best" section. I ain't gonna lie!!

Okay. It's getting late here in L.A. This "clear the clutter" date was exactly what I needed to clear my head, and I hope reading this letter has helped you clear yours a bit, too. I'm going to sign off now, but in a few minutes when I get down on my knees to lift it up to the Lord, I'm going to pray that you exercise your God-given strength

to make all of your decisions with purpose and with pride. I'm going to pray that you continue speaking to and about others in truth
and with honor. You are a
magnificent, shining light. So
act accordingly. And will you
please hit me back soon? Oh,

> You are a magnificent,
> shining light.

and keep tutoring and mentoring other kids in your school! You are
doin' the right thing and I am proud of you. And you know what? I
know you will, 'cause you got it like that! Good night.

Much Love,
Hill

Date: February 20, 2007 12:13 AM
From: Young_Sistah@home.net
To: Hill@manifestyourdestiny.org
Subject: Gossip Girls

Hill, how come girls feel the need to have to talk about each other?

Date: February 27, 2007 8:45 PM
From: Hill@manifestyourdestiny.org
To: Young_Sistah@home.net
Subject: Re: Gossip Girls

I decided to go to the source. Did you ever watch the television series *A Different World*? Well, on that show was a beautiful Southern belle, Whitley, who couldn't help herself when it came to pointing out other people's flaws. Well, the actress who played her is the talented artist, writer, and activist Jasmine Guy—who is the exact opposite of her famed television character.

As Jasmine and I were campaigning in Iowa together I shared your e-mail with her.

HH

----------Begin Forwarded Message----------

Even though we know it is hurtful and at times devastating, we still gossip. I have been talked about behind my back and it really burned, especially when the ones talking behind my back smiled in my face. The pain of this deception affects our trust in others and makes us feel bad about ourselves. Boys don't seem to do this to each other. Where they punch or kick, puff up their chests and stomp one another . . . girls lash out at their victims like vicious vipers with evil and nasty words. This is a mean and divisive technique that leaves the victim alienated and isolated. Girls beat up on other girls' self-esteem . . . but why?

I think putting other people down is a way for some girls to feel better about their own lives. When these gossiping girls talk about another person's problems or flaws, it makes them feel bigger than that person. Of course, this is a lie and a false feeling because we are all flawed and we all have problems. By focusing on someone else's issues gossipers do not look at themselves. It is a way to avoid dealing with their own challenges.

It is incredible how girls follow each other even when they know this behavior is bad. They laugh and partake in putting down another girl and don't have the courage not to follow the leading bully. Bullies and bitches are sad, mean people. They have not yet learned the power that lies in respecting others. They have not learned how different their lives could be by embracing what is good in other people. Seeing what is wrong with other people is easy . . . recognizing the good in others may take more effort. It takes inner strength not to follow the crowd and to think for yourself.

Over time I have learned to forgive and dismiss hurtful gossip. But the greatest gift in my life has been the ability to embrace. Embrace all the wonderful women around me who are gifted, talented, beautiful, smart, funny, and brilliant. I celebrate the light within other women and in turn they celebrate mine. Evil forces exist but I believe compassion, understanding, and forgiveness are stronger, more powerful forces. What is important is that you don't let meanness and ignorance poison the fabulousness in you.

Your Friend,
Jasmine Guy

The Parent Trap: You Can Choose Your Friends, but You Can't Choose Your Family

March 19, 2007
Los Angeles

Dear Young Sistah,

Hey. I just got back from Aspen, Colorado . . . visiting my mom. Your letter about being raised by a single mother came at the perfect time. I felt such a connection to you when I read about some of the difficulties you and your mom are going through.

Don't get me wrong, I love my mom, but sometimes it's tough spending time together. To her, I'm always going to be a kid, and if you think that's frustrating at your age, imagine what it's like from where I'm sittin'! No matter how successful I become, or how old, to her I'm still the child she birthed into the world . . . which means she's looking over my shoulder and questioning every decision I make. After a few days of visiting, I'm dying to get back to my life where people treat me like a grown-up. So even though I may have a different relationship with my mother than you do with yours, I can definitely relate.

The first difference is that your mother is raising you, and I spent most of my childhood living with my dad. Not to mention that you're so far ahead of the game having an online social network where you can talk to friends going through similar things. Wow, saying that just reminded me of my pastor, who always says "*growing* through" instead of "*going* through" things. He says that if you're simply going through something and not using it as an opportunity to grow and learn, then you will spend your life going through things. On the other hand, he promises that if you pay attention to the experience you're having and learn from it, then you're growing and you won't have to "go through" it over and over again. It's weird how certain things can trigger memories out of the blue, huh?

Okay. Back to you now. Clearly I'm not a female and I had a different experience from yours when it came to curfews and dating. My father was strict, and he warned me about being careful in the streets when I would hang out with my friends, but I was basically a good kid, so there were a lot of things he didn't have to worry about. All my girlfriends had a different set of rules, too. I don't think it's fair, but now that I'm older and I'm watching these kids who I knew as babies get their driver's licenses, I understand why parents worry.

I'm not siding with your mom, but I don't think it's you that she's worried about. The fact that she yells at you to wear longer skirts or to cover up isn't about her trying to make you look ugly or old-fashioned. When she tells you that she doesn't want you to end up like her, I think that's her way of loving you. Her not wanting you to turn out like her is probably what drives her to be strict and to not allow you as much freedom as your friends. Parents don't always know how to talk to us and tell us that they're just afraid for us.

> Parents don't always know how to talk to us.

I have a friend who grew up with a single mother in a rough section of Philadelphia. Renee had three sisters, and her mother wouldn't let them go anywhere unless she was with them. She said her home felt like prison. But the worst part of it was that her mother was incredibly cold to them. She hardly ever hugged them and she never told them that she loved them. Years later Renee talked to her mother, who admitted that because the streets were so rough she was scared of raising soft girls. Her girls grew up with a desperate need to be loved; one rushed into a bad marriage, one took drugs, and the other, like her mother, had a hard time letting anyone get close. I'm sure if there were a bible on parenting that guaranteed perfect, happy children, your mom would be first in line to buy a copy. Unfortunately, like most parents, she can only do her best, and since you said she had you when she was young, she's probably trying to protect you from some of the mistakes she made.

And then you said something else, and I'm trying to figure out if you said it because you were mad at your mom or because you absolutely meant it. You said that you wouldn't care if the same thing that happened to your mom (having a baby young) happened to you. Were you being for real? Knowing you through our letter exchanges, and hearing you talk about all of your goals and dreams, I gotta believe you were just trying to upset your mom, but either way, it still makes me worry. While you've said that you'd like to have a family of your own someday, would having a baby now really fit in with everything *else* you've talked about that you want to do? Career, travel, the things you've written in your journal that you haven't shared with anyone, not even me?

I'll bet you if you ask your mother, she might tell you about her dreams. The ones she buried in the backyard when she had a child in high school. That is not to say any parent regrets having a child, but I know a lot of them wish they had put it off until they had experienced and explored more of the things they wanted in life.

Did you know that only one out of three teenagers who has a baby graduates from high school? Or that 80 percent of teenage mothers end up on welfare? Between 1991 and 2002 there was a 42-percent decline in African American teenage pregnancy. This means that young Black women are making smarter choices about when to have their babies. Having to take care of children when you're not far from being a child yourself is a huge setback to have while you're still trying to get off the starting blocks. And even when a young guy says he loves you, not many are mature enough to handle the responsibilities of being a teenage father. I have guy friends in their thirties who are still terrified of the idea of being parents. It's a huge amount of pressure and worry.

And no matter how much you love your children, they are expensive. Say you have a summer job this year and you make $6 an hour working forty hours a week. That makes your pay for that week $240 before taxes. If you take out 25 percent for taxes, you'd bring home a paycheck for $180. A box of fifty diapers costs about $25, which might last you a week. You add up all the expenses and rent, gas, electric, phone, clothing, etc. . . . and believe me, you are better off going to college first and making sure you're pulling down better than fifteen cents over minimum wage before taking on a lifetime of responsibility for another person. Yeah, I get that you were mad, but please don't even joke about making decisions that last a lifetime.

I know I mentioned before about talking to your mother. Sometimes it's not that parents don't want to talk, it's just that they don't know how to communicate with their children. Because your generation has things like Facebook, you're learning how to say what you feel to people and still have the safety of not having to say it face-to-face. Maybe you can talk your mother into getting her own Facebook page where you two can communicate? Wouldn't that be great if parents and their children had a Web site where they can say all the things they want without worrying about the other person getting mad or disappointed in them? You'd log on and open your mother/daughter chat room and you could tell your mother all the things that are bothering you. Then you'd each have to separate for a few hours to calmly process everything you've said to each other. Until that happens, maybe you could try writing each other letters, like you and I do.

I would have given anything to have had a way to talk to my father when I was younger. There are so many things about a one-parent household that make it hard. (Though truthfully, there are also some pluses to having only one parent, like when you mess up, they're not able to gang up on you.) But the hard part is that you don't have a second parent to go to when you're having problems with the first parent. I know you said you want to get that second job to take the stress off of your mother, and it's great that you're worrying because it shows that you care. So do her a big favor and don't give her anything more to worry about with regard to this Nasir you've mentioned or any other boy for that matter. Cool? When you're mad at a parent it's normal to want to turn to someone who makes you feel better. My only concern is that you're also really vulnerable and you need comfort and maybe there is an aunt or a girlfriend of your mother who you can talk to.

My friend Renee, who I was telling you about, and her sisters all had different dads because when her mother was a teenager she didn't feel her mother loved her. One of the boys who liked her told her he loved her and she was so desperate to be loved that she wound up getting pregnant. As soon as the guy found out she was pregnant, he took off. Then she met another guy and the same thing happened. Here she was at seventeen, stressed out with two kids with no fathers, and then another guy came along and it happened again. Well, after three kids with three different men, Renee's mother struggled raising her daughters and never dated another man again. This was more than thirty years ago, and this woman gave so much of herself as a teenager that she never trusted love again, when in reality she simply wasn't ready to get into heavy adult relationships. I'm not saying anything like this would ever happen to you, but what I am saying is that sometimes you have to trust your mother. At your age, it's sometimes hard to look at life and imagine that you'll ever feel another way, but I promise you it'll happen. Probably soon.

Maybe it's the thing about girls maturing faster, but when you talk about your father and missing him and feeling you want someone to love you like he did, I am so impressed. No, really, I could never have put that feeling into words like that at your age. Maybe it's a guy thing, but I dealt with my parents' divorce by shutting down and not allowing myself to be open enough to love in that pure way we are born with. After my mother left, my brother and I lived with my father. I thought that I just accepted it and my life went on. Now that I'm older, I can really see how parts of my life stopped when my parents got divorced. I was a kid and I just didn't grasp the reality of suddenly, instead of coming home to both my mother and my father, I was only going to come home to my father. It didn't make it easier that the few friends I had whose parents were divorced all lived with their mothers. Here I was feeling weird because now I lived with just my father. It wasn't like today, when kids live in all kinds of families. I'm talking about living in a conservative neighborhood where this was downright strange. I went from being the golden child in this happy marriage to being a latchkey kid living with my dad and my brother.

At first, I saw my mom regularly, but eventually we moved to another state, and I only saw her on long weekends and holidays. And I just pretended that this new life was normal by shoving all my feelings deep down inside. I knew things weren't easy for my parents as it was, so I never wanted them to see me hurting. Eventually, I got used to pretending to be okay and that's how I stayed, kind of. But now, years later, I look at my life, and while I have a great career, plenty of close friends, and a strong relationship with God, the one area of my life that I can't seem to make work is a romantic relationship. I know this is grown-people business, but I promised you I'd give it to you straight. I guess what I'm trying to say is that if you figure out how to talk to your mother in a way that I couldn't, maybe you'll wind up having a more balanced life. Missing my mother every day when I was your age led me to close myself off. I used to think that if my own mother could leave me when I was a child, how could I ever trust another woman? So don't just ignore your feelings about your father being absent and think that they're going to go away. If you asked me back when I was young how I felt about my mother having to leave, I would have said it didn't bother me, but I can admit now that it wasn't true. My mother was, and still is, a beautiful, successful woman, and all the women I date are, in some ways, versions of her: beautiful and successful. I hope to have that wife and family of my own someday, and believe me, "growing through" to the other side of my issues is something that I'm working on every day.

I know you are capable of great things, and I believe you can use this obstacle you're having with your mother as an opportunity to ultimately build a stronger relationship with her. It'll only make your life better in the short and the long run.

> I know you are capable of great things.

Well, I got to run, but before I go I just want to thank you for all the ways that your honesty helps me to grow and to be a better person. Your mother brought you into this world and she's doing a great job raising you so far, so you have to think she's doing something right. Let's talk soon.

Much Love.
Your Big Brother,
Hill

THE PARENT TRAP

Date: March 25, 2007 12:31 PM
From: Young_Sistah@home.net
To: Hill@manifestyourdestiny.org
Subject: OOOOHH BABY!!

Hill, is it OK to have a kid at a young age?

Date: April 5, 2007 2:34 PM
From: Hill@manifestyourdestiny.org
To: Young_Sistah@home.net
Subject: Re: OOOOHH BABY!!

To be honest, young sister, I have yet to have a child, and since I'm not a parent yet, I don't think I'm the best person to give you sound advice. So instead of me trying to answer this question I'm going to pass this e-mail on to actress, celebrity, and mother of four Shar Jackson. Shar had her first child while in high school and went on to star as Brandy's sidekick Niecy in the hit sitcom *Moesha*. Shar is truly an inspiration to me!

HH

----------Begin Forwarded Message----------

I don't recommend becoming a teenage mom, but seeing how sometimes it's a reality, I think those in that position CAN and WILL definitely make it! You are simply forced to make the best of it! I definitely can't judge anyone for being or becoming a teenage mother, as I was one. But the fact that I was one and still able to accomplish everything that I wanted, in regards to a career and education (I am a successful actress and a college graduate), should at least inspire other girls who find themselves in a similar situation.

Shar Jackson

Date: May 5, 2007 8:32 PM
From: Young_Sistah@home.net
To: Hill@manifestyourdestiny.org
Subject: Make Me Beautiful!

Hill, I want to be attractive! Doesn't everybody? So how can I be attractive?

Date: May 11, 2007 3:23 PM
From: Hill@manifestyourdestiny.org
To: Young_Sistah@home.net
Subject: Re: Make Me Beautiful!

C'mon, you know what I think about this—I believe true "attractive qualities" come from within. But I also know that an answer like that is not necessarily what you want to hear; so I decided to have another young sister, Chanel Iman, a teenage runway sensation and top teen fashion model, answer you directly. Chanel has appeared on the cover of *Vogue*, *Teen Vogue*, and *CosmoGIRL!* and inside hundreds of magazines as well as many advertising campaigns, including one for Gap. She is perhaps the #1 teen model in the world. Not only is she an amazing model, she also has a good head on her shoulders.

HH

----------Begin Forwarded Message----------

Being attractive is not about how much makeup you wear or how fly you think you have to look. To me, being attractive is about glowing. I mean being happy from within because you are free to be yourself. On the runway I put on many faces and wear fashions that are as far from my personality as you can get, but I try to put a little bit of myself in my walk and my attitude so that I not only try to sell the collection, I also sell myself as a confident and attractive model.

My mom always taught me "always put on your best and live your life in style." That's what I try to do. I'm talking about your best being a good and positive attitude and style being class!

I see many young ladies with really bad attitudes and thinking negatively all of the time. That's neither attractive nor does it set you up for happiness or success. There's good in everything if you just take a minute extra to see it. Think positive, have a good attitude, be yourself, and when you look in the mirror you will see how much you shine and how absolutely attractive you are.

Chanel Iman

R.E.S.P.E.C.T.:
How a Boy Should
Treat You

> Boys frustrate me. I hate all their indirect messages, I hate game playing. Do you like me or don't you? Just tell me so I can get over you.
>
> **Kirsten Dunst**

May 19, 2007
Los Angeles

Dear Young Sistah,

Let me get this straight. You want me to give you the "guys' point of view" on the rules of dating? Hmmm . . . I don't know about the "guys' point of view." I can give you *my* perspective, which I'm sure is representative of the opinions and beliefs of some men but definitely not all of them. Even though it may not always seem that way, men (like women) are as individual and unique in our opinions as we are in most everything else. At least, that's what we like to tell ourselves!

Dating is one of the most dazzling—and dizzying—dances that two people can do. Have you ever heard the saying "Opposites attract"? I doubt that's always the case, but the saying itself is a testament to the unpredictable nature of our emotions when we're dating or involved with other people.

The amazing poet Nikki Giovanni wrote: "We love because it's the only true adventure." Dating is, you could say, the beginning of that adventure. The purpose of rules is to regulate behavior. How we choose to demonstrate the emotions that we have toward the people we choose to date is part of "the workings of the human heart," and the reason it's "the profoundest mystery" is that there are very few rules that *can* regulate it.

As far as I'm concerned, when it comes to dating there is only one real rule, and it supersedes all the other so-called rules. That rule can be summed up in a single word: respect. It's the end-all and be-all. Without respect, dating has more to do with controlling other people than it does with caring for them. The things you mentioned in your letter—like who should pay for the date, whether a guy should open doors and pull out chairs for you, whether he should ask before he tries to kiss you—they're not really governed by rules. Those things are personal preferences, stuff that can be modified or altogether changed, depending on the situation.

Let me break it down another way. You wanted me to tell you what the rule is when it comes to paying for a date. People assume that when a man and woman go out on a date, the man should be the one to pick up the tab, no matter what. That arrangement suits a whole lot of people, both men and women, just fine—but not everybody. Just a few weeks ago, I went out on a date with a woman whom I'd always found interesting and wanted the opportunity to get to know better. I was the one who asked her out, and I was the one who chose the restaurant, so I naturally thought that I should be the one to pay. When the waiter brought the check, she snatched it up before I even had a chance to look at it. She insisted on paying. We went back and forth for a little while and then finally I gave in and agreed to let her handle the bill. Why? Because I wanted to respect her wishes. Incidentally, my initial offer to pay was also made as a show of respect.

Both you and I have written about respect before in our letters, but I really feel the need, with this subject, to break it down. When I say the word *respect,* especially in relation to the boys and young men in your life, I'm referring to the behavior and language that somebody uses to show that they hold you in high esteem. It's when somebody speaks and acts in a way that says they accept, acknowledge, honor, and value your humanity. So this means that anything they do with or to you will be an indication of the respect they have for you.

My initial offer to pay for my date was made as a show of my respect, not as an obligation of my gender. Back in the day, people assumed it was a man's responsibility to pay for everything because most women didn't earn their own money or, if they did, the man had a higher income. In those times, women were financially dependent on the men in their lives, and that sometimes placed these women in potentially exploitive situations.

A number of my female friends have told me of times when they have agreed to go out on a dinner date only to find out the guy actually believed that paying for their meal meant that they should go home with him. A few of the women reluctantly gave in to that expectation because they felt they didn't have any other choice.

Crystal Jefferson is one of those female friends. Every time she and I would talk, Crystal seemed so bitter about dating. She really wanted to have somebody special in her life, but she was suspicious of everyone who asked her out. More than that, she was suspicious of men in general. She felt that their kindness was usually inspired by an ulterior motive.

I remember once, several years ago, I mentioned to Crystal that I'd bought a gift for the woman I was seeing and that I was planning on giving it to her during our date later that evening. Crystal said, under her breath, "And what's she supposed to give you in return?" I was stunned. I had never given Crystal, or any of my friends, any cause to believe that I was the sort of person who gave to get. I asked Crystal why she would say something like that.

"It seems like you all are only nice when you want something," she explained. "Who's you all?" I asked, trying to make a point. I don't remember what Crystal said, but she didn't answer right then, and soon I had to leave for my date.

The next time Crystal and I caught up, I asked her what that was all about. Turns out, she'd had some bad experiences. One time this guy she was out with wanted her to come back to his place. He'd treated her like a princess the entire evening. He'd picked her up, given her a flower, taken her to a fancy restaurant, told her she was pretty, and that he was falling for her. He was a colleague at her job—her first job out of college—and she'd had a crush on him since day one. And yeah, they'd said hi and bye every day in the hallways and elevators. Still, she didn't feel she knew him, really knew him, at all.

The idea of going back to this man's place with him, even if it was only for a little while like he'd promised, set off Crystal's alarm bells. It made her think of the many "date rape" lectures and "no means no" seminars she'd had to sit through during high school and college. Deep down, she knew that she had no business going over to his house, and she didn't really want to go anyway. The only reason she eventually agreed to go was because he was persistent. He wouldn't let up. He said they wouldn't stay long, he just wanted her to know where he lived, and he wanted to show her some of his books and CDs and stuff.

As soon as Crystal got inside his apartment, all of those promises he'd made went straight out the window. The guy pounced on her, started kissing her, feeling her up, and trying to take off her clothes. For Crystal, it was too much, happening too quickly. She refused his advances, politely at first, but that didn't work. He kept on. Finally, she had to put her foot down, raise her voice, and be real firm about it. That's when he cussed her out, accused her of teasing him and leading him on. "How?" she wanted to know.

"All of that money you made me spend on you tonight," he told her, "just so you could say no? Don't try to play me for a fool. I know you know that ain't how it works." Crystal felt terrible. She was also confused. Had she led him on? How could he have gone from being such a gentleman to being such a mean and nasty person? He wouldn't even drive her home or call a cab for her. She had to walk the three blocks to the main road to hail one (and use her "mad money" to pay for it). By the time she got in, it was almost midnight.

Crystal had a handful of stories about incidents just like that one. Each one was proof positive of her theory that almost all men were out to get something, and the few who weren't, the good guys, ended up with girls who were a lot luckier, or prettier, or smarter, or sexier than her. In any case, Crystal—who, for the record, earns an impressive salary as a graphic designer and is plenty smart and sexy—decided that the best way to avoid any future situations like the ones she'd had was to pay whenever she went out. That way, she'd always be in control, and no man would ever again be able put her in a position of powerlessness or use money to try to manipulate her.

These days, more and more women are financially independent. With that comes the freedom of choice. Some women, like Crystal or the woman I recently went on a date with, will choose to pay. Other women won't. There's nothing wrong with either option, or any of the other choices in between the two. Whatever works for the two people who are out on the date. To be honest, I'm not sure who's going to end up paying the next time I go out with that woman, but we'll discuss it and find a solution that works for us. Obviously, paying for dinner does not entitle someone to anything except the pleasure of the other person's company during the meal. To many people, having the money means holding the cards. It can give rise to a false sense of power. Folks start trippin' and think that if they're forking over their money, it means the other person needs to give them something to make it come out equal. Respect is what tells us we are not being controlled or manipulated by another person and that what we say and how we feel actually matter to them.

The famous English critic Cyril Connolly wrote, "The friendships which last are those wherein each friend respects the other's dignity to the point of not really wanting anything from him." Had the guy who took Crystal out truly respected her, he wouldn't have done any of the things he did to her, from pressuring her to go home with him, to touching her inappropriately or making her find her own way home. That's not the way you treat somebody you respect.

Crystal was shocked to learn that some of the guys she'd dated had only pretended to be nice and generous. I'm sure, though, that there were signs, "red flags" pointing to that person's real personality. For instance, do you ever meet a person who is really nice to you but you've seen them be mean to waiters in restaurants or service people? People who they believe are below them in some way? This is what I refer to as a "red flag" because one day that person will wind up treating you the same way. People announce themselves from the very beginning. They tell us who they really are. It's in the things they say and the things they do, but we often dismiss these signs because we're so invested in the images and ideas we've created in our own minds.

Even in the story Crystal told me, there were several signs pointing to the behavior she was met with later that night. Were you able to recognize any of them in my retelling of Crystal's story? One of the main signs was the guy's complete disregard of Crystal's growing discomfort. Most of us can sense when we are doing something that is making another person uncomfortable. Though Crystal had flatly said no, and she'd been openly hesitant about going to his house, he kept pushing anyway.

Crystal confided something else to me about her interaction with that guy, something that also could have been seen as a sign. During the brief conversations and flirtations that they'd had before going on that date, he'd made comments about her body that were too direct, too crass. He'd said things like, "Look at that big ole booty you got on you" and "Mmm, can I have some of that?"

Comments like that made Crystal feel awkward and uncomfortable, but she liked this guy and she didn't want to be "bitchy" or do anything that would make him not like her back. She was willing, then, to accept that sort of flirtation even though it was not in keeping with the standards that she'd set for herself. The standards we set for ourselves are the barometers other people use to gauge our sense of self-worth. And like it or not, people will usually attract who and what they feel they deserve.

If you conduct yourself in a way that suggests you don't feel you're worthy of respect, it will invite a certain kind of person into your life. It's like when you see a young sister dressed with all her stuff hanging out. You don't need me to tell you that if you dress in a way that shows you respect your body, men won't come at you in the same way they will if you walk around half dressed. Now, that may not be right, but it's real.

You shouldn't ever disregard your self-respect because you're afraid some guy won't like you. If he decides he doesn't like you simply because you tell him to treat you respectfully, then I don't care how nice or cute or funny or charming he seems—he's not. He's told you in no uncertain terms that at some point he plans to treat you badly. The best thing to do in this case is to keep moving. Show him that you have set a higher standard for yourself and then . . . "See ya, wouldn't want to be ya."

Okay, I'm gonna get a little philosophical with you for a minute, but bear with me 'cause I think it's worth it. Dr. Albert Schweitzer was an Alsatian philosopher and the recipient of the 1952 Nobel Peace Prize. Extremely smart dude, and he was quoted as saying, "Only those who respect the personality of others can be of real use to them."

What do you think Dr. Schweitzer meant by "real use"? I wondered about that the first time I read the quote because it seemed like an odd choice of words. I mean, I wouldn't want to think that somebody was using me, especially somebody whom I respected. But there is a difference between use, misuse, and abuse. What I came up with is that the people in your life who are of real use to you are the people who inspire you to grow, encourage you to be more, not less, of the brilliant, dynamic, unique individual you are. When someone is of use to you, they are a positive addition to your life. To be of "real use," then, is to enhance somebody's life in practical and direct ways.

A couple of the situations you wrote of, some of the things you've observed with your friends, are examples of how a lack of respect can actually lead to abuse. You can ask the following question about anyone in your life: Does that person add to your life or drain energy out of it? For instance, the way your friend Jessica's boyfriend talks to her—telling her to shut up, purposely cutting her off midsentence in a way that makes it clear he has no interest in what she's saying, and making fun of the things she does say—is offensive and demeaning. The reason it makes you so uncomfortable is that you recognize it for what it is, verbal abuse. Jessica might brush it off and tell you that he doesn't mean it because she doesn't think she *is* worth listening to, or for some other reason. But that doesn't make either his behavior, or the fact that she allows and accepts it, a good thing.

I have a confession to make: It did not, sadly enough, surprise me to read in your letter about the many female students in your school who you suspect are being physically abused by their boyfriends. There is a high rate of physical and sexual violence among young sisters. Abuse does not always happen in the ways we are made to think it does from watching television and movies. I know that a lot of schools educate young sisters and brothers about date rape, so there is an increased awareness of it. What is still being talked about in whispers, though, if it's talked about at all, is habitual abuse. Like when a young sister's boyfriend is punching or slapping her around or, worse, intimidating her into doing things she is not ready to do. Maybe he's controlling what she wears or who she is able to hang out with. A lot of this type of abuse goes undetected, mainly because the young sisters are too scared or ashamed to tell anyone. When others do find out, they have a tendency to ask, like you did in your letter, "Why is she putting up with that?"

The reasons why people find themselves in those circumstances are many and varied. When we start trying to guess at the reasons why some young women end up in such situations, we can sound as though we're blaming the victim of abuse for the abuse that she has suffered, almost suggesting that she brought it on herself. I don't want to do that, or encourage you to do it.

When it comes to dating, always be on the lookout for those red flags, or your intuitive signs that tell you what you need to know about who a person really is, as opposed to what they want you to see. When we first meet people, we usually put our best foot forward, but as we get to know someone we start to relax, and that's when our flaws and issues show up. Look, we all have flaws and issues, and that's part of what makes us human, but the real question is, are these issues dangerous? Are we mean or cheap or controlling or abusive? I have a friend, Mena, who married a guy we all thought was great. He couldn't have been any nicer . . . except we all started to notice that she never went anywhere alone anymore. At first, we thought it was because they were in love. But then we realized that on the rare occasions we saw her when he wasn't around, he would text and call her every few minutes. Mena thought that all his concern meant he cared, but what she saw as caring was a giant red flag. He was a control freak, and when she started to take back her independence, he freaked out on her. Needless to say, they are no longer together, but she failed to take those red flags seriously and now she wishes she had.

> You have choices when it comes to how people treat you.

Remember that you always have choices, especially when it comes to how people treat you. Speaking of which, there are lots of resources and support networks available to people like your friend Jessica who want to get out of abusive situations. Let me know if you want a list of those places so you can pass the info on to your friends who might need it.

Oh, and I have a date tonight, a really intelligent and beautiful sister named Nichole. Fingers crossed!

Stay safe, you. And write me back soon, okay?

Much Love,
Hill

Date: May 30, 2007 1:19 PM
From: Young_Sistah@home.net
To: Hill@manifestyourdestiny.org
Subject: Boys, Boys, Boys . . .

Hill, what should I look for in a boy I want to date?

Date: June 15, 2007 6:52 PM
From: Hill@manifestyourdestiny.org
To: Young_Sistah@home.net
Subject: Re: Boys, Boys, Boys . . .

I sent your question to one of my great friends, who is a mother and a fantastic actress, Nia Long (yeah, the beautiful sistah from *Boyz n the Hood, Big Momma's House,* and *Alfie*). She's always given me great advice, so I truly trust her to do the same for you.

HH

----------Begin Forwarded Message----------

What should you look for in a boy you want to date? I think friendship is the key to all healthy relationships. Spending quality time together, sharing common interests, and having clean fun is essential. Learning to love one another through a budding friendship is key. If a boy is pressuring you for sex, he's not the one for you. There is plenty of time for sex. Sex is not love! Developing a great friendship will be more valuable in the long run. Everybody needs a good friend.

With Love,
Nia Long

Date: June 23, 2007 2:26 PM
From: Young_Sistah@home.net
To: Hill@manifestyourdestiny.org
Subject: Dating My BGF

Hill, I think I have a crush on my best guy friend. Is that weird?

Date: July 2, 2007 9:20 AM
From: Hill@manifestyourdestiny.org
To: Young_Sistah@home.net
Subject: Re: Dating My BGF

It's totally natural to develop a crush—especially your first big crush—on someone you're friends with or have known really well for a long time.

I think you falling for your friend is a sign that you are a healthy young woman. You didn't develop a big crush on someone who makes you feel bad about yourself, who doesn't get you or doesn't care about you. The first person you decided to like in that "boy meets girl" kind of way is (your words) "your biggest fan." So when you really think about it, it's fantastic that you think so highly of yourself. There's nothing wrong with having a crush, and a lot of the time it can be a lot of fun to feel that way.

Friendship is the basis of everything. It's the first and most impor-tant step to every lasting relationship. We often fall for people not because we're really in love with them but because we like the way they make us feel about ourselves. If that's the way you feel about your BGF, then I think that's great!

Does he accept and respect you for who you really are? Does he allow you to be your true self no matter what? When you think about one person who always makes you feel good about being you, does it happen to be him? If the answer to all those is Yes, then I say "Cool"!

HH

Okay, okay . . . so I sent your e-mail to Kim Porter (one of my costars from *Mama, I Want to Sing!*). She's a model, actress, and proud mother who understands relationships between men and women very well! She will definitely give you an alternative point of view.

----------Begin Forwarded Message----------

I don't think it's weird at all to have a crush on your best guy friend. I have found myself in this situation a few times. Obviously, he's your best guy friend for a reason! He possesses those qualities that you are attracted to (i.e., great personality, smart, sensitive, loyal, caring, etc.). So the attraction is apparent and makes sense!

Crushes are good because they are innocent!!!! HOWEVER, I don't advise crossing the line between best friends, because it will indeed jeopardize the friendship. Once those lines are crossed, then things will never be the same. If you are willing to take that risk, then GO FOR IT!

Kim Porter

LETTER 9

The Taboo Topic: SEX

[Don't even try it. . . . I'm not giving you a quote on this one!]

July 6, 2007
New Orleans

Dear Young Sistah,

In your last letter you asked me about sex. Wow! I really feel like a big brother for you to trust me with this conversation. I've been pacing all up and down the floor of my new loft space. It's all wide open without many doors or partitions. So, picture this large room, with big windows, that runs the length of a large building . . . and me walking a hole in my carpet with all this pacing up and down. Well, actually I don't have a carpet, it's a hardwood floor, but you know what I mean. . . . (Man, I haven't even started talking about this stuff, and already it's got me all discombobulated!)

You really want to talk about sex? Now I know I said you could ask me *anything*. Somehow I pictured you being older when this conversation came up, but I guess that would be naïve of me in today's evolving fast-paced world. Maybe I just pictured me being older when this conversation came up! Either way, things are happening so fast in technology, why wouldn't that spill over to other areas in your life? Or maybe it's also the impact of the media, television, videos, magazines, and Internet that constantly shoves images of sex at young people and makes them believe they need to do it in order to feel current.

Okay, instead of me staying all up in my head and worrying if I'm going to be able to really help you or have a positive impact on your life in this area, why don't I just answer your questions? I do want you to know that it's not the easiest or simplest subject for me, but it probably wasn't the easiest or simplest subject for you to ask about either . . . and it's definitely something we should talk about. I'm going to be completely honest, but I need you to know that my only hesitation comes because you are my *Young* Sistah and not one of my *grown* surrogate sisters.

There is one thing I'd like to know before we really get into this, though. Are you asking me questions about sex because you're considering having it, or are you asking me because you don't have anyone else to ask and you just want some information? Why is that question important? It's not so much for the answers I'm going to give but more for me to get a sense of where you're at. But no matter where that is, I'm glad you wrote and asked me my advice, "Young Sistah to Big Brotha."

Remember what I said about there being no coincidences? I think part of the reason I'm so nervous writing to you now is because the same day your letter arrived asking me about sex, a friend of mine called and asked me have a talk with her daughter, Kiana, whom I've known since she was a baby. She told me they were having some very serious communication problems, and she knew that Kiana felt comfortable talking to me. She warned me, though, that there was something very serious I needed to talk to her about—her daughter was thirteen years old and had gotten pregnant. I had to stop right there and take a deep breath because I really was about to wear a hole in my imaginary carpet. THIRTEEN! She was still a baby to me. Ever since I had known her, we would laugh, and kid around, and joke together, and now she was going to have a kid of her own? To be totally honest, heading out to the park where we were going to meet, I was scared. Well, I guess *afraid* is a better word. I was afraid because I didn't know what was going on in her head. I had looked for some more information on this Web site called TeenPregnancy.org, where I found statistics like: Only about 2 percent of teen mothers have a college degree by age thirty. That didn't make me any less afraid for her, but it did help me put that fear aside. I knew having an adult she could talk to would be really important, now more than ever.

As soon as I saw her sitting on that bench, waiting for me, all I wanted to do was to give her a hug, tell her everything was going to be okay, that there is a way to handle every so-called obstacle that life presents. As we sat together I could see her small body trembling in fear; I knew it was fear because it wasn't cold outside. We talked, and we also just sat in silence sometimes, neither of us knowing where the conversation would take us next. But finally it came, perhaps the most honest moment we have ever shared. I asked her why, at such a young age, did she think she needed to have sex? After a long pause she looked me dead in my eyes, and her eyes began to well up with tears and she said, "I just wanted someone to love me."

And in that instant I felt responsible for her pain because somehow the adults in her life, me included, had failed her. She had always been close to her mother, who would work two jobs to make sure that Kiana had every advantage, and I knew she was aware how much her mother loved her. I started thinking, trying to read between the lines of what she wasn't saying. Clearly she had plenty of other women in her life: aunts, cousins, a grandmother who were all devoted to her. But where were the men? Her father was not around to love her in the way that she needed to be loved. He wasn't there to validate her and let her know how important and unique she was. So she sought out someone who she thought would provide male love and attention. Chances are he was probably the first boy who told her that she was incredible and lovable. Now her entire future was at stake because of choices she made before she was ready for the consequences.

I know that the questions you're asking are nowhere near what Kiana is going through. I don't want you to think that I'm telling you this story to lump you two together. I am clear that you are not where Kiana is and that you're making healthy choices and that's good. I like that you're exactly where you need to be and you're not rushing down any roads you aren't ready to be on.

There is definitely value in developing a long-term relationship, and it sounds like you have a best friend in Nasir. He knows you well and you trust him, and you feel valued in the relationship. In your letter, you said that some of your friends said, "Girl, you've made him wait long enough . . . if you don't do it with him now, you're going to lose him." First of all, talk about someone else projecting their fears and insecurities on you! Whenever anyone is telling you what to do, rather than asking you questions about what *you want* to do, ask yourself: Is this person truly a friend looking out for my best interest, or is she for whatever reason attempting to coerce me into taking the action she wants to see me take? Throughout your life, I want you to take actions that *you* want to take. There is no such thing as "making someone wait too long" in any area of life. If there is something that you do not want to do or some action that you are not ready to take, it's no one else's business but yours. And that's in terms of sex, relationships, career, children, investments, purchases, everything.

You did mention that Nasir has started to hint around about the topic of sex, but he's "being sweet about it" and not putting any pressure on you. I'm glad to hear that. I know that even if he did, you would have the inner strength not to let him talk you into anything you aren't ready for.

And one more thing, and this is really hard for me to say: There are a lot of women and girls who, because they have had issues with their fathers perhaps not being around or loving them in the way that they should, they have made mistakes in attempting to "please men" to get them to love them. And hear me when I say this: *Having sex with a man will not make him love you.* In fact, it might have the opposite effect. In the magazines and on talk shows, they say that women and girls who exhibit this behavior might have "daddy issues." We can talk more about that later if you want to, but since you asked about sex, I want to make sure that you know that you should *never*, under any circumstances whatsoever, feel or think that you have to have sex with a guy to keep him around or to make him love you. If a man truly loves you, he does so without placing conditions on that love, *any* conditions. If any boy or man ever makes you feel you have to have sex with him for him to love you, or to prove you love him, he just proved that he's not worth loving. And that is someone I don't want you to be around, because he is not loving you the way you deserve to be loved.

You are beautiful, magnificent, brilliant, and a gift to this world. You are "the newest perfect model" of the human species and you deserve to be treated magnificently . . . with love, respect, and admiration. You deserve that and should always require it.

> You deserve to be treated magnificently.

Never, ever think of yourself as *less than*. So as you read this, right now know that you are *more than* enough.

Okay, my ride to the set just got here, so I've gotta go. But that does remind me of one more thing. You mentioned that you and Nasir went to the movies and he made a "romantic" comment about one of the love scenes that was in the movie you saw. Well, those sex scenes you see in the movies? Not real. Not even a little bit. Think about it. They're filmed under these bright lights in front of a huge crew of people, and then a dozen different shots are all edited together months later to make the final scene. Sex in movies is about looking good, not being real. So don't be fooled. Real sex in real life comes with real consequences—that you never see in the movies. And as a woman, you bear the brunt of a lot of those consequences. I know I probably haven't had time to address even half your questions, so write me back soon, and we'll talk some more. Okay?? Have a good night, my friend.

I look forward to your response. Until then—SMILE!

Much Love,
Hill

P.S. I'm gonna go see Beyoncé perform tonight at the Essence Music Festival. Front-row seats and backstage passes! I know you have a massive collection of concert ticket stubs; I'll save mine for you.

Date: July 17, 2007 1:27 PM
From: Young_Sistah@home.net
To: Hill@manifestyourdestiny.org
Subject: No Hook-Up/Hurt Feelings

Hill, if I don't want to do "anything" with a boy but just be friends with him and he wants more, how do I tell him No without breaking his heart?

Date: July 20, 2007 5:17 PM
From: Hill@manifestyourdestiny.org
To: Young_Sistah@home.net
Subject: Re: No Hook-Up/Hurt Feelings

That's a typical male mind trick. To be blunt, not having sex does not break hearts! You should not do anything that you do not want to do. His broken heart (and believe me, his heart will not be broken) is NOT YOUR CONCERN! Your concern is YOUR heart and YOUR body. Do not allow any man, or anyone for that matter, to manipulate you into doing something that you do not want to do. You have the right to choose what you want to do with your body!

I wanted my good friend, Blair Underwood, to add his thoughts regarding this question. We costarred on a television series, *City of Angels.* Blair is not only an award-winning actor, he's also a successful coauthor of *Casanegra: A Tennyson Hardwick Novel*, and a producer and director. The brother is Bad!

I have so much respect for him and admire how he respects and treats women. Considered a sex symbol (named one of *People* Magazine's Sexiest Men Alive) he still maintains an incredibly stable and happy family in "Hollyweird." He considers women "queens" of the earth and calls them such—he is someone who can teach us all a thing or two about the proper way to treat a woman.

HH

---------Begin Forwarded Message----------

Dear Young Sister,

Don't worry about breaking his heart, sweetheart. Your body is a gift from God that has been entrusted to you to protect and take care of AND for you to share with, ultimately, the one that God has chosen for you. To determine who that "boy" is will take time and a great deal of trust. Don't rush into anything, and trust your instincts.

If he doesn't respect you enough to understand how you feel and not pressure you, then he definitely is NOT the right one. Also, watch out for the "game" that some boys will try to run on you. For you to ask this question, it is very evident to me that you have a huge heart and you are able to empathize with others.

Some "boys" will take advantage of that and pretend to have their hearts broken when they're actually focused on becoming more intimate with you. Stay true to your beliefs and he'll respect you more for it. If he doesn't, he's not worth the trouble.

Blair Underwood

Date: August 8, 2007 5:18 PM
From: Young_Sistah@home.net
To: Hill@manifestyourdestiny.org
Subject: The Dating Game

Hill, how do you get a boy to like you if he doesn't?

Date: August 15, 2007 3:12 PM
From: Hill@manifestyourdestiny.org
To: Young_Sistah@home.net
Subject: Re: The Dating Game

I want you to focus on being (and putting) yourself first and foremost. And as long as you do that, then the boys who are truly attracted to your authentic "you" will come. You should never "change" who you are in order to receive the attention of a boy. You are an amazing, magnificent, and beautiful young woman with a huge future in front of you. Any boy worth having would recognize your qualities from the jump—if he doesn't, then move on.

But that's just this boy's opinion. There is a friend of mine who is liked by almost every boy she meets, so I'm going to forward your question to her so you can get her "expert" opinion. You probably know her from movies like *ATL, This Christmas*, and on the television shows *Entourage* and *Everybody Hates Chris*. And I also want you to compare her answers to a young man's opinion. So I asked one of the hottest young actors in Hollywood to respond to you. Evan starred in *Pride, Life Support* with Queen Latifah, and much more! He also knows a thing (or two) about women, especially given the strong, positive women he is surrounded by on a daily basis—his mother, the Majesty herself, Diana Ross, and his sister, star of *Girlfriends*, Tracee Ellis Ross. He can definitely add his two cents.

Let's see if they have different answers!

HH

```
----------Begin Forwarded Message----------
```

Dear Young Sistah,

I am a true believer in the power of self. And without self-love
there's no self-confidence. Without self-confidence there's no
respect. When dealing with matters of the heart, being yourself is
all that anyone can truly do to win the affections of a boy you're
interested in. And if he's truly worth it u can take it 1 major step
further . . . by being your "best" self. That's a rare gift that someone
gives another person. In the end—leave it to the universe. If he
accepts you for who you are . . . u will be respected at least as
a human being, as a friend, and maybe even more. (And who's
to say . . . maybe he's simply shy).

Lauren London

```
----------Begin Forwarded Message----------
```

That's hard. But it's definitely not to keep trying. I think it's more to
let go and see how time can change his liking you when he doesn't
know he can have you. We want what we think we can't have. Boys
want a girl to be her own person. For the girl to have her own thing
going. It's sexy and we end up wanting the girl more 'cause she is
less available to us, 'cause she is doing her own thing. So we can't
ever get enough. Because as bad as it sounds, we get bored when
it's just there.

Evan Ross

LETTER 10

Sex, Lies, and Texting: The Lies Boys Tell

Honesty is probably the sexiest thing a man can give a woman.

Debra Messing

September 10, 2007
Santa Barbara

Dear Young Sistah,

It took you a little while to write me back and now I'm the one lagging. Sorry, but I have been swamped preparing for this weekend. You'll never guess where I have been. You remember I told you earlier that I'm on the National Finance Committee for the Obama campaign? Well, we held an amazing event in Santa Barbara yesterday . . . at Oprah's house! I had to keep pinching myself, saying, "Wow, I'm at Oprah's house. Oprah lives here."

The dinner was amazing. It was outdoors and there were two long tables and in front of each seat was a name card. I was seated next to Gayle King, who I had never had the chance to really just talk with at length before, and let me tell you, I love me some Gayle King! It is a night that I will never forget. I'm still on cloud nine!

As much as Oprah is this very humble person who is totally genuine about her desire to give and to be of service to others, when you are standing next to her, you are completely aware that you are in the presence of greatness. Everything about her resonates truth, compassion, and also a lot of fun. But more than anything, she's a truth sayer. She always tells the truth and she has incredible integrity. Reading your letter made me think of Oprah, asking myself, "How would Oprah answer these questions?" And you know what I decided? Oprah would tell it to you honestly.

You asked about the things guys say and how much you can and should trust guys when they tell you certain things. Here's the deal. And here's a big statement that I'm going to make that is probably going to get me into trouble. But I promise you, it is true: *All guys will at some point in their lives lie for sex.*

Now I know this is a very broad, sweeping statement, but take it from me, a guy with a lot of guy friends, it's true. And yes, maybe the word *lie* is a little harsh. We could call it "stretching the truth" or "exaggerating" or "falsely implying"—but at the end of the day, it's lying to a girl for sex. Men mislead women in the area of sex all the time. I'm not proud to say that I, my friends, and even some of the greatest leaders in history have done and said things that we later realized misled a woman about our true intentions. I'm not really talking about brothers who are conscious, purposeful liars. You know I don't think you should waste your time with anyone who's just using you for sex. But when a feeling overwhelms a person, he might say something that is not what he truly feels. Sometimes a boy's hormones can lead him to say words like "I love you" without really understanding the impact those three simple words can have. It's almost as if the boy's hormones justify it in his mind. I want you to cultivate the self-confidence and intuitive ability to be able to know when a boy is misleading you versus when he is telling the truth. Yes, even when he can't tell the difference himself! But even if he is telling the truth, and your intuition tells you that he *does* love you, that still doesn't mean that you have to take any physical action with him. This is important, so I will say it again: Just because Nasir "likes" or "loves" *you* doesn't mean you have to be physical with *him.* Even if *you* "like" or "love" *him*, it doesn't mean you need to be physical with him.

In your letter, you told me that Nasir texted you:

"u r my #1 & only, i luv u so much . . . & if u luv me 2, u wld do it wit me."

Now, I'm not saying that Nasir is lying about loving you. I'm sure he does love you in the way he's defining it at this point in his life. But he is lying to you and misleading you by saying that if you loved him, you would hook up with him. Any boy or man who truly loves you the way you deserve to be loved will never ever truthfully say, "If you loved me, you would do _____." That is putting a condition on your love, just as I talked about in my last letter. It's a lie, it's misleading, and it's wrong, and I'm glad you said you called him on it. I also think you have good instincts when you tell me, "He said he didn't mean to do that, but I don't think he's that dumb."

Wow, did you nail that one on the head. Another one of the biggest lies that we men use is to pretend that we don't see the same things that you see. Men do this to women not just in relationships but also in the workplace, at school, in almost any environment where we think it might work to our advantage. What do I mean by that? Guys will often *act* oblivious. For instance, when you tell them your view of something, a classic guy move is to pretend we have no idea, when all along we may have known how you felt about or viewed that particular situation. Here's another example, and I'm not proud to admit it, but I have done this exact thing. Let's say a guy you're dating is attracted to another girl. So the guy will hang out with this other girl one-on-one but tell you, as Biz Markie says, "She's only just a friend." Yeah, if they'd known each other for years before you came on the scene, I might buy it. But, as a guy, I can tell you that a good nine times out of ten (unless she's his mandatory lab partner), if your intuition is telling you that a new so-called friend is more than that—whether you want to admit it to yourself or not—you're probably right.

I'm not saying that guys are lying all the time; you can trust a lot of what a guy says, but what I need you to be able to do is to *really* trust that intuitive voice *you* have inside *your* head. Because the problem for most of us isn't in the information, it's in our reactions. The late great singer Aaliyah had a perfect song about this called "Read Between the Lines" on her self-titled album. In that song, she sang, "Lies are gettin' told, look in his eyes, gotta read between the lines."

Usually, we can tell when someone is lying to us or not treating us the way we deserve to be treated, but we just as often ignore our intuition because we really want to believe that other person is truthful. Especially if we like them or are attracted to them. It happens to all of us.

A few years ago, I went away to Toronto to shoot the movie *The Skulls*. I was going to be gone for at least three months. I also had a girlfriend in L.A. at that time who I was so "in love" with. After I got to Toronto, I missed her so much that I wanted to see her as soon as I could, so I invited her to come up and visit. She said she didn't want to come. Then, after a couple weeks, she started accusing me of having an affair. I was *so* confused . . . she didn't want to come visit me in Toronto, and now she was picking fights on the phone, claiming that I was having an affair? My intuition was working overtime, telling me something was wrong, but I completely ignored it. After finishing the movie and returning to Los Angeles, the truth (that deep inside I already knew) came out. She had met someone else, was cheating on me, and to assuage her guilt, told herself that *I* must be cheating on *her* up in Toronto. The karmic irony of this whole story is that I *had* cheated on a girl I had dated before, but with this girl I didn't have even the slightest interest in looking at another woman. But, like Timbaland and Justin Timberlake say, "What goes around comes back around." It's really true. As we walk through this journey, we *must* treat people the way we would like to be treated. *And* have enough clarity and confidence to be able to listen to and act on our intuition.

This may sound stupidly obvious, but I have to say this once again: Just because a boy wants to have sex with you doesn't mean you should feel you have to have sex with him. I was nineteen years old and a sophomore in college when I lost my virginity. During high school there were numerous times that I could have had sex, but I chose not to, because I wasn't ready. But no matter how old you are, you can still make mistakes in the area of sex. I've made them, and you will probably make them, but we can be courageous and attempt to minimize mistakes because sex is a big deal, and irresponsible sexual activity has ruined many, many lives.

You're an individual, and I can't control your actions, but I would rather you didn't start having sex at this point in your life. Fear and coercion should never dictate choices you make, especially in a sexual context. So I ask you, even if you felt Nasir had "waited long enough," do you think it would be a responsible choice for you to have sex with him? If both you and Nasir decide to have sex (which I don't think you should do), have you considered all of the components and issues that go along with that choice? In other words, have you discussed sexually transmitted diseases with him? Have you both been tested for STDs? Have you talked about protection—using condoms? And that means using condoms whether you are taking birth control pills or not, because condoms are about more than just not getting pregnant. Condoms are about protecting the health and safety of you and your partner. Have you gone to the doctor to check into the newly available HPV vaccine that's supposed to work well for young women and can help protect you from this fast-spreading virus? These questions are essential for responsible sexual activity. Clearly, I think the best choice is for you not to have sex with Nasir. And if that means he feels he has to get with Monica, then, although it will be difficult, you should stop dating him and say, "We should just be friends, then" (and mean it when you say it, and act accordingly). You do not need to rush into having sex at this point in your life. There are a whole lot of steps and a number of conversations you need to have if you decide you want to be sexually active. But if you are not willing to do all the things that responsible sexual activity entails, you should not have sex. Period. I want you to wait and exercise complete control over who you allow to touch you and in what way you allow them to touch you.

Now, I don't mean to sound preachy, but one other thing that's unfortunate but essential for you to know: In terms of sex, the potential negative consequences of irresponsible sexual activity fall disproportionately on the female. *You* are the one who gets pregnant. *You* have a much higher chance of catching a sexually transmitted disease from him than he does from you. It's something you need to be aware of, because you can't trust that a guy will think about it for you.

I know a lot of guys who think of sex as just an act, with no connection to or respect for the woman. They are just trying to have their pleasure or rack up what they call "notches on the bedpost." Truth is, most of these guys are so insecure about themselves that whatever woman they are able to convince to have sex with them they respect even less than the women they complain about for turning them down. It's kind of like this old quote from Groucho Marx, who said, "I refuse to join any club that would have me as a member." What he meant, in his own satirical way was, since he doesn't think highly of himself, if a club he was trying to join let him in, then that club must not be very good. A lot of those guys who are out there bragging about all the women they've slept with are the same. They think so little of themselves that they can't respect any girl who would let them "hit it." I'm not saying Nasir would treat you that way, but I am saying give yourself the opportunity to continue growing and maturing before you rush into anything with him or anyone else.

There is one more thing that I want to warn you about that we guys do. And it is particularly prevalent in this "high-tech/low-touch" society we are living in today. I call it *New-School Game Playing*. What do I mean by that? Well, unfortunately, modern technology makes it easier for boys to lie. Because so many of us today are using technology (texting, e-mails, AIM, Facebook) to communicate rather than being face-to-face, it allows us men to lie much more easily. Attempting to have a serious, real conversation with someone using technology is not the way to do it. You can't look them in the eye, see their expression or their body language, or all those other things that allow your intuition to get a feel for whether what you're hearing is the truth or a lie. I'm not saying that just because someone e-mails or texts you "I love you" that they don't mean it. No, a guy can use technology to tell the truth, too. But if you find that it is mostly through technology that a guy "says" stuff like that, it's possibly a sign that he's not doing it from the most genuine place. This new-school world of technology is allowing for a new type of game playin' and hustlin'. So be careful, be aware, and let your intuition be your guide—even through that web of technology.

I hope all this stuff doesn't scare you and lead you to be totally mistrustful of guys. I'm not saying that all men are liars. There are some great ones out there!!! Okay?? I just want you to be aware so that the ones who aren't so great won't be able to take advantage of the most wonderful Young Sistah a guy could have. Okay?? Good.

And before I go, I want you to know that I'm proud that we can have an open, honest exchange about serious stuff like this. I hope it's helpful for you and I know you don't believe me when I say this, but you are helping me, too. If you don't figure it out by then, one day I will tell you how.

I got your back and I know you got mine and that's a good feeling. Good night, my friend. Good night.

Much Love,
Hill

Date: September 11, 2007 8:02 PM
From: Young_Sistah@home.net
To: Hill@manifestyourdestiny.org
Subject: Cheating and Lying!?!

Hill, why do boys cheat and lie?

Date: September 12, 2007 7:23 AM
From: Hill@manifestyourdestiny.org
To: Young_Sistah@home.net
Subject: Cheating and Lying!?!

Often a sister will hear something from a brother that raises a
red flag of concern, but instead of following her intuition and
confronting him, she remains quiet, thereby teaching this brother
that it is acceptable to lie to her. When you train another person
to believe that he can treat you badly in any way, then you must
understand that he's not going to suddenly do the right
thing.

I also wanted you to have an answer from a female perspective so I
asked Terri J. Vaughn to answer this one, too. As well, I turn again
to my fellow actor and friend (as well as one of the most recogniz-
able talents in film and television) Blair Underwood.

HH

----------Begin Forwarded Message----------

Dear Young Sister,

Too many women allow men to cheat because they always take
them back into their arms and give them another chance. If you
don't want a man to cheat, you must make it clear, in no uncertain
terms, that if he wants to be with any other woman, then he'll have
to leave you. Oh, that sounds scary, doesn't it? Many women are
afraid to be alone and without companionship; this is why they
unintentionally ALLOW their men to cheat.

Again, MEN CHEAT BECAUSE THEY CAN; THEIR WOMEN ALLOW IT!!

The question then becomes, what kind of woman are you going to be, one who allows her man to cheat on her or one who is confident enough in herself to know that YOU are "The Prize." If he can't see that, then he is not worth your time.

Blair Underwood

----------Begin Forwarded Message----------

To My Dear Sister,

Boys are very competitive creatures. We (girls) are nurturers and boys are competitors. Usually boys lie to cover up what they feel are their shortcomings or inadequacies. They overcompensate for where they feel they are lacking. They want you to see them as the best. So if they want to be your boyfriend, they'll say whatever it takes; they want you to do their schoolwork, they'll say whatever will make you feel compassionate enough to do it; they want to have sex with you, they'll say what will make you see them as your knight in shining armor. You are intuitive, most of the time. You can tell when a boy is pouring it on thick. The best thing you can do for them and yourself is call them on it. Whether he's just a friend or someone you really like, make him be honest with you. Make him talk to you about your concerns and his concerns. Tell him he doesn't have to lie; he doesn't have to try to trick you. Assure him that he can be free to be himself with you and you are smart enough and loving enough of a person to accept him as his true self.

That way you empower yourself to make a decision based on truth and you help him to know that he is perfectly him and he shouldn't try to cover that up. Oh boy, he will respect you, appreciate you and want to have you in his life as a friend or more for always. You also have to be in a secure place within yourself to require him to be honest with you. Know if you compromise yourself and your values, you just end up hurting yourself and shorting him on a chance to grow from what you have to give. I Love You!

Terri J. Vaughn

Date: September 13, 2007 8:43 AM
From: Young_Sistah@home.net
To: Hill@manifestyourdestiny.org
Subject: Love, Sex, and STDs

Hill, I hear people talkin' all the time about the danger of HIV and AIDS, but I don't think any of my friends have it and I'm not gay or a drug user or anything. Is it for real something I really need to worry about?

Date: September 13, 2007 10:21 AM
From: Hill@manifestyourdestiny.org
To: Young_Sistah@home.net
Subject: Re: Love, Sex, and STDs

I really can't believe that with all the education and information out there regarding HIV and AIDS that you would take such a nonchalant perspective on this REAL disease.

AIDS is now the leading cause of death in African American women ages twenty-five to thirty-four. This is a real number. Those are real deaths. AIDS does not discriminate. It is not a "gay" disease or a "drug addict's" disease. However, it is a disease that can be avoided by being responsible.

I want you to listen to someone who can speak truthfully about the effects of this disease and why you need to be informed!

HH

----------Begin Forwarded Message----------

To My Young Sister—

People perish for lack of knowledge. . . . People are also dying due to the lack of knowledge concerning the issues surrounding HIV/AIDS. Take in all the information people are saying; yet do your own research as well, for such a stigma has been placed upon this disease for twenty-seven years that people sometimes may make comments or give information that is not true. You must be able to distinguish the facts from the myths; this way, you will be able to not only protect yourself, but treat those who you may come into contact with who are living with this disease in an understanding way.

What makes you "think" that none of your friends have it? Because they haven't told you or said anything to you? Rejection is something no human being wants to experience, whether it's telling someone you stole the cookie out of the cookie jar or you once slept with your best friend's boyfriend/girlfriend. Whatever the situation may be, nobody wants to be judged or criticized or made out to be a sympathy case because of something that has occurred in our life. Believe that you may not only have a friend but maybe a close relative who may be HIV-positive but never said anything to you because she might not know how you may respond.

You do not have to be gay or a drug user to be living with this disease. As long as you are a human being, containing blood, semen, or vaginal fluids . . . then you are qualified for this position. If you know that you have or you are engaging in any type of unprotected sex, then you need to be tested and continue to get tested every 3–6 months until it becomes a part of your routine checkup. Should you be worried? More likely concerned, because if you are not infected, then you are affected because HIV affects us all!

Shahdae Janelle Holland
The Family Planning Council

LETTER 11

Daddy's Little Girl: How Shadows Can Loom Large

I know that I will never find my father in any other man who comes into my life because it is a void in my life that can only be filled by him.

Halle Berry

September 14, 2007
Somewhere over Nevada

Dear Young Sistah,

It's just after midnight on the West Coast. I'm almost 30,000 feet above ground, about a half hour into a flight that I've become oh-too-familiar with, the red-eye from Los Angeles to New York. Takeoff is my favorite part of flying. I've loved it ever since I started flying, when I was a little kid. I love that feeling you get in the pit of your stomach the instant the plane's wheels lift off the ground and you know that you're in the air, defying gravity. I used to have dreams about flying. Not in an airplane or anything, just me, out there like a bird, surrounded by sunshine and clouds. But the first time I got in a plane, I was terrified. I didn't want to be up in the sky. I wanted to stay on solid ground.

Before my parents split, I remember my mother would hold my hand, gently kiss me on the forehead, and say, "Everything is going to be fine." Her tone and smile were so warm that I automatically believed her. And you know what, she was right.

Everybody around me is fast asleep. As soon as we got to our cruising altitude, they dimmed the lights in the cabin. This flight is called the red-eye because you don't get very much sleep on the plane, and when you land, your eyes tend to look all tired and blood-shot. We left L.A. at around eleven thirty at night and we'll arrive in New York at six thirty A.M. tomorrow. It seems like an entire night, but when you factor in the difference in time zones, the flight really takes only four hours. So after I settled into my seat, I turned on the overhead light and took out your letter.

I really liked how confidently and knowledgeably you wrote about three-point shots and touchdowns. I told you I played football at Brown, right? (You're probably saying, "Yeah, Hill, a thousand times . . .") Well, I loved football. Sports is one of the most incredible things you can take part in—as a player or as a spectator. It's such a uniting force. It's been used to break racial and gender barriers in this country. And it's bridged political and cultural differences all over the world.

A lot of the women I know don't particularly like sports, but I think that's because they didn't have anybody to properly introduce them, to teach them the rules and to tell them about the players and the history. Of course, that's changing, but I wish it'd hurry up and change a lot faster. You were lucky to have someone there to indulge your interest in sports and teach you all about the games you liked.

I like hearing about the time you spent with your dad on the courts playing ball and then watching the big games on TV. I espe-cially liked the part about how the two of you used to go up against the other fathers who were out there with their sons and beat them real bad. It served them right for underestimating how good you were just because you're a girl. I would have loved to see the two of you in action.

Do you know who Mia Hamm is? She's one of the most famous women athletes in the world. She was a forward for the American women's soccer team, and during the time that she played, she scored more international goals than anybody. That includes male players, too. Mia Hamm once said, "I am a member of a team, and I rely on the team. I defer to it and sacrifice for it, because the team, not the individual, is the ultimate champion."

It sounds like another reason you and your dad used to win all the time was because you played really well together. You were a good team. Teamwork is about much more than moves, though. It's about timing, and trust, and being in sync with each other's emotions. Team members feed off of one another's energy. They come to know one another so well that they can predict what the others are going to do before it happens. It's a symbiotic relationship.

Reading about those times with your father made me think back to some of the special moments I spent with my own father. Some of them were just snapshots in time, but they really shaped my life and my idea of the kind of man I wanted to be. My father passed away in May 2000, and I miss him very much. Not a day goes by that I don't think of him and the influence he had on my life.

Of course, when I talk about the positive relationships I had with my mother and father, I'm speaking about what those relationships have become. But keep in mind that they weren't always like that. In the past, those relationships have each had more than their fair share of highs and lows. So when you talk about how hard it is to grow up without one of your parents, I get it. My parents split up when I was young, too, remember?

When you told me that you've learned not to miss your dad anymore and you don't care if you ever see him again, I wonder if you really feel that way, or are those just words you use to protect yourself? Sometimes it seems easier to hate than to hurt. *Hate* is a powerful word. I was surprised to read it so many times in your letter. *Hate*, like *love*, is used a lot of times to mean more than one thing and to convey more than one feeling. It's not unusual to despise a situation or a set of circumstances and then to transfer that emotion onto the person we feel caused it.

In my case, since I was living with my dad, my mom got a lot of those feelings, and for a long time my relationship with my mother was painful and confusing. I can't say I didn't love her, but I wasn't convinced that she really, truly loved me. I envied all the other kids

I knew who lived with their mothers. I wanted what they had. I wanted to see my mother every morning before I left for school and every night when I came back home, but I couldn't because she didn't live with us anymore. I resented that my life had been turned upside down.

I'm not saying that it was my mother's fault or that it was my father's fault. It wasn't any one person's fault, but I was too young and too afraid of all this change and uncertainty. If the parents who gave you a secure and safe home life can suddenly take that away, then how safe can you feel in the world? It was just the way things were, but it was easier to blame my mother because that gave me a place to direct my anger and pain. I felt that her physical absence in our home was an empty space, a loneliness, and instead of dealing with my feelings, I let my anger and bitterness become my best friend, to fill the space that had belonged to my mother.

You and your father were tight. The two of you shared a deep bond. What I learned when my father passed away was that those ties don't just vanish because the person is no longer alive or in your daily life. Every time I share a memory about my father, it makes me remember how much I love him and how much he loved me. The same was true of my relationship with my mother (even though she is alive and well) while she was living apart from my brother and me. I found that the more I thought about all the things we used to do when we lived together, the more I felt my love for her. Believe me, I did my best to ignore those thoughts and push them out of my mind. I felt abandoned and I didn't want to love my mother because I thought that meant I was accepting this new life that had been forced onto me. But try as I might, I couldn't stop caring about her.

That's what I think was most confusing to me. I knew that deep down I loved her, yet I didn't know what to do with that love. I didn't want to own or show my love for my mom because I was scared that it might be rejected. After all, it "appeared" to me she had rejected me, my brother, and the love, that she and my father shared, and that was the love, that had created me. So it stood to reason that she could reject my love, too. Except all that reasoning wasn't based in logic but in fear. And I was wrong—but I had the mind of a five-year-old. Because I was a five-year-old.

By the same token, the fears I hear you expressing about your dad can become self-fulfilling prophecies. My cousin is the head pastor of a great church here in L.A. called Agape. Everyone calls him Rev. Michael. He often speaks about fear, and he believes that the outcomes that any of us fear most are usually the ones that are unknown, so we start compiling information that we then use to substantiate that fear. We look at the lives of others, take their experiences out of context, and turn them into the so-called evidence we need to rationalize our fears. What I mean is that we often decide how other people are feeling in our own minds, and then we take that assumption and use it to decide how they will react to what we say or do. We think if such-and-such happened to so-and-so, then it stands to reason that it'll happen to me, too. In truth, we have no way of knowing. What's worse, the longer we let those false and unfounded expectations guide our emotions and actions, the greater the risk that we will actually create the outcome we most fear. In fact, that's kind of what I did with my mom. I believed that she didn't want to be with me, so I put up a wall that, as it turns out, was what kept her from being able to get close to me.

The journalist Helen Rowland, who was something of an expert on relationships, wrote, "When two people decide to get a divorce, it isn't a sign that they 'don't understand' one another, but a sign that they have, at last, begun to." My parents' decision to get a divorce was based on the fact that their way of relating to each other had changed. How my mom and dad felt about my brother and me remained the same, but the decision they made to get divorced brought so many other changes into our lives, it was hard for me to hold on to the fact that we were still a family. And all of my assumptions, as logical as they seemed to me in those days, made it even more difficult for me to feel their love and support.

I'm worried that the same might happen to you, especially after reading about the conversation you and your friend Starr had. Especially that she told you, "Men leave; it's what they do best." Yeah, some men do leave, but more stay. Getting divorced shouldn't be interpreted as leaving. You might feel abandoned because you don't get to see your father as often as you did when he lived with you, but keep in mind he may be dealing with his own sense of loss about being away from you.

Author Joe Cucchiara talks about girls and self-esteem in his book *What All Little Girls Need & What Most Women Never Had.* "There are certain things that only the men in our lives can teach us, just as there are certain things that only the women in our lives can teach us. Through those lessons, we learn how to interact with members of the opposite sex, how to negotiate our romantic relationships. Without a father's loving guidance, girls have a greater chance to grow up with low self-esteem and self-worth, make poor choices when it comes to choosing men, hate their bodies, and often develop eating disorders. Fathers must prioritize their daughters if they want them to become successful, happy, confident, loving, good people with high self-esteem." So it makes sense that you are having all these feelings about your father; you just need him. Parents don't always understand that our needs are really that simple.

I grew up in a house full of men, so for the longest time, women seemed like foreign creatures to me. That was all right in my younger years when I didn't really have much interest in them, but as I grew older and started becoming curious about and attracted to women, I wished that I knew more about how they were, what made them tick. My friends who had the best insight were always the ones who were surrounded by women in their homes, the ones who lived with their mothers or their aunties or their sisters. They'd talk about how they'd had to wait to use the bathroom because their sister was holed up in there putting on her makeup, or about being dragged around from one lingerie department to another as their mom searched for the right bra. They knew about relaxers and flat irons, braids and hair extensions. For someone like me, who didn't have a clue about any of that stuff, those guys were a well of wisdom.

Then I met Anisa. You remember her? We first met when she was my lab partner in chemistry class. She was smart and pretty, and over the course of my sophomore year in high school, the two of us grew close. She was the first real female friend I'd had since elementary school, and those friendships didn't count because the only things we ever did together were paint or draw or play kickball during recess. Anisa was different. And as you know, she wasn't a girlfriend; she was a friend, someone I'd hang with and talk to about almost everything. She lived with her mother. Her father had died when she was young and she didn't have any brothers. She was three months older than me, and boy did she like to rub it in. She called me the little brother she never had but always needed.

Over the years, Anisa and I have remained friends. She's married with two children now. She's told me more than a few times that I helped her to learn the language of men. I can definitely say the reverse about her. Because of being around her, I didn't feel as intimidated by women. They no longer held a fearful mystery. The countless hours she spent on the sidelines cheering me on made her develop a fondness for football which, she tells me, has come in handy in her marriage. The countless hours I spent watching *The Wizard of Oz*, which was her favorite movie, was good preparation not only for my career but for all the lazy Sunday afternoons I've spent at the movies with girlfriends.

By the time Anisa came into my life, I had already started breaking down that wall I'd built between my mom and me. If that process hadn't been in motion, I don't think I could have let Anisa into my heart the way I did. Between her and my mother, I became more comfortable around other women. I found the confidence I needed to ask them out and to let them get close enough to know me and, if I was lucky, to love me.

You asked whether I thought it was stupid of you to wish your parents would get back together someday, even though you know that's never going to happen. No, I don't think it's stupid at all. Lots of kids of divorce share that same wish. I know I did. Even after I'd made peace with the *idea* of my parents being divorced, I still felt they belonged together. And I still wanted to be magically returned home, to the place and time that existed before everything seemed to break apart.

But what I've come to realize about home is that like most things that bring us security and strength, it's inside of us. That's why you hear people saying things like, "I feel at home here" or calling each other "homey." You said your place stopped feeling like a home after your dad left. Maybe there are things that you could do to get back some of the warmth of the home you remember. It may not be as simple as clicking your heels together three times like Dorothy did with those ruby slippers, but it might very well be as simple as just picking up the phone.

DADDY'S LITTLE GIRL: HOW SHADOWS CAN LOOM LARGE

Call your dad. Or better yet, when you see him on the courts with his buddies shooting hoops, don't turn around and take a different route. Maybe the reason you've been seeing him around lately is because he's been hoping to run into you. It may seem awkward at first, but don't let your fear of being hurt keep you from your father. Who knows? Soon enough, the two of you might fall right back into the habit of being a team again. In

> Sometimes another point of view can make a big difference.

the meantime, I hope it will help that you're letting me be the big brother you don't have but have always needed. Sometimes just having another point of view can make a big difference.

Dawn is breaking. The darkness is gradually fading, giving way to sunlight. My cabinmates are rousing from their sleep, yawning and stretching and rubbing their eyes. Pretty soon, the airline hostess will announce that we're making our final descent into New York. It'll feel strange to see streets and skyscrapers again.

It's weird that no matter how many times I arrive in New York City, when I approach the skyline and see those skyscrapers of Manhattan, I get energized. I get energized driving across the Triborough Bridge or approaching the Midtown Tunnel from Brooklyn. I just get revved up. So even though I didn't sleep much on the flight, the view makes me feel like I am ready to go. I hope you feel ready to go today! We are gonna change the world!! Ha-ha. Have a great day, and smile a lot today, all right!? All right. Big Hug.

And hey: Your mom *and* your dad love you. And so do I.

Your Friend,
Hill

Date: September 16, 2007 7:43 AM
From: Young_Sistah@home.net
To: Hill@manifestyourdestiny.org
Subject: Quality Man

Hill, a lot of my friends and people on TV say that boys are liars, boys are jerks. . . . What do you think I should look for in a boy?

Date: September 18, 2007 9:21 PM
From: Hill@manifestyourdestiny.org
To: Young_Sistah@home.net
Subject: Re: Quality Man

Wow, that's a pretty broad and tough question to answer. And I must start by saying that all of us are unique, and all of us respond to different things from different people. But for me, there are two requirements: trust and honesty. To answer your question more specifically, I think that you should look for a boy who you're truly, truly, truly attracted to for the right reasons. What do I mean by "right reasons?" Well, I believe that most of us end up dating people we think we are attracted to, or who we are told we should be attracted to. People who look good in person or on paper, or have all those "things" that advertisers and music videos say you should be attracted to. But I want you to develop friendships with boys first. And if, once you have the basis of trust and honesty in friendship, it develops into something more, then you already know how and why you're attracted to that person.

As a guy, I also want to tell you a very simple thing you should look for; this will give you clues into a young man's personality and whether he also likes you. I want you to look and see if he treats you (and other women he interacts with) with politeness, respect, and chivalry.

But I wanted to give you a more complete and specific list, so I asked a group of my surrogate sisters to compile a list. And here are some qualities that Anisa, Tanya, and Serene look for in a guy.

- Honesty/Trust
- Giving of self
- Friendship/Companionship
- Sexual chemistry
- Intimacy
- Mental stimulation
- Morals/Values
- Sense of family
- Spirituality
- Growth
- Nurturing/Sensitivity
- Levels of commitment
- Compatibility
- Goals/Aspirations
- Willingness to sacrifice or compromise
- Romantic
- Partnership

I think that's a pretty awesome list, and you deserve a boy in your life who has all of those qualities. But for those extra-golden nuggets of advice—I forwarded your initial question to the incomparable Ruby Dee. Her fifty-seven-year "partnership" and marriage to Ossie Davis is legendary and proves that it is possible for all of us to find a life partner who elevates us while we in turn elevate them. To say I have respect for this genius woman would be an understatement. I am in awe of her. Read her simple yet powerful words of substance regarding dating and choosing a life partner.

HH

————Begin Forwarded Message————

As you start dating, you should look for a man who is concerned about humanity and life issues. Someone who is consistent and will search with you for the profoundly satisfying ways to live and love each other.

Ruby Dee

PART THREE

Overcoming Obstacles

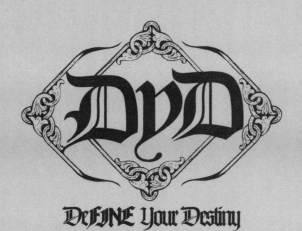

DyD

DeFINE Your Destiny

LETTER 12

Breakup, No Makeup

People think, because we're young, we aren't complex, but that's not true. We deal with life and love and broken hearts in the same way a woman a few years older might.

Rihanna

September 20, 2007
Los Angeles

Dear Young Sistah,

I'm sorry if I can't give you the best advice in this letter today because to be totally honest with you, I'm just not 100 percent. However, I have to say it makes me feel a little bit better to be able to write to you. You know in that song when they say "walk it out"? Well, for me it's "write it out," I guess.

You talked about a lot of things, but it seems that you are mostly upset because you and Nasir are having problems. I am so sorry you are hurting over this. Have you asked him what's going on? You say he's being distant and avoiding you, but you don't have any idea why. You and Nasir have been best friends for longer than you've been a couple, so don't you think he'd tell you if he was going to break up with you? Maybe he's just going through something that isn't about the two of you. The only way that you can know for sure what's going on with Nasir is to ask him. Trust him to tell you the truth.

You think that because he's acting normal around other people, it isn't bothering him, too. Well, as someone who has been through way too many breakups, I am here to tell you that chances are he's going through something, too. We guys generally don't wear our feelings on our sleeves, but it's just because we don't want to look like punks or whatever in front of other guys. Can you imagine a guy walking around crying because he's having problems with his girl? The brothers would clown him out of the neighborhood and take away his "guy" card. So don't assume that just because Nasir is hangin' with the fellas, laughing and playing around, that he's not upset that you're having problems. It's got to be hard on him that you two are having trouble communicating. I sound like I know what I'm talking about there, right? Except now I'm going to tell you a story to explain why I'm not sure I'll be able to help you with your problems with Nasir. It doesn't make me seem like anybody's relationship role model.

Last night I had to go to this television black-tie event, some awards gala fund-raiser thing. And there, I ran into this woman I used to date. That might sound casual, but it was more than that. When we were together I got to the point where I found myself checking out wedding rings. Before I actually bought one, though, we started having all these problems and next thing I know it was over. It seemed like we went from love to done in a matter of weeks. And seeing her last night brought everything back. Here I was, running into this woman I had imagined spending the rest of my life with at this big Hollywood soiree, and I had to pretend everything was fine. And I did. I stood there acting all regular as if seeing her didn't mess me up at all. But the truth was, it brought back the hurt like it happened yesterday. I think that a lot of people believe that the person who does the breaking up does not hurt at all, or at least not as much as the other person. Well, I can honestly tell you that it's not true. Just because a relationship gets to a place where it has to end doesn't mean that it feels good to be the one who ends it. Right now, I feel like there's a fire in my stomach. As if I'm sick with a nervous and sad feeling at the same time. I really loved her, but I never fell *in* love with her. Does that make sense? And what's most ironic is that the next morning I get your letter asking for some advice in your dating life while here I am reliving the effects of a breakup. The fact is, I am far from an expert on romantic relationships. So I can't just sit here giving you advice and acting like I know everything.

What I can do is talk to you about my experiences in dating. I've been in a whole variety pack of relationships, from healthy, positive ones to drama-filled, not-so-positive ones. And the ones that were the most drama-filled? I was just as responsible for that drama as the woman in the relationship. Many of us don't have the full tool kit that you need to have healthy relationships. I'm still learning, and I'm twice your age. I even bet that if you ask your mother, she would say she's still learning about relationships. Like so many things, often the best guide you have for deciding if a relationship is healthy or not is, guess what. Yup . . . your God-given intuition.

Each and every relationship is unique. And you have to treat them that way. The only thing other people can really do is just share their experiences and hope that in sharing them, there is a positive effect. For instance, I've found that the few things that are essential in a relationship, and this is *any* relationship, whether it's dating, family, or friendship are: honesty, trust, respect, positivity, and love without conditions. To me, these elements are the essential foundation. But just because they exist doesn't guarantee a successful relationship. For instance, all of those things existed in the relationship with my ex. However, our relationship got to a point where it had to go one way or the other; it was time for us to get engaged or move on. She deserved to be in a relationship that was moving toward where she ultimately wanted to end up. In her case, married with children. For whatever reason, I wasn't ready to be in that level of relationship with her. And just because we loved each other dearly, we respected each other, and we treated each other with honesty and dignity doesn't mean we had to stay together forever.

> Each and every relationship is unique.

But it also doesn't mean our relationship was a failure. I was talking to a friend about whether to break up with my girl or not, and she asked me, "Well, why do you think the relationship failed?" And that word *failed* really struck me. Because as I looked back over the year and a half we had been together, there is no part of our relationship that I would consider a failure. We had shared laughter, joy, and romance, and had taught each other so many things. We truly enjoyed each other's company. I couldn't see having a year and a half of that level of joy as a failure. But, it also came time for it to end. And there is nothing wrong with that either, and that's nobody's fault.

So remember that in your life you don't have to approach every relationship as if it's the last one you'll ever have. As if this person has to be the one you're going to marry. Instead, treat it as its own individual experience and allow it to grow in a natural and organic way.

What does all that mean? Well, I did warn you that I didn't have all the answers. And anybody who tells you they do is wrong. Affairs of the heart are individual and unique. But the one thing we can always do is follow our intuition. If we end up giving our heart away to people who don't treat it with care, then when the person who would treat it well comes along, we're not able to trust.

So there you have it. I want to thank you, though, because writing this letter has made me feel a little bit better. I hope reading it helped you in some small way as well. Hit me with an e-mail so we can talk about this further. Okay?

I hope to hear from you soon.

Much Love,
Hill

Date: September 21, 2007 7:56 PM
From: Young_Sistah@home.net
To: Hill@manifestyourdestiny.org
Subject: Heartache

Uuugh! Hill, I'm sad!! Please make me laugh! I mean a part of me wants to get back together with him, but deep down I know it's not what I want. Should I go back?

Date: September 23, 2007 3:18 PM
From: Hill@manifestyourdestiny.org
To: Young_Sistah@home.net
Subject: Re: Heartache

This is one of those times when I realize that I'm a little too attached and would probably answer this question as a protective older brother and believe me it won't have a bit of humor. Instead, I am going to forward your e-mail to someone who always makes me laugh! Niecy Nash is one of the smartest and most honest sistahs I know! She can be seen on Comedy Central's *Reno 911!* as the hysterical Raineesha and as the host of Style Network's *Clean House.*

E-mail me back after you stop laughing.

HH

————-Begin Forwarded Message————

My dearest sister,

You don't have to eat a whole side of a cow to know that it's beef . . . all it takes is a bite! Over and over and over again you've been hurt, disappointed, misused, and abused. You keep thinking that somehow this person will change . . . will be different. Baby, please! You got to believe a man when he tells you who he is the first time. Why? Because he knows himself better than you do. Don't allow yourself to be balled up in a knot, rubbing your bangs across the carpet, crying enough tears to wash twenty cars over something you can't change! We've been duped into thinking that love hurts. On a good day it should be like getting your eyebrows waxed. When the tape is snatched off, it stings for a minute. But, when you experience the smooth, silky skin you are left with, ooh, you know it was all worth it!

Many songs have been sung about heartache—"What Becomes of the Brokenhearted," "Where Do Broken Hearts Go?" "What's Love Got to Do with It?" Quite frankly, some of these songs simply lie! What becomes of the brokenhearted? Brokenhearted little girls become women who are seasoned at navigating their way though solid relationships. Where do broken hearts go? Broken hearts end up in a well of friendship, surrounded by other women who understand your pain and provide comfort and support. What's love got to do with it? Not a damn thing if you don't first love yourself! No one is ever going to be better to you than you are to yourself. Ever. Never. Ever!

I believe you should celebrate whenever a relationship ends. You can never have a new love unless you are rid of an old one! My twelve-year-old daughter was sad on Valentine's Day and started to cry because like her friends, she didn't have a boy to celebrate with. I said, "Well, let's stop the tears cause this ain't the first Valentine's you'll be without a man. Keep on living. Second, you don't need a man to celebrate how good and loving you are. You get your friends together and exchange gifts with them. Love on each other. You don't need a man to love yourself!" When the boys at school saw my daughter and her friends sharing, laughing, and having a good time . . . baby, they were all over them like maggots on a dead piece of meat! Why? Because they were enjoying being themselves. My sister, you will attract what you are. So remember, the next time you taste meat of a relationship, if it's tough, spit it out and move on . . . if its tender and rare, baby, chew it to the bone!!!

With Love & More Love
Niecy Nash

Date: September 23, 2007 9:05 PM
From: Young_Sistah@home.net
To: Hill@manifestyourdestiny.org
Subject: I Don't Wanna Look Like a Clown

Hill, I've noticed that my friends wear way too much makeup (some simply don't wear it very well)—which may mean that I don't. I really don't want to look like them, can you help?!

Date: September 24, 2007 6:45 AM
From: Hill@manifestyourdestiny.org
To: Young_Sistah@home.net
Subject: Re: I Don't Wanna Look Like a Clown

Although they put some powder on me on my show to knock down the shine, I am definitely not an expert when it comes to makeup, but thankfully I have some amazing friends who can help me out on this one!

I sent your question to a woman who is an expert. My friend, former Miss USA Kenya Moore! She knows quite a bit about how to use makeup properly and successfully.

HH

————-Begin Forwarded Message———

Your inner beauty is what you should strive to project, so makeup should only be worn to enhance your physical features. The great thing about being young is that your supple skin doesn't need much coverage or foundation. Always remember, Less is More. A few products go a long way.

If shopping for foundation, to be used only on special occasions or if you have numerous discolorations, my favorites are Bobbi Brown and Prescriptives cosmetics found in department stores, and CoverGirl and Maybelline found in local drugstores. I love Prescriptives because they expertly match your makeup to your complexion. Always buy a liquid foundation that is oil free and apply with a makeup brush, NOT a sponge. Brushes are best because they don't apply too much of the product on your face, giving you that mask look. You can find some inexpensive ones at CVS or Walgreens. You always want to appear to have a "no-makeup look" even if you are wearing foundation. And always test a color in the daytime before buying it—on your face, not your hand or arm. If it blends into your skin and disappears, then it's a winner.

Powder is not necessary unless you have oily skin. Try the makeup blotting papers instead. If you have some blemishes, try using a dab of your foundation just on those spots. If your skin is dry, I love tinted moisturizers. They add a little sheer color and provide moisture at the same time and subtly even out your skin.

Next, try one coat of a little black mascara on your eyelashes to bring out your eyes—more than one coat can look clumpy. Then try a great sheer lip gloss in soft pink, rose, or bronze shades that compliment your complexion to make your lips "pop." You don't need a lip liner. It can look "drawn on" if applied too heavily and that is what you want to avoid. You want to always look naturally beautiful, especially at school. Avoid colors like very dark browns, or dark reds; these are too sophisticated and are often worn incorrectly by beginners. The same is true for blush; find sheer shades in the same tones as your lip gloss and apply a small amount to the apples of your cheeks only. You can find them by smiling. To finish your look, you can try a bronzer powder and lightly dust your face to give it a healthy glow.

Finally, always remove makeup before going to bed. Makeup will clog the pores and promote pimples and breakouts. Remember, LESS is more. You don't need a lot of makeup to enhance your features. No one wants to see the makeup you are wearing on your face. They want to see YOU!

Kenya Moore

LETTER 13

Words Have Power: The B, H, and T Words

I used to want the words "She tried" on my tombstone. Now I want "She did it."

Katherine Mary Dunham

September 25, 2007
Baton Rouge, Louisiana

Dear Young Sistah,

Hey there, I'm down in Louisiana now, on location shooting the movie *Mama, I Want to Sing!* with Ciara. It's an amazing project for her. I wish you two could meet; you'd get along great and probably be friends for life. Just like you and your girls, she hangs out with her friends, goes to the mall, goes out dancing and checking out the latest flicks. Sometimes we'll get to talking, and I can't help being struck by the dignified way she carries herself for someone so young. She reminds me of you in that way. She's also one of the nicest people I've ever had the pleasure of working with. Believe me, I've worked with people with a lot less talent than Ciara who walk around the set without an ounce of humility. They demand things, and then have tantrums that hold the entire cast and crew hostage until they get their way. Ciara is the star of this movie and her character is in almost every scene of the film and never once has she treated anyone as if she were above them or doing them a favor. And I'll tell you this; she is not the kind of girl a brother would come at using disparaging words like *bitch* and *ho*. Trust me when I say they would know better.

Thinking of that reminded me of a letter you wrote a while back where you said that you and your friends sometimes use the words *bitch* and *ho* when referring to one another. You told me that every time you hear those words, an unsettling feeling comes into your stomach. Much more than an unsettling feeling came into my stomach when I read that. Words have power, but they also have meaning. Meaning is the very thing that creates a word, isn't it? Without meaning, words are nothing more than a collection of sounds grouped together. And the words that we choose to call each other have extra meaning. These words affect our image of self, our psyche, and the way we relate to each other. I find it disturbing enough when the word *ho* is thrown around casually by some young men, because it's such an offensive and abusive way to label a person. But it's even more disturbing to me that more and more girls and women are using that word to refer to other females, and to themselves.

Some musicians have definitely encouraged the casual and widespread use of words like *bitch* and *ho*, as well as the objectification of women. As much as I love rap, and respect many of its makers, that aspect of it is one that we can't ignore. When you answer to words like *bitch* and *ho*, or words that are even worse, *you* are granting those words power. If a brother steps to you and says, "What up, ho?" and you giggle or laugh, or get annoyed but still respond to his attention, you're giving him tacit permission to call you that, and by extension to think of you that way.

Don't buy it? If I'm walking down the sidewalk and as I go by someone yells out, "John! Hey, John! John!" would you expect me to stop and ask what he wanted? Of course not, because my name's not John. It's Hill. Why would I acknowledge someone who is calling me the wrong name? So would you expect me to stop for someone yelling, "Hey, asshole!"? And if I did, aren't I saying, at some level, that I think the label "asshole" applies to me?

My Female Legacy

This is me as a baby in South Carolina with my maternal grandmother, Eugenia Ashmore Hill, and my older brother, Harry.

Eugenia Ashmore Hill, my maternal grandmother, as a young woman.

Here's a close-up of my beautiful maternal grandmother shortly before she passed.

And here's a close-up of my equally beautiful paternal grandmother, Lillian Grinage Harper.

This is me as a toddler in Iowa with my paternal grandmother, Lillian Grinage Harper, and my brother.

My Mother

Here is my mom with her school books at Howard Medical School, beginning her uphill battle toward becoming an anesthesiologist.

This is my mother's graduation picture. So proud of her!

This is my mother at about four years old. Wasn't she adorable? This is me when I was around the same age. The fruit doesn't fall far from the tree, huh?

My Day Job

JOYCE WESTERGAARD

ROBERT VOETS / CBS

On the set of *CSI: NY* with my castmates Gary Sinise, Carmine Giovinazzo, and our show's Executive Producer— Pam Veasay. Most people don't know this, but the head person in charge of my show, the "showrunner," is this amazing African American woman. She is a trailblazer!

Looking far too serious on the set of *CSI: NY*. C'mon, I gotta catch the bad guy! Lol.

On the Road

I'm on the road, teaching a classroom full of eager young minds in Jamaica.

RODNEY DIXON

That's me speaking at the historic and beautiful Big Bethel AME Church in Atlanta.

DARRELL SMITH

Signing copies of *Letters to a Young Brother* at a school in Jamaica.

RODNEY DIXON

Here I am taking notes for *Letters to a Young Sister* from super teen model, Chanel Iman, and her best friend, Qeona Perti. We talked about everything that day.

SHANA MANGATAL

There Are Good Brothers Out There

Me with one of the most brilliant men in America, the amazing Princeton professor, Dr. Cornel West.

RACHEL GOLDEN / THE BRITTO AGENCY

DARRELL SMITH

Me and one of the classiest men in Hollywood. My man Blair Underwood truly represents the best of brothers.

Me with another amazing brother, Usher Raymond and his beautiful new wife, Tameka Foster.

DARRELL SMITH

Uplifting Women in Entertainment

Me with Deborah Lee, the CEO of BET, at the 2008 BET Honors. She is numero uno at a 6-billion-dollar corporation!

DARRELL SMITH

Sitting down with the lovely Lauren London. She is a beautiful spirit and a rising star!

RACHEL GOLDEN / THE BRITTO AGENCY

Me with Ciara at a publicity event while we were filming our movie *Mamma I Want to Sing.*

DARRELL SMITH

DARRELL SMITH

Above, left. Me with the incredible Kerry Washington. She is smart, beautiful, and passionate about improving the lives of others. **Above, right.** Catching up with Keyshia Cole. **Below, left.** Backstage with my friend India.Arie. Whenever I feel a little down, I put on one of her CDs and my mood instantly shifts. **Below, right.** Me with the amazingly talented and inspirational Mary J. Blige.

DARRELL SMITH

LISA SORENSON / LSPR

A Holly Robinson Peete and Nia Long sandwich, two of the most beautiful and classy women in Hollywood, at an event where all three of our charities were being honored.

Yes We Can!

ANASTASIA ALI

Working the phones and calling potential voters and caucus goers at the Obama campaign headquarters in Iowa. The energy on the campaign trail is amazing!

Me with Tatyana Ali in Iowa cheering for Barack Obama before his victory speech, after we won in Iowa!

STAND FOR CHANGE

Me with the next president of the United States. My former classmate, the amazing and honorable senator from Illinois, Barack Obama!

IAN FOXX

Same is true for the words *bitch* and *ho*. Anyone who uses them, including musical artists, comedians, your friends, are not calling you by your name. *Bitch* and *ho* should no more refer to you or any of your friends than someone calling me John. Therefore, you shouldn't answer to them or acknowledge them, except insofar as to explain to your friends that if they continue to use those words around you, they will cease to be welcome. Of course, the name John does not bring with it the negative, sad, and dangerous historical connotations of those words.

A bitch is a female dog. And a ho is the *h* and *o* taken from the word *whore*, "a woman who engages in promiscuous sexual intercourse, usually for money; prostitute; harlot; strumpet" (dictionary. com). And we both know that doesn't describe you any more than *female dog* does.

We're taught early in our childhood that "sticks and stones may break my bones, but words can never hurt me." But ask anybody who's ever been on the receiving end of abusive language, and they'll be quick to tell you that it's just not true. Words can wound as deeply as any other weapon, especially words that are meant to describe, characterize, or label you negatively.

It must have stung when you finally confided to Starr that you were thinking about joining the debate team and she said, "I know you're not turning into one of those tired type of hos, are you?" But you did the right thing by going home and giving yourself time to figure out what you wanted to say to her.

Don't feel bad if you didn't or couldn't say anything back to her right then. I know when I've been insulted or cut down by somebody, my brain's often too busy being hurt or surprised to come up with anything to say at all. Of course, then I'll obsess about it for days afterward, going over all the things I could have or should have said. Naturally, by then I can come up with a hundred perfectly worded responses that have just the right amount of bite and defense to match what was said to me. For a long time, I'd always be kicking myself for not being able to think of them in the moment. Then one day I realized that when it came to issues I felt that strongly about, maybe it was better to take the time to properly choose the words that I wanted to use to explain or defend my position, rather than just coming back with a witty retort. It was better for my words to carry weight and intention, not to simply sting or hurt the other person in the moment.

So I stopped with the self-kicking and the next time someone said something that really bothered me, I waited until after I'd had some time to think about it, then told the person I wanted to talk to them. Over time, I found that people were better able to listen to what I was saying when I did it that way. It also didn't feel like an attack, and I know when I am attacked I can forget to be a caring and considerate friend. I've noticed that when I use words to hurt another person, I always wind up feeling terrible for much longer than they do. The next time you find yourself in a position where you are tempted to say something negative or hurtful, ask yourself, "Will that language make me feel better or worse about myself?" It's not just turning the other cheek; it's learning to turn a negative into a positive.

I'm glad you decided to say something to Starr, because otherwise your silence might have been interpreted as an acceptance of her language. If you just stay silent on something you know isn't right, you become a silent accomplice in their messed-up behavior, and you know what happens on *CSI: NY* (and in real life) to the accomplices in a crime? They get the same penalty as the ones who actually committed it. Because you know what? If you stay silent in the face of wrongful behavior, then you have committed a crime, too.

Ultimately, choosing the type of language you use is not really all that different from choosing the type of clothes or hairstyle you wear. It's all right to follow a trend as long as it suits your taste and style. It's you who determines your style, not anyone else, and it's you who decides the words you are comfortable using.

Yeah, that's right, words are a personal style choice. I'm serious. It all goes back to your definition of self. By using words that are unflattering, negative, or abusive, you are, in essence, telling others that those are labels you find acceptable. But using language is about more than just not choosing words that are abusive, profane, or otherwise negative. You should be choosing words that can actively empower you. Words that are transformational, that take thoughts and turn them into positive action. Winning words. Think of how much better you feel about yourself when someone refers to you as a winner, or smart, or talented, or beautiful. And the truth is, you are all of those things and so much more.

In fact, I started thinking about your talent when you wrote that you may "try to be a singer after all." Anybody who knows me (and that includes you) is aware of my tremendous dislike and disapproval of the word *try*. It places a barrier between you and the thing you desire. It leaves room for the possibility of failure. Instead of saying that you're going to try to be a singer, why not simply say that you're going to be a singer? Do you see how much more assertive the statement is without the word *try*? *Try* is one of a bunch of words that I call "fillers," because they fill sentences with doubt and hesitation. *Think* is one of those words when it's used to create distance between an individual and an action she's claiming or a choice she's making, like saying, "I think I'll try out for track," instead of "I'm going to try out for track!" I want you to be just as conscious of the words that you use as you are of the words others use. Words don't have just any power; their power can elevate us or bring us down to nothing. So in the future when we write to each other I want us to stay conscious about the words that we are inviting into our lives.

I know you're probably saying, "C'mon, Hill, there's all these words and sayings that you don't want me to use, like *try*, *need*, or *think*. Does it really matter?" I'll admit that, at first, being conscious of the words we use takes a little bit of effort. But you'll see that very quickly those words will be eliminated from your vocabulary almost automatically. In fact, there will come a time when you won't even notice they are gone. Words have power, and if we frequently use words that don't empower us, we will become un-empowered. And I don't know about everybody else, but you and I are going for Empowerment 3.0!

Carol Moseley Braun, the first African American female U.S. senator, once said, "Defining myself, as opposed to being defined by others, is one of the most difficult challenges I face." You and I have written back and forth quite a bit about self-definition and how it contributes to the process of creating and sustaining a vision of yourself, especially one that surpasses all boundaries and limitations. You, Young Sistah, are limitless, and I want you to remember that each and every day.

So the next time someone, whether it's a male or female, jokingly or seriously, refers to you in a way that you are uncomfortable with, I want you to remind them who you really are. I want you to be clear that you are not a *b* or an *h*. But rather, you are an *M*, for *magnificent*. You are an *A*, for *amazing*. You are a *W*, for *wonderful*. You are a *Q*, for *queen*. Those are your definitions. When people say to you, "Hey, Wonderful! Hey, Amazing! Hey, Magnificent! Hey, Queen!" then you can answer, because they will be describing who you really are.

Write me back soon. Okay? We on a roll now!! Ha-ha.

Much Love,
Hill

Date: October 2, 2007 5:03 PM
From: Young_Sistah@home.net
To: Hill@manifestyourdestiny.org
Subject: Nappy-Headed, Well, You Know!

Hill, recently there was a scandal with the radio DJ Imus insulting Black women by calling them "nappy-headed hos" and he put the blame on hip-hop. Do you believe hip-hop is to blame?

Date: October 10, 2007 7:11 AM
From: Hill@manifestyourdestiny.org
To: Young_Sistah@home.net
Subject: Re: Nappy-Headed, Well, You Know!

Hmmmm . . . this topic still makes me quite angry and I might write some things that the Lord wouldn't like, so I'm gonna allow my friend and poet, Devynity, to break it down in the way only she knows how.

HH

----Begin Forwarded Message----

They told me I was ugly,
Something like Pecola, undeserving of love—no kisses, no hugs
"Go scrub my floors!" they said
"Nurse my children and when they grow up they will call you ugly too, because ugly's what you are . . ."
They said the lighter, the better, but still not good enough
Made me hate myself and my sisters
Showed me thin white ladies with narrow noses
Striking elegant poses
Accentuating their emaciation, then they told me I was fat
They put Hottentot Venus on display; with thick hips, thick thighs and supple behind
And proclaimed her a freak of nature
They called me mammy
And nanny, jigaboo, sapphire, jezebel, harlot, skeezer, slut, chickenhead, nappyhead and

Too proud and independent
Too loud and too relentless
The Black male's emasculator
But still a welfare mother
With one baby on each hip, 5 walking behind
Legs spread open and wide
To keep those checks coming
They probed my insides
Mutilated my body in the name of science
When I complained, I was reprimanded and called defiant
They made me hate myself and
My Blackness
My African-ness
My natural curves
With a nose like your father
A smile like your mother
African—yes!
Before American ever was
And beautiful
Strong, yet delicate
Like the dandelions
They put Donyale on the cover of *Vogue*, but made her
cover her face
They've denied us Oscars and accolades
Told us we should hate ourselves
Told us we should have no pride
Hate our heritage, our culture, our lips, our nose
Then Imus got on the air and called us nappyheaded hos
Told us hip-hop made him do it
As if the word whore was somehow created by our music
As if we criminalized ourselves
They showed me Shirley Temple dancing with Bojangles
Showed me Marilyn Monroe, Raquel Welch, Elizabeth Taylor
as Cleopatra
Then they gave me Aunt Jemima, gave me ashy knees and
swollen feet DAX grease, straightening combs and
bleaching cream
My kinky hair the crown God gave me to wear
And so I permed it
Twisted it out of shape and I pressed it to make it straight
I burned it and colored it blonde

They called me exotic
At once marveling at my beauty and making a mockery
of my humanity
And I've been made an exposition
They greased me up and stripped me down
Til there was nothing mo'
Still they copy my style—from my braids to my wrap to my fro
Still they sing my songs
And envy my complexion
Still they put me down
I'm so yellow, so red, so black, so brown
So beautiful—it's true
They almost convinced me I was ugly
Til I saw you
My sister
Your radiance resonates in my reflection
With cornrows and thick lips
And the backside that switches like a pendulum
Jumping double Dutch in the school yard
Color confident
Almond shaped brown eyes
As if we enslaved ourselves
As if we segregated ourselves
As if we were brought here hating ourselves
Well this is my Black girl manifesto
For my sisters in the suburbs and the ghettos
For Nikki, Alexis and Keisha
For Jessie, and Khalilah
For Black girls who beg their mommies for white Barbies
Looking in the mirror, hoping that their faces will change
For the mikas and the iquas and the aquas and the fiyahs
You are beautiful the way God made you
The sun loves you
Can't you feel it embrace you?

Devynity
Emcee.poet.blackgirl

LETTER 14

Double Jeopardy:
Racism and Sexism
as Obstacles to Success

> I was raised to believe that excellence is the
> best deterrent to racism or sexism. And that's
> how I operate my life.
>
> **Oprah Winfrey**

November 1, 2007
Los Angeles

Dear Young Sistah,

In your last letter, you told me that Camilla, your girlfriend Starr's older sister, had come home for a visit and that she was all upset because she hasn't "made it" yet. Apparently, she hasn't gotten as far with her job at the bank as she thought she would by now. Boy, do I understand that frustration. Each one of us knows, better than anybody else, how long we've studied and how hard we've worked, so when things don't happen in the way we feel they should, there is the tendency to feel slighted, or overlooked. I think everybody who's ambitious and determined has moments like that.

It's nearly impossible for me to answer your question about whether I agree with Camilla's belief that sexism is the reason why she hasn't been promoted in her job. More often than not, sexism in the workplace occurs in such subtle and understated ways that only the person who is being directly affected by it is able to immediately know that's what's taking place. This is not to negate or dismiss Camilla's perception of her experiences. Both racism and sexism are based in prejudices that are so long-standing and pervasive that they've become deeply ingrained in the fabric of our society. They've become institutionalized. This means that they are practices that people pretty much take for granted as a part of our culture.

For example, for many years, and not so long ago either, women were not compensated as much as men, at the same company, doing the exact same job. It was an accepted practice, one that people just took for granted. Men got higher salaries because, well, they were men. Sometimes people tried to justify the practice by saying that a man worked because he had to support a family, while a woman was more likely to be working to earn "extra" money, but somehow those people didn't pay single men any less, or single mothers any more. Sexism like that (it's called wage discrimination) still occurs today, but not as frequently, and that's because a lot of people challenged the status quo. They raised public awareness, they took to the streets, they protested, they wrote to newspaper editors and lawmakers, they sang about it. They even went to court over it. A good number of the laws we have now came into being because people took a stand against what they felt was unjust.

But that doesn't mean it's easy to distinguish between what is a real injustice and what is a seemingly unfair response. The story you shared about Camilla illustrates that point perfectly. As much as she might want to blame not advancing in her career on either racism or sexism, your suspicion that her poor work performance played a large part in her lack of success might be right on. Showing up late almost every day and calling in sick multiple times a month will almost always result in some sort of penalty. Even if it was a small, part-time job that she took to make extra money on the weekends, her employers hired her because they needed help. They had a set of tasks that needed to be fulfilled, and they were relying on her to do them.

Even if Camilla was the only Black female at her job and, coincidentally, the only one to not be promoted, it doesn't automatically mean it's a racist or sexist act. One has to take into consideration all the other factors that influence a supervisor's judgment of your work performance, especially whether or not you're getting the job done. When all is said and done, that's often the first and most important question that bosses ask. Based on what you said, Camilla might have found it easier to say that she was overlooked because of her gender or her race. Instead, she might have been the only employee who was not putting forth the effort that the decision makers at the company felt was needed to help them meet their goals. When you don't apply yourself fully to the things you do, you can never know for certain why you didn't succeed in the way you thought you should have. If Camilla had showed up on time every day and focused her attention and efforts on her job, and only her job, and they still did not promote her, she would have known without a doubt that their reasons had nothing at all to do with her skill, proficiency, or commitment as an employee. Then her assertion that she was a victim of racism and/or sexism might be seen as a valid explanation instead of just another excuse.

> If you don't apply yourself fully, you'll never know why you failed.

You know, as much as we'd like to believe that racism and sexism are all but nonexistent in this modern day and age, they are both still present and being practiced on both an individual and an institutionalized basis. To deny their existence is to deny the struggle and the progress that have been made by people who have been courageous enough to strive for the goals they were destined and determined to reach, regardless of the obstacles that blocked their path. People like Harriet Tubman and Sojourner Truth and Madam C. J. Walker and Dr. Maya Angelou and Oprah Winfrey. People like my mother, Marilyn Hill Harper.

I can't even begin to fathom the opposition my mother must have faced when she decided to become an anesthesiologist. I'm sure there were people who told her, during each and every stage of her journey, that she would not make it, that she *could* not make it. Even if they didn't come right out and say it, they probably found ways to let her know that's what they believed, or wanted, or hoped for. There might even have been times when she got sick and tired of feeling like she had to prove them wrong, times when it might have been easier to see herself in some lesser capacity, achieving some smaller dream.

One of the ways that institutions like racism and sexism are kept alive is through the manipulation of images. I've written a lot to you about the vision that you have of yourself, how important it is for us to define ourselves with our own words and through our own eyes. Henry Ford said, "Whether you think you can or you think you can't, you're right." I felt strongly about this before I became an actor, but working in the entertainment industry has really made me see how vital this mind-set is to our survival.

To be a working actor, no matter your race or gender, is a blessing. There are a whole lot of people out there who are struggling to get noticed and to achieve in this field. It seems like the farther away you are from the idealized mainstream identity—which is usually white and blond, American and thin—the fewer opportunities there are for you to work. At least, that's the belief held by many people in my line of work. It's a belief that basically leaves folks who look like you and me undesired and unemployable. History has shown us that it is a belief based in fact, not fiction. The roles that have traditionally been reserved for actors of color have not necessarily been the most desirable, nor have they realistically portrayed the experiences they claim to. But just because something is based in fact doesn't mean that it's representative of the whole truth. If that were the case, people like Hattie McDaniel—who won the Academy Award for Best Supporting Actress in 1940 for the part she played in *Gone with the Wind*—would never have been able to break down the barriers she did.

Hattie McDaniel was not only the first African American to win an Oscar but also the first African American woman ever to receive that recognition of excellence by her peers. Her victory was an inspiration to millions of young Black women in the arts. Though there have been numerous brilliant performances given by top-rate actresses—such as Cicely Tyson, Beah Richards, Diahann Carroll, Ruby Dee, Diana Ross, Alfre Woodard, Angela Bassett, and many more—it would take another fifty years for the Academy to award another African American woman an Oscar for acting. In 1991, Whoopi Goldberg was awarded Best Supporting Actress for *Ghost*.

It can be confusing, frustrating, and sometimes deflating when you take your cues from external sources, from the messages that are sent out by society at large about what your capacity for success can or cannot be, should or should not be. Some people become so paralyzed by those messages that they stop giving the world their best because they feel it's a wasted effort.

It's one thing to see and understand what the struggles have been in the past; it's quite another to allow those struggles, whether they resulted in victory or in defeat, to be the standard by which you measure yourself.

I guess what I'm trying to say is that regardless of the frustrations that Camilla feels, and even regardless of how the people she works with regard her, be it positively, negatively, or indifferently, if she relies on the *internal* messages that she is receiving, on her intuition and her own definition and vision of herself, she will find herself in a league of her own, much like my mother and all of those other African American women I listed earlier did.

You asked some tough but important questions, questions about why racism and sexism exist in the first place, why some people feel that they are superior to others because they are of a different race or gender. Those are things you could spend your whole life trying to analyze, figure out, and make sense of. What I *can* tell you is that any amount of time you devote to that venture would probably be time better spent elsewhere.

When I was little, I would spend my summers at my grandparents' house in Seneca, South Carolina. This particular summer, I was six or seven years old and a group of white teenagers chased me down the street, calling me Nigger. I hadn't said or done anything to them. I was just minding my own business, walking around my grandparents' neighborhood like I usually did. (This was before Halo 2 and MySpace, when kids actually played outside.) Our neighbor, "Aunt Tiki," saw me huffing and puffing, running as fast as my tiny legs could carry me. "Like a bat out of hell," she told my grandmother. The boys had ducked out of sight as we approached my grandparents' house, so Aunt Tiki had no idea what was wrong with me and why I was hopping over flowers and sprinting through people's yards.

"Hill, you all right?" she asked me as I passed her by. She was a soft-spoken old woman, but she was also stern. When she spoke, I listened. We all did. "No, ma'am," I told her. I walked up to her front steps so she'd be able to hear me as I explained what had happened. I asked her why those boys had called me that name, why they were being mean to me when they didn't even know me. Aunt Tiki chuckled a bit, then turned serious, looked at me, and said, "Don't you pay them any mind, boy. They're actin' crazy, that's all." It wasn't the response I was expecting, but I let it be and moved on.

Aunt Tiki had been around and dealt with prejudice long enough to have learned that trying to understand it would be tantamount to trying to invent logic to justify the illogical. What she said let me know that while I may have been the target, I was not the cause of their behavior. And it wasn't my responsibility to try to figure them out. My responsibility was to keep being myself and to keep living my life. But be that as it may, the next day, I spent the afternoon in my grandparents' yard. I was scared that if I went out, those boys might be there.

After watching me for a little while, Aunt Tiki got up, walked down the street, and came to my grandparent's house. She opened the gate and said, "Hill, how about you keep me company while I walk to the store?" I followed her, and she and I walked and walked. We walked farther than I had ever ventured on my own. She told me stories about the people who lived in the neighborhood, people she had known and admired for years, some of whom had passed on. Whenever we'd come to an intersection, I'd turn my head and look back, and Aunt Tiki would say, "You got it in you to keep going?" I'd nod, and we'd cross the street and walk another block. In fact, we walked past the store and kept going. We even walked into this pristine area of town with manicured lawns and long, winding driveways. And no one dared bother Aunt Tiki. We walked and walked.

Though she didn't say a word about what had happened the day before, following Aunt Tiki taught me a valuable lesson about what to do in the face of bigotry. She showed me that the entire town was just as much ours as anyone else's and that there will be times when people try to limit you, but you must not let them. What you must do is hold on to your history. Don't look back. And keep walking.

One time when I asked my mother how she had managed to

make it through all the potential setbacks in her education and career, she admitted to me, "Whenever I was tempted to stop, I'd ask myself if I could really go on." This reminded me of my afternoon with Aunt Tiki, how she'd look over at me and ask me if I had it in me to keep going on. Because of women like her and my mother, my answer has always been an emphatic *yes*.

Remember that list I asked you to write up a while back? To list those people who said *yes* when the world was telling them *no*? I want you to take it out and add your own name to the list. Doing it might feel strange at first. You might wonder, "What have I done that's so great? How have I said *yes*?" By adding your name to the list of all the others who have gone before you and proven that it can be done, in spite of racism, sexism, or any other prejudice or problem they may have faced, you're not only applauding their accomplishments, you're accepting the truth of who you are—a person who has what it takes, a person who can and will keep going.

XO
Much Love,
Hill

P.S. You might even want to encourage Camilla and Starr to write their own lists, too.

Date: November 3, 2007 11:35 AM
From: Young_Sistah@home.net
To: Hill@manifestyourdestiny.org
Subject: Million-Dollar Baby

Hill, you say I am so amazing and I can do anything, anything, ANYTHING I want in life, but come on. . . . For me, a girl from a family that has hardly any money and lives in the projects, do you really think it's possible for me to become a CEO of a multimillion-dollar company? Get Real!

Date: November 6, 2007 8:12 AM
From: Hill@manifestyourdestiny.org
To: Young_Sistah@home.net
Subject: Re: Million-Dollar Baby

There is no better person in the world to answer this question than Ms. Cathy Hughes. Ms. Hughes founded Radio One, a $400 million media company owning a television network, magazine, and radio stations across the country. She is one of the most successful and powerful women in the history of business!

Take it all in, as Ms. Hughes knows the true deal!!

HH

————Begin Forwarded Message————

Most women aren't taught that they are in many ways already CEOs. I am not sure what you do in your spare time, whether it's braiding hair, tutoring, mentoring, being active on student organizations or whatever—just know that you are already serving as a CEO. Even if you give advice to your friends—you are a CEO of a consultant business.

Embrace the fact that the skill set you use for managing your personal life is transferable for managing in the corporate world. Most of us, particularly girls and women, are never taught that principle. Balancing a budget is balancing a budget, whether it's a billion-dollar corporation or a ten-dollar weekly allowance.

Growing up, my family lived in the projects, but I knew I was an entrepreneur at a very early age. Why? Because every Friday was trash day in my neighborhood. I knew we had a lot of elderly people in our building, and every Friday I would walk up and down my building to knock on every door and ask a simple question, "Ms. Jones, do you need me to take your trash out for you today?" Sometimes for simply reminding people it was trash day they would give me a nickel or a dime—and luckily, if I took out their trash, I might get a quarter. At the age of nine, I knew I was the CEO of my own business that was open every Friday.

So embrace that reality—particularly since you are a young, intelligent woman! Just look around you; at your mom or in your friends' homes there are many "young" sisters who are heading up their households. They are all CEOs!

Ms. Cathy Hughes
Founder and Chairperson
Radio One, Inc.

LETTER 15

Food for Thought

I lived the skinny b*tch lie for too long. No
more. I'm here to say I am phat and phat is
where it's at.

Mary-Kate Olsen

November 9, 2007
New York

Dear Young Sistah,

Okay, I'm not going to mince words on this one. I was reading your last
letter and all kinds of alarms went off in my head. A few letters ago you
talked about dieting and losing weight in order to be more attractive to
Nasir, and now you're talking about it again. Then you "joked" that you
felt like taking a shortcut and throwing up or taking laxatives like
some of your girlfriends because "at least they were able to stay thin."
And then you followed that with a "(jk)." You better be 'jk'! Because if
not, you are gonna have me getting on a plane to come and find you
and hug some sense into you. People are always talking about how
quick fixes and shortcuts don't work. Quick fixes and shortcuts, for real?
Come on, you and I are not quick-fix and shortcut kind of people. We
are long-term, self-esteem-building, Empowerment 3.0 kind of people.

You remember that time when you and your girl Caroline went

and "got your nails done"? You got the pink with sparkles that spelled out your name, but you had a hot attitude because one of the letters came off almost immediately? And I told you that if you made an attitude adjustment and went back to that nail shop, they would probably work with you. An hour later you were texting me telling me about how they redid that nail for free and how they were so nice to you. You sounded shocked, but it's like I've been telling you, if you put out the right energy, people will give you that energy back, and if you put out the wrong energy, folks will throw it right back to you.

I mention the nail shop because I want to use it to show you how you can make better decisions. When you go to the nail shop the manicurist doesn't just slap some polish on your nails. First, she clips your nails and shapes them to encourage them to grow longer. Then she soaks your nails in a solution that strengthens them. After that, she cuts back your cuticles, so that your nail base will be healthy. And once she's done all those steps, she applies two coats of nail polish. Now, if you want some sparkly bling or some fabulous design, she'll do that before she adds a clear top coat to both strengthen the nail and add shine. The reason she did all these steps was that she cared about the health and appearance of your nails first. That's the way I want you to see yourself. Healthy first as your base, and then you add the sparkly jewels. So the next time your girls try to tell you the benefits of weight loss by practicing an eating disorder "shortcut," don't believe the hype.

Truthfully, I've dated many women who I could tell practiced disordered eating. That's defined as troublesome eating behaviors, such as restrictive dieting, bingeing, or purging, that occur with less frequency or are less severe than would meet the full criteria for the diagnosis of an eating disorder. Sounds technical, but it's real. My girlfriend Yolanda (I sometimes called her Yo for short) and I were in law school together. For the longest time, I didn't understand why she took so long in the bathroom or why she ate some of the things she did. The signs were there, but I didn't see them at first. She went from being healthy and eating normally to suddenly starving all day long and then bingeing at night. She'd slip off and disappear into the bathroom and when she'd come back, she smelled like mouthwash and her face was flushed from throwing up. If we went out and ate junk food she'd have to stop by her place afterward, and if I tried to make a stop at the video store or a movie she'd bite my head off. Half an hour later she'd come back to the car, and she'd always look exhausted, like the life went out of her. If we did go to a movie after that, she'd be so tired, and if I ordered popcorn, she'd start eating like she was starving, like she couldn't even stop herself.

Then there was the other Yolanda, who wouldn't eat anything and ran six miles a day. She'd pick at her food or only eat diet food, but it was as if she was afraid to eat. She obsessed about her weight and was dieting all the time. If she gained one pound I could tell, not from her body but by the way she upped her workout. Instead of just doing six miles, she'd go to the gym and work out and *then* run six miles.

It wasn't long before I realized that something was really wrong with her. I didn't know why her teeth were discolored, but I learned later that the acid from throwing up was eating away at the enamel. Although she had brown skin, it seemed a washed-out color. Her eyes were frequently bloodshot, but I figured it was from pulling all-nighters studying for law school exams. She looked exhausted, with heavy bags under her eyes and her normally chiseled face expanded by her puffy cheeks. And no matter how she tried to pretend she was upbeat and happy, that's exactly what it looked like, pretend.

It took me a little more than a minute but finally I realized what was going on. And I confronted her about her eating disorder. As her boyfriend I felt close to her, and I knew I couldn't wait for someone else to say something. After denying it for a while, she broke down and confessed her bulimia to me. Instead of offering her any solutions, I simply listened. Eventually, Yolanda went to an outpatient treatment facility and she started to get better, but for the longest time I worried not only about her health but about her life. I saw how much an unhealthy relationship to food almost ruined her life forever. While Yolanda was practicing an eating disorder, she couldn't think about anything other than food, eating, starving, and eating again. An unhealthy relationship with food can also happen in the reverse, with overeating and obesity.

So do me a favor and don't even joke about having an eating disorder. It's not funny. When people are starting to practice an eating disorder they think it's temporary or that they have it under control. They see the pictures of women who look gaunt or obese and they always say the same thing, "That couldn't happen to me." But while they're in it, they can't see it and they can't stop it.

One of my surrogate sisters, Stephanie Covington, has a book coming out called *Not All Black Girls Know How to Eat*, chronicling her own experience with eating disorders. Steph and I have been close for years so I saw firsthand what "throwing up" did to her life, and I would never want anything that horrific to happen to you. She told me recently, "Hill, I lost ten years of my life between throwing up, starving, and trying to have a healthy relationship with food again. I ruined my health and my teeth, not to mention friends, jobs, a career, and the ability to have a healthy relationship. I would give anything to have those ten years back." You say your friends are practicing eating disorders in order to stay thin? Maybe they don't realize that the short-term solutions lead to lifelong problems.

I have another friend, Nancy Redd, who has an amazing book out called *Body Drama*. The book is a photo essay about real women who have real issues with their bodies. It's the first time I've ever seen a book address real women and not just celebrities who have been airbrushed to look perfect. The women in the book are keeping it real, and as a brother who's heard similar statements from sisters, I can't wait for you to have a copy. It's amazing to be able to read the truth and to tell the truth. I'm going to get Nancy to sign a book and send it to you, and when you get it, I want you to share it with your girlfriends. I'm not saying that so I can help my friend sell books either. The reason I want you to let your friends read your copy is because I believe it will help them. If you help one person, that person will go off and help at least one other person; it's the cycle of life and the "law" of exponential growth. One helps two, two helps four, four helps eight, and on and on. We are talking about a movement of change and uplift and prosperity for everyone—but it *starts* with you and me. Okay?!?

Although I've known many women struggling with weight and body image, I'm still a man and in no way do I consider myself an expert. Society constantly sets up a yardstick of attractiveness that women work to measure up to regardless of their genetics or the kind of body type they have. I do not want to see you go down a road of yo-yo dieting, bingeing, purging, laxative abuse, starving, or any of the other ways people "control" their food. I want your relationship with food to reflect your relationship with yourself: healthy, loving, nurturing, and whole. So many times, women focus on the man in their lives or the man they want in their lives. "Does he think I'm fat?" "Do I have a big butt?" "Does my hair look right?" "Am I wearing the right outfit?" And what I want you to focus on is, "How can I be happy with myself?" "How can I love myself today?" "How can I become my best self?" Those are the questions I want you to ask yourself today. Looking outside of ourselves and picking ourselves apart and comparing ourselves to others is a no-win exercise. It serves no value and can at times be very debilitating. I want you to choose a life that is about being greater than, not ever being less than.

This whole letter keeps going back to your girlfriends. Chances are they haven't begun to understand the consequences of their actions. And as much as I want to help you with this, I am not an expert. So I did what I have done my whole life when I needed information. I researched it. Man, your generation is so lucky to be born in the age of the Internet. At your age I had to get up, get on a bus, go to the library, and then start to look through the card catalogue and hope they had the book in stock. Wow! You guys are absolutely blessed to be here right now. The National Eating Disorders Association has a great Web site full of information. Check them out at www.nationaleatingdisorders.org.

This may make you want to talk to your friends about their behaviors around food; if you do, that's great. Try to be supportive, nonjudgmental, and there for them. And try citing specific instances when their behavior toward food has scared you. Ask them to speak to someone knowledgeable on the subject of eating disorders. You could even offer to go with them to their first appointment. You can't force them to do anything they are determined not to do; it's not your job. Your job is to be the best friend you can be, and that includes taking care of yourself, staying healthy, and being the best mirror possible for your friends. Be the honest and caring person that you are, and I know you'll do fine.

Li'l sis, I'm proud of you for trusting me with your thoughts and your real feelings. I want you to remember that you are perfect just the way you are, and I am so proud of you.

> You are perfect just the way you are.

Hit me back and let me know how you and your friends are doing.

X (and a big ole) O
Hill

Date: November 10, 2007 9:49 AM
From: Young_Sistah@home.net
To: Hill@manifestyourdestiny.org
Subject: Is My Fat Phat?

Hill, I get a lot of mixed messages about my weight and body. Some people say being overweight is unhealthy, while a lot of boys say they like girls with big breasts and phat bootys. What's the real deal?

Date: November 10, 2007 7:15 PM
From: Hill@manifestyourdestiny.org
To: Young_Sistah@home.net
Subject: Re: Is My Fat Phat?

Asking a question about what is "unhealthy" or not is really a medical question so I am going to forward your question to one of the smartest doctors I know. She also happens to be the district health director for DeKalb County, and that means she is overseeing the health of millions of people in and around the city of Atlanta. So she truly is an expert with regard to your question. However, before I forward your e-mail to Dr. Ford, I want to address the second part of your question, when you talk about what types of bodies "boys like." I would much prefer you think about what kind of body YOU like, and hopefully it is one where you are the most healthy, energized, dynamic, and vibrant and happy version of yourself. Take it from me, a "boy," that we are attracted to women who exude those qualities whether their breasts or bootys are big or small. Make sense?

HH

----Begin Forwarded Message----

While a few extra pounds might not be such a big deal, weighing significantly more than you should can lead to serious problems, both now and later in life. Obesity, or weighing more than 10 percent over what is recommended for your age and height, increases risk for heart disease, high blood pressure, and diabetes. Overweight people tend to have more problems breathing and often have joint problems and trouble sleeping. A teenager who is obese by the age of thirteen has an 80-percent chance of becoming an obese adult.

Overweight teenage girls may also have lower self-esteem and therefore have fewer reservations about being sexually active, which could lead to sexually transmitted diseases (STDs) and unwanted pregnancies. Those pregnancies become even more dangerous because of the risks that the excess weight adds to the mother and the growing baby.

Poor eating habits, overeating, lack of exercise, and even stress and depression are contributing factors to obesity, which is responsible for more than 300,000 deaths each year. Adopting and maintaining healthy patterns of eating and exercise can keep you healthy for a lifetime.

S. Elizabeth Ford, M.D., M.B.A.
District Health Director
DeKalb County Board of Health

Date: November 11, 2007 6:46 PM
From: Young_Sistah@home.net
To: Hill@manifestyourdestiny.org
Subject: The Not-So-Celebrity Fit Club

Hill, I think I want to start exercising but I really don't know what to do. How do I get started?

Date: November 14, 2007 9:00 AM
From: Hill@manifestyourdestiny.org
To: Young_Sistah@home.net
Subject: Re: The Not-So-Celebrity Fit Club

Well, it sounds as if you have the right attitude—which is simply that you WANT to exercise. That's the first step. And since I'm definitely not the expert as to how you should begin your program, I'm consulting with my personal trainer, Chariesse Griffin. Whenever I need to get my body ready for a role or just staying fit day to day, I go to Chariesse. She's the best health and fitness expert! She has trained some of the biggest actors and musicians. You're about to get some advice that people pay big bucks for!!

HH

————Begin Forwarded Message————

Well, I may sound a bit biased, but I think that everyone should start a "get in shape" regimen with a good trainer. I know that may not be realistic for everyone, so a great start would be to identify the top three activities that you like to do and then start doing them. You can mix them up within a week's time or do one for about six weeks, then move on to the next favorite. The key here is to start with simplicity. You're moving. Great! One day and one step at a time. Before you know it, you will be in better shape than you were just weeks before. No need to overanalyze your results or compare yourself with others by thinking, "Why don't I look like her?" It's your body, and it will adapt and change as it is supposed to.

For fine-tuning your body, you will definitely need to do weight-bearing exercises—using dumbbells, resistance bands, even soup cans if you have to. Weight training is the best way for a woman to shape her body; and, no, your body will not look like a guy's body. You will just be a beautiful, trim, and shapely young woman. So embrace it, and go for it!

Chariesse Griffin
Personalized Motivational Fitness
www.chariessegriffin.com

LETTER 16

Hillified Hugs:
Dealing with the Blues

It's not the load that breaks you down, it's the way you carry it.

Lena Horne

November 17, 2007
Crossing the Mississippi!

Dear Young Sistah,

Yes, I'm writing you from another airplane. I'm on my way to Charlotte, North Carolina, to give a speech and do a book signing tomorrow. I got your letter, and I was so happy to read that things are looking up for you in your relationship with your math teacher. That's you controlling school, and not letting school control you. Of course, I wasn't happy to read that you're not feeling so positive right now, and that you're feeling kind of down.

Sigh. I hear you, though. It's amazing how our moves mirror each other so much. I'm kind of sad today, too. Because of the WGA strike (the writers of our show are part of a union and the union called a strike to get fair pay), today was the final day of shooting for me on *CSI: NY* this year. After the final scene, I packed up my dressing room and said good-bye to the cast and crew. And I had the same feeling I used to have on the last day of school. I drove home feeling so happy, with a sense of completion, accomplishment, and satisfaction for a job well done. The sense of completion, no matter how small the task, can feel so satisfying. But after a while, I start to feel the empty space that isn't full of work anymore.

While I was riding to the airport, just staring out of the window, I found myself getting completely lost in thoughts . . . and each one seemed to bring me down deeper and deeper, and now I'm on the plane staring out the window 30,000 feet above the ground, and I don't feel much better than I did when I was in the car.

You know that really sad feeling you described in your letter? That's how I feel right now. For me there's a sad feeling in the middle of my stomach that grows and grows until it fills up so much space inside my stomach that I'm not even hungry—just sad. Is that how you feel? I guess you could say that we have "the blues."

You've heard that expression before, haven't you? It's an old one. As a matter of fact, that's how that style of music, "the blues," got its name. People used to write songs about challenges in their lives, and when they sang those songs, it was called "singing the blues." Jimi Hendrix, the legendary singer and guitarist said, "The blues is easy to play, but hard to feel." And he was so right!

I've gone through the blues several times. There was one time, during college, when it seemed like my life was cursed by Murphy's Law. You know, the one that goes "Anything that can go wrong will" . . . and in my case you could add, "and it will do it at the worst possible moment." I'd get to the bus stop as the bus was pulling away; I'd spend hours studying, only to find out that I'd studied the wrong information. Even the young sister I was dating seemed to feel the bad vibe coming off me. She broke up with me and started going out with a guy who, it seemed, had it all together. He had "the Midas touch," turning everything he touched to gold. Me? Whatever I touched seemed to turn to dust.

For weeks, I walked around with what felt like a huge weight on my shoulders. What made it all the more stressful was that I felt like I couldn't talk about what I was going through. I did try, a few times. I confided in my friends, like Anisa and Taylor, but they didn't quite get it. Not that I could blame them. When I listened to myself talking about my problems, they didn't sound the way they felt. They sounded trivial, not worth the effort or emotion that I was putting into them. But to me, they were huge. And they were wearing me down, and making me miserable.

And you know what was worse? You know what was *even* worse? The worst part was this: I felt guilty about feeling sad. Isn't that crazy? Well, crazy as it might sound, that's what happened. It's been happening tonight, too. I start to feel sad, then I get mad at myself for feeling sad, and that makes me feel worse!

Why feel guilty? Because there's a part of me that deep down somewhere inside thinks I'm not allowed to feel sad. There's this voice (which is really a mixture of other people's judgmental voices) that says, "How can you feel sad? You're on a hit TV show, you own property, you've written a successful book, you make a great living. . . . There are so many people in the world who are suffering. . . . I'll slap you if you say you feel sad."

Seems like you've got a voice like that invading your thoughts, too. Now, I know you expressed to me that there are a lot of people out there who don't have a roof over their heads, who don't even have *one* parent raising them, who don't even have food to eat. So is it wrong for you to be down and feel sad sometimes? You know what? It's *not*. We all get the blues. It doesn't matter how much money you have or don't have, how good your job is, how cute the person you date is, or whether you have the latest clothes, handbag, or shoes. You're not always going to be happy, and so you are allowed to be sad sometimes, because sadness is a part of our journey. . . . But only a part of it.

We don't smile or laugh all the time. And we don't expect to, so we also shouldn't expect to be sad all the time either. Being sad all the time could mean that we're falling into depression. And there's a difference between being sad sometimes and actually being depressed. Life is about moderation, so there is nothing we should be all the time, except for thankful and faithful. But you're still allowed to be sad while being thankful and faithful. So don't beat yourself up about it. Just experience it, and learn from it.

At the end of the day, I've found one of the best things that I can do to deal with sadness—and you're going to laugh at me now, when I tell you—is get, or give, a really good hug. I mean it! A hug can be more powerful than any drug, better than the funniest movie you could watch, and more spirit-filling than the greatest sermon. Sitting on this plane, I feel like I could use a hug from you. And if you were here, I'd give you a big ole hug, too.

One of my favorite pastors was Pastor Cecil "Chip" Murray, and let me tell you, he gave out the best hugs. I think I got more and learned more from his open-hearted hugs than even his sermons. (And his sermons were nothing to sneeze at, either!) His hugs were not too tight, not too soft, but full of love. So know this: Whenever you need a hug, just stop what you're doing, close your eyes, and imagine me, your mom, or someone who loves you there giving you a big tight ole hug. Mental hugs work almost as well as the real thing. I'm serious. You don't believe me? I'll explain.

Actors do this all the time. It's called sense memory. What that means is that you recall and use an experience you've had before through each of your five senses. You think about what it tasted like, looked like, smelled like, felt like, and sounded like. You know how sometimes a song will come on, and it'll remind you of a particular time and place when you heard that song, and then you start to feel in your body how you felt then in that time and place? That is what sense memory is, and it's at our disposal all the time. So when you're feeling down or sad, you can let your senses take you back to a time when you felt great and happy. Which is just to say that you and I don't have to fall victim to feeling down and sad. We can change that condition.

My friend Senator Barack Obama said it best: "It doesn't mean that you can't get down sometimes. Everybody does. But always remember that being defeated is a temporary condition. Giving up is what makes it permanent." So you and I need to make a pact. Number one, we're not going to allow other people to project negative energy onto us. Number two, we're not going to beat ourselves up if we get down sometimes, or if we make so-called mistakes. And finally, when we do feel down, we're not going to wallow in it. We're going to use our sense memory to help pull us out of it. You and I are too wonderful to be held back

> You are too wonderful to be held back by sadness.

by temporary sadness. I lift you up, I celebrate your magnificence, and I love the fact that you're in my life. And you know what's a testament to all of that? This letter. Writing to you on this plane has elevated my sprits. I'm no longer anywhere near as sad as I was when I began writing, and it just proves to you that giving and receiving mental hugs works. So as you read this letter, know that this letter is a huge hug from me to you. I hope to hear from you soon, Young Sistah, and don't take so long to write me back!

Much love and blessings.
Your Friend,
Hill

"It Really Hurts": Dealing with More Than Just the Blues

I always want people to—to get the message that I'm trying to send out. You know, I've been through some things, so when I get up there and sing my songs, I'm like, hey, I've been through it, and I want to encourage somebody else that if you're going through it, you can come out.

Fantasia Barrino

November 25, 2007
Los Angeles

Dear Young Sistah,

I was relieved to get your letter. Since I hadn't gotten an e-mail from you since my last letter, I suspected something was wrong. Now I know that my intuition was right, as intuition usually is. Many of the things you wrote in your letter concerned me, like how you said you'd "checked out of life" for the last week and just stayed in bed because everything had just become "too much to handle." And from the way you broke down what that "everything" was, I can definitely understand how it could seem overwhelming: the constant arguments between you and your mom; your father's absence and the pain that it's been causing you; finding out that Nasir has a new girlfriend; sensing that you and your friends are growing apart; being frustrated with your weight; and feeling, as you put it, "a growing loneliness" in your life.

When I told you in my last letter that I understood, I'm wasn't just paying you lip service. I really do. Sometimes it feels like you're standing in front of one of those automatic tennis ball servers. The problems and issues come at you one by one and, at first, you tackle them that way, in a steady pace. Even though it's challenging, it's still doable. Then, suddenly one day, it starts to feel like the server has gone haywire and the problems are being pelted out too quickly and with too much force. They're coming from left, right, and center. You can't keep up, so you throw up your hands, not so much in surrender but in self-protection, and you stop moving; you simply stand still. Is that an accurate description?

I was feeling that way, and although you may not know it, you've been giving me a whole lot of mental hugs lately. Not too long ago, I had this callback for a Will Smith movie called *Seven Pounds*. I read a lot of movie scripts but it was, hands down, one of the best I'd ever read. I was to play the part of Will Smith's character's brother, who was dying of cancer. I did all my work, studied real hard and, man, I wanted this job so bad I could taste it.

My agents were excited. I felt so connected to this role that I couldn't imagine anybody else playing it but me. The friends I told totally thought Will and I looked like we could be brothers. I was so excited about the entire thing. Everything seemed to be going my way, and I thought I had nailed my audition. I gave them everything I had, and I walked away thinking this job was mine for sure. Man, the next few days were full of anxiety. I was walking on air one minute and then freaking out the next. Finally, my agent called to tell me I didn't get the job.

I have to tell you, as anxious as I had been, I didn't see that coming. I was devastated and even though I did things, like the mental hugs, to get out of the funk, I'd find myself right back in it not long after. And then I got your letter, saying that you're having a hard time, too. Even though it wasn't a "happy" letter, it came to me as a blessing. You'll find out why soon enough. Now let's talk about what's going on and how you're really feeling.

When you wrote about how you'd "checked out of life," you said you stayed "holed up" in your room, in bed, not really sleeping but not really doing anything else. You said you cried a lot and when your mom asked you why you were crying, you couldn't tell her because you didn't know why; there wasn't any one reason. There were lots of reasons and there were no reasons. Some of them seemed so small that it felt embarrassing to admit them out loud. You saw how hard she was working, and you didn't want her to think you couldn't handle things in your life that should have felt normal. Now, I'm no doctor (yeah, yeah, I know the saying "even though I play one on TV"), but seriously, what you described sounds to me like a lot more than the blues that I went through that time in college. It sounds like you could be dealing with what's known as clinical depression.

Back then, when I was dealing with the blues, my friend Taylor suggested that I go and talk to one of the counselors on campus, and I almost did. I got as far as the building where the counselors were, but when I saw the sign that said "Psychological Services," I got scared, turned around, and went back to my dorm. What if somebody saw me going in there? Brothers would have straight-up punked me. Guys are supposed to be able to handle their problems, so I told myself to toughen up and deal. I kept imagining how horrible it would have been if I had walked into that office. It would basically have been like admitting I was a "psych case," and there was no way I was about to do that. I'd heard the sort of language people used; I'd even used it myself. To say that somebody was a psych case was bad enough, but the other terms that people used, terms like *basket case* and *nut job*, *loony* or *crazy person*, were worse.

Mahalia Jackson, who was indisputably one of the greatest gospel singers in the world, once said, "Anybody singing the blues is in a deep pit yelling for help." And that's true, you know? But I reacted to my fear by shutting up, and not getting help, which didn't make my problems go away. Instead, I learned how to walk around pretending I felt better then I did. It got so I'd practice a happy mood in front of the mirror just so people didn't see that I was blue. But the only thing all that pretending did was cut me off from the very people who could have been a source of help. I don't want you to do that.

You're probably wondering what the difference is between the blues and depression. Well, the short answer is that one is a temporary emotional response to a set of situations or circumstances, like my response to the audition; the other is a more prolonged condition. It's still an emotional response, but it lingers because of the chemical changes that have taken place in our bodies.

In other words, all those challenges that melted into each other to create that huge "everything" you wrote about may have been what brought you down, but what's keeping you down and "checked out of life" may be a chemical imbalance. I know those two words together, *chemical imbalance*, sound like something that should happen in a science class experiment, not in your body, but it does happen there, too. The mind is part of the physical body. Every hormone or chemical that exists in our bodies affects our moods, in other words, our mental state.

Every mood change that we have is either caused by or will bring about a shift in our body's chemical levels. When we're mad or frightened, our adrenaline levels increase, making the heart race. When we exercise or play sports, our body releases endorphins, which have been shown to spark a certain type of happy feeling.

I want you to know all of this because you were awfully hard on yourself. Those things that you wrote about yourself—"I'm hopeless," "I'll never amount to anything," "Nothing good ever happens to me because I'm a bad person"—were difficult for me to read because I know they're not true. And I know you know they're not true. And that's what bothers me most, the fact that whatever you're going through is hindering your ability to see yourself as you really are.

Mental health is as important as physical health. Maybe more so, because if you can't function mentally, how are you supposed to go on with your life? When we're not feeling well, like if we have a cough or a migraine, we immediately take stock of our condition. We start adding up all our symptoms and try to match them to an illness. We start monitoring those symptoms to figure out if we're getting better or getting worse. And if we suspect that we're getting worse, we go to someone who can help us get better. When it comes to our mental health, we're conditioned not to pay the same kind of attention or to have the same set of responses. We're told by people around us to "cheer up" or "stop complaining and deal," but no one suggests we go to a doctor who can help us like when we've had a bad cough for weeks. So what I'm saying to you is that since you've been feeling bad for so long, maybe it's time for you to go see a doctor so you can figure out, with a trained professional, what you're going through.

Whatever you choose to do, and whatever you eventually find is going on with you, whether it's the blues or clinical depression or something entirely different, I want you to know that you don't have to feel like you're alone and misunderstood. At any given time, one in five young brothers and sisters is dealing with the blues or clinical depression. I'm not gonna bog you down with a bunch of statistics and figures, but take a quick second to think about that. How many students are there in your school? A fifth of those young sisters and brothers could very well be feeling exactly the way you've been feeling. But you'd never know it, because people don't really talk about it. They get up every day and go through the motions. A lot of other people, like Janet Jackson, Jennifer Holliday, Brooke Shields, and Halle Berry, have all battled depression.

Okay, enough about what could be wrong. Let's focus now on what you can do to make it right again. When I was going through the blues, one of the things that kept me going was working those muscles and breaking a sweat. I'd go out and play football, shoot hoops, whatever I could do to get those endorphins traveling through my system. I know you said the only thing you feel like doing is staying in your bed, but you might need to figure out a way to motivate yourself to do it, even when you don't really think you're up to it. I've come to realize that the times when I least feel like exercising are the times when I need to the most.

Another thing you can do is talk about what you're going through. Therapy makes a lot of people uncomfortable, though. There's the whole issue of stigma, which I've already admitted stopped me in my tracks during my first experience with the blues. Some people are also uncomfortable with the thought of talking to a stranger about their private business. Most of us aren't used to being that vulnerable in front of strangers, but it's no different from taking your clothes off in front of your physician for the very first time. The awkwardness doesn't last long, especially after it becomes clear that they're seeing you through professional, and compassionate, eyes.

"IT REALLY HURTS": DEALING WITH MORE THAN JUST THE BLUES

While we're on that subject, I've got one more thing to admit about why I didn't go into the Psychological Services office that day. My dad was a psychiatrist, and a well-respected one at that. Knowing my dad as I did, I became immediately judgmental of the therapists in the Psychological Services office, even though I'd never met them. My dad was a wonderful father who did his best by my brother and me—I'm aware of that now. I was even, on some level, aware of it back then, but his flaws were equally prominent in my mind. The fact that he was fallible made me wonder how useful any of the therapists in that Psychological Services department could really be. After all, weren't they fallible as well? The answer, of course, is yes, but so are we all. It's part of being a human being.

Phew! I know I just threw a whole lot at you. My friend Kelvin once told me that things have a way of working themselves out, and I never forgot that. And you know what? He was right. Sometimes it's hard to see that when everything feels wrong, but there's nothing wrong with just consciously saying that to yourself, even though the evidence around you seems to say the opposite. I'm not sure if Kelvin knew his simple words would one day have a profound effect on my life—but just like most things, our biggest blessings often come from the most unexpected places. Like my friendship with you. You have become a wonderful blessing in my life, and who would have ever guessed that after I didn't even answer your first two letters right away? Ha-ha. Remember that? It seems like so long ago. But that's in part because you and I have both evolved, just as our friendship has. So let's keep changing for the better! Okay. And hey, things have a way of working themselves out—so keep that beautiful chin of yours up—okay?

Write me back soon.

> Our biggest blessings often come from unexpected places.

XO
Much Love,
Hill

Date: November 28, 2007 2:17 PM
From: Young_Sistah@home.net
To: Hill@manifestyourdestiny.org
Subject: Lonely and Depressed

As a young spiritual woman, I sometimes feel alone and wonder how God can help me in the midst of loneliness and depression.

Date: November 28, 2007 5:36 PM
From: Hill@manifestyourdestiny.org
To: Young_Sistah@home.net
Subject: Re: Lonely and Depressed

That's a complex yet not uncommon question. And you being able to be sensitive, intelligent, and self-aware enough to ask such a question tells me that your feelings of "loneliness and depression" will only be a temporary condition. I'm still single and still get lonely and depressed now and again as well. And there is a perfect person that I can think of to help both of us, by answering your question. I am going to forward your question to one of the great spiritual leaders of our time, Bishop Noel Jones. I look to the lessons Bishop Jones teaches to help me guide my life and I know he would love to help answer your question.

HH

——————Begin Forwarded Message——————

All single people have the experience of "loneliness" from time to time. Particularly in a culture that extols the virtues of marriage or being with someone. However, if you are married to someone who is not suited to you, you can be just as lonely as you are now, and more depressed than you are now.

The answer is in your definition of yourself as "spiritual." You must find strength in the word of God and His promises. This infuses hope and expectation, which is an antibody for loneliness and depression. Hope energizes you to serve others while you wait expectantly on God to supply your needs. You will decrease the lonely spells as you serve others. You see, this will take the focus off you and your needs as you seek to embellish the lives of others. This will give you a sense of value, and you cannot serve others and not be noticed by God or man, unless you have your true sense of your own value.

Bishop Noel Jones

PART FOUR

Your Future

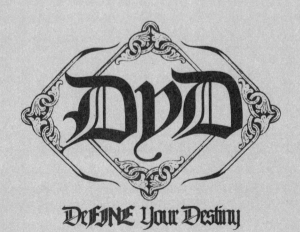

DeFINE Your Destiny

LETTER 18

Educatin' Excellence

To be able to be caught up into the world of thought—that is to be educated.

Edith Hamilton

December 1, 2007
Los Angeles

Dear Young Sistah,

Hey, you! Care package! You're kiddin' me! Thank you so much for all the goodies you sent. I don't think I've gotten a care package since I was in college. Don't get me wrong, the things that fans send in to CBS are great. I love fan mail—but a real live honest-to-goodness ole-fashioned *care* package—As Lil' John would say: Yeahaaah!! I'd almost forgotten how exciting it is to find an unexpected surprise like that in the mail. It's the best feeling, knowing somebody cared enough to take the time to pick out everything, pack it all up, and drop it off at the post office. Guess that's why it's called a *care* package. It serves as a reminder that somebody special really cares about you. And that somebody special is you. So thank you very much!

You know, the first care package I ever got was filled with snacks, gum, stationery, stamps, a fancy wool sweater, and cold hard cash. It was from my mom. I knew how hectic her work schedule was, so it was especially moving. That's how I felt when I got your care package. Oh, and the new pictures were great. I see you got your braces off and . . . "got your hair did," too. It's grown out a lot since the first picture you sent me. I especially like the picture where your hair's pulled back in a ponytail because it shows off your pretty face and that new, million-dollar smile!

Speaking of smiles, there was a huge one on my face when I saw the copy of your Algebra II test. B+, huh? Go, girl—it's your birthday!!!! Ha-ha! I am so proud of you, almost as proud as you must be of yourself. But you made it sound in your letter like you got that B+ through some stroke of luck instead of through hard work by working smart. Now, I hope you really don't feel that way, because it's just not true. There's a big difference between hard/smart work and what people like to call "luck." The thing about luck is that it's random and it can run either good or bad. The results of hard work may not always be predictable, but one thing you can be sure of, the output is always pretty much consistent with the input.

You *earned* that B+. You *chose* to excel. The fact that you did excel is not a coincidence—it's not an accident—it's not random—it's purposeful. Remember, that's exactly how I want you to approach all things in your life. *Purposefully!* I know you said you didn't bother studying that hard because math hasn't been your strongest subject and you thought you'd do poorly on the test. I guess you proved yourself wrong, huh?

You know what the grade you earned means? That you had the material *down*! And that doesn't just happen instantly or through luck. So, girl, keep doing what you're doing! And remember the three ways to work it: hard, smart, purposeful. You know what else is really effective in school? Study groups. Yeah, I learned about those when I went to Harvard, but I wish I would have known all along through school. A study group is when you get a few friends together who are studying the same subject. You guys meet after school, make an outline and an overview of your work, then share your notes from class and help each other with the homework. But it's gotta be all about school and studying. You can't hang out and gossip or talk about other stuff. If you stay disciplined and actually STUDY in your study group, it winds up being a case where the total is greater than the sum of its parts. You know, like when two heads are better than one? Working together and joining information allows you to learn more and faster than if you worked separately. And it's fun, too. So study groups are a win-win-win.

I saw you threw a few college catalogues into the care package, and I was excited about some of the schools you're considering sending applications to. I kept it small and only applied to three schools, two of which were state schools, one in Colorado and the other in California. Luckily, I made it into my first choice, Brown University. Each of those colleges you wrote about has something unique and interesting to offer its students.

You said some of the kids in school already know which colleges they want to apply to, but you can't narrow down your choices because you're not yet sure what career you want to have. Let me tell you a secret. Most people don't know before they go to college. And even if they think they do, a lot of times it changes. I had no idea I wanted to be an actor when I went to college. I even went to grad school for something completely different! A friend of mine, Margaret, who's now a writer, once told me she signed up for her first college writing course because she was trying to fill a hole left in her class schedule after she was placed into a higher-level math class than she had been expecting. That one class opened a whole new world for her. (Bet her high school math teachers never saw that one coming!)

Each of the potential careers you listed sounds promising. I can definitely imagine you as a teacher or a psychologist because of the compassion and sensitivity that shines through you. I gain a lot of insight from reading your letters, and that's helped me with some of the difficulties I've faced in my own life since our friendship began. Then again, I can also see you as a writer. You have a distinct way with words and descriptions. It's a definite gift, which you've already started using and developing. Of course, seeing as how I'd already had you pegged as a singer from the get-go, I wasn't shocked at all to see that on your list as well.

It did throw me off, though, to read that if you do decide to pursue singing as a profession, you'll maybe skip college altogether. C'mon, what's that all about? I know there may be times when you're just not feelin' school, but those times will pass. So don't write off the entire experience of college because of them. You might not think so, but going to college is a real benefit to any, and every, career you choose, even singing. And moreover, college is *fun*. And for that reason alone it's worth going.

The education you get from college goes beyond the classroom. Because teachers and textbooks aren't the only ways we learn, you know? Most college students are young, and it's their first time away from home and on their own. You'll meet people whose backgrounds are vastly different from yours, people whom you might never have encountered had you not attended college. For instance, I never would have become friends with the next president of the United States had I not gone to Harvard Law School. The guy that I opened my hotel with in New Orleans, I met in my dorm at Brown University. Shahid, the roommate of the kicker on our football team, was from Pakistan. He and I became close friends. Down the hall from me lived a girl named Jennifer who was from a Jewish community in Westchester, New York. She invited a few of us who couldn't go home for Easter to her house for Passover. It helped me learn how alike we were when her rabbi talked about how they had been slaves and were freed from bondage. I loved learning about it. Shoot, it made me wish we all could celebrate Passover. What I'm trying to get across is that college expands your life experience. I met people and got to do things that would not have been possible had I gone straight to work. Through those types of interactions, you get to learn not only about others but also about yourself. You get to encounter, and sometimes even adopt, new cultures, new languages, new hobbies, and new habits. All of these experiences will inevitably influence your character, how you view the world, and help you decide how best to participate productively in it. That's all part of the overall education you get when you go to college. There are clubs, athletic teams, and sororities you can join, things you may not have the time or money to consider doing if you're out there trying to find work and establish yourself in a career. Alicia Keys went to school even when she had a record deal. My friend Tatyana Ali was on the *Fresh Prince of Bel-Air* for years and had a super-successful acting career and decided to go to Harvard just to learn more. She wanted to be educated simply to enrich her life. Oh, yeah, and an added benefit is college is a great place to meet *boys*. So yet a another reason to go! LOL.

The most obvious reward of college is the formal education you get. Sure, it's not impossible to do on your own, but it is incredibly challenging to acquire the wealth of information that students are exposed to by attending classes and seminars every day for four years, getting to listen to lectures given by individuals who are at the top of their field and well respected by their peers.

You and I can both name people that run around talking about "I'm gonna do this . . . then that . . ." And what's wild is that they think it's just gonna magically happen. But it's not their fault; our culture is not good about teaching journey, we only show result. That's why most people don't ever reach their dreams—they were never taught to build their foundation first. I call it the "Hittin' the Lotto" mentality. We all want to think that we can go from the sidewalk to the limo overnight. But there is a big journey of foundation building in between. And the best part is, that journey is *fun* if you are passionate about what you are learning. Shoot, even Paris Hilton, as ridiculous as she is, spent months and months in front of her mirror perfecting her signature red carpet pose! (And, truth be told, her grandfather is the one in the family who *really* built the foundation.)

Let me tell you about a brother I know, very intelligent brother, good businessman, very successful, named Kanye West. Now Kanye put out an album called *The College Dropout*, right? It's a good album, isn't it? But what's the message he's tacitly sending with that title? He's basically saying he didn't need a college education to be successful. Right?

Now, what's interesting about Kanye talking about being a college dropout is that Kanye's misleading us. He's not lying, he's just leaving out a lot of information. And can I explain to you why and how? It's false evidence appearing real. And how is that false evidence? Because what Kanye doesn't tell you with the title of his first album is that his mother, who raised him, was a brilliant and celebrated college professor (may she rest in peace). So since the day he was born he'd been getting a college education. He didn't go to college for four years; when he was living up in her house he went to college for eighteen years! And so the title of his album, if it were factual and not false evidence, would read: *College Dropout, but Unless Your Mom's a College Professor, You Need to Take Your Butt to College!*

Education not only strengthens your foundation, it buys you

options. It lifts you up and gives you a steady place where you can access and absorb various points of view. Liz Murray said, "One point of view gives [you] a one-dimensional world." Have you ever heard of her? A few years ago, I watched a movie about her life story called *Homeless to Harvard: The Liz Murray Story*. Both of Murray's parents were drug addicts. They lived on welfare and whenever the check came in, her parents would cash it and use the money to buy drugs. When the money ran out, they'd resort to selling anything they could to support their habit. They even sold their children's winter coats.

Because of their drug use, Murray's parents contracted HIV. When Murray was fifteen, her mother died. She, along with her father and older sister, became homeless. She ate out of Dumpsters and sometimes, since she didn't have anyplace else to go, she'd ride the subway all night. Still, Liz Murray dreamed of a better life for herself, and she started to realize that, with an education, she just might be able to get it. She enrolled in high school when she was seventeen, even though she was living in New York City parks and subway trains, and she was so determined that she finished in two years. She visited Harvard on a school trip and made it her goal to go there. And guess what. She did.

Even as a homeless teenager, Liz Murray had big dreams for her life, and she was able to achieve those dreams because of the education she earned. If your friends and the other kids at school are telling you that college is too expensive and not worth going to, they are so off track. *Not* going to college will cost you a whole lot more money! Trust me.

Oh, and while it's good that you're feeling out different careers, really there's no rush, either to choose one or to start one. What's most important is that you become comfortable claiming the passion you have for what you like to do. And that can be many things. One question I used to get asked over and over again in high school was "What do you want to do when you get older?" It always left me a little tongue-tied because I wasn't sure. What if I picked the wrong thing? Would I be stuck with it for the rest of my life? I realize now that most of the adults I know are still searching, too. Ha! But for real, when I packed up and went off to college, all I knew was what I loved doing: playing football. When I was out there on the field, I felt awake and alive in a way that was indescribable. Probably the same way you feel when sing. But I enjoyed my classes, too. I could take classes about any subject I could imagine and some I'd never heard of before. Like semiotics. I still don't know what that is, but I knew people who got degrees in it! The material I was learning was interesting to me. I didn't know how, or if, I'd be able to use it in whatever I ended up doing after graduation, but I did recognize that simply learning how to be a critical thinker could only help me in anything I did. Knowledge really is power. So I studied hard, as hard as I played.

That's why I'm so happy to hear that things are turning around for you in math class, and why I want you to start learning good study skills. It's one of the most important tools you'll ever have, and it will serve you in many areas of your life, whether that is school, work, sports, or relationships. It's studying that turns *effort* into *expertise*. And excellence tends to replicate itself in every area of your life. What I mean by that is, you know how a lot of people who are really good at something tend to be good at a lot of things? It's not coincidence. They tend to have the same commitment to excellence in everything they do.

I'm sure you've noticed that travel is one of my passions. I like going to different places, exploring the landscapes, and seeing how other people live. I especially like when I connect with someone who is from a different world, has a different lifestyle, and yet we always find something in common. Last week I was in Hamamatsu, Japan. I went jet-skiing on Lake Hamana and watched a group of workers who were eel farming. Then I took a bus into Inasa to go see Ryugashido, which is a limestone cave that has a huge underground waterfall.

Everywhere I go, I always make it a point to visit a school because it gives me a clearer sense of the place and the culture than any of the literature I read or the tourist attractions I see. So while I was in Hamamatsu, I stopped by a couple of elementary schools. In some ways, I could have been standing inside any elementary-school classroom in the United States. But one thing I noticed that was different from anything I've observed here is that whenever a class ended, the students would all stand and bow and then thank their teacher. The memory of that has stayed with me. If I were to see any of my teachers today, I'd do just what those students in Japan did. I would stand, bow, and say, "Thank you."

When you're looking through those college catalogues, have any of them jumped out at you? When I received my Brown University catalogue I immediately started to visualize myself attending the school. There was a picture on the cover of a group of kids standing in front of one of the buildings, and I used to imagine myself on that cover with those kids. I see you, just as I saw myself, in those college catalogues. I'm guessing that you do, too. Why else would you have sent them to me—in a care package, no less—if you didn't "care" at all?

And I know you are probably saying, "Yeah, Hill, I get that education is a foundation-building tool, blah, blah, blah . . . tell me something I don't know." Well, okay. How about MONEY? Did you know that most people think about money as a result and not as a tool? How many times have you heard someone say, "I'm trying to get that money"? As if money were the goal or end, instead of thinking about money exactly the same way we view education or training, as a tool. But more on that in my next letter—Oohh, I'm excited. Hurry up and write me back!

You know, there's something else that I discovered in all my experiences: We each take turns being the teacher and being the student. I always learn so much from your letters. If you could see me now, you'd find me standing, then bowing and saying, as they do in Japan, "*Arigato.*"

Much Love,
Hill

Date: December 3, 2007 2:13 PM
From: Young_Sistah@home.net
To: Hill@manifestyourdestiny.org
Subject: Do I Really Need to Go to School??

Hill, you talk about education all the time, but for real—how important is education for women?

Date: December 8, 2007 4:45 PM
From: Hill@manifestyourdestiny.org
To: Young_Sistah@home.net
Subject: Re: Do I Really Need to Go to School??

You know how I feel about this! Education provides a woman (and a man for that matter) with the best chance of creating a life for herself that is satisfying personally, professionally, and romantically. So I'm gonna forward your question to one of the most "educated" sisters I know. She is an amazing professor at M.I.T.—Dr. Melissa Nobles.

She knows a lot about the importance of education—especially for women.

HH

—————————Begin Forwarded Message—————————

It is really hard to overemphasize the importance of education for women. Although the phrase "education is key" seems overused, it is overused for a reason. The reason is it captures a fundamental truth about human development. Through education, a woman learns how to think. She learns how to process information, solve problems—just imagine the possibilities. These basic skills are developed while she is learning substantial subjects, like English, chemistry, history, business administration, nursing, or acting. The point is that they all require the ability to reason and to think clearly. Education provides these tools.

Education opens doors. With a high school diploma, a young woman can attend college. With a college degree, she can attend graduate school, medical or law school. Or she can work, and successfully compete with others who have not only the degrees, but the thinking skills and substantive knowledge that I spoke about earlier.

This leads to my last point. Education allows a woman to be independent. She either knows what she needs to know or is confident in her ability to find out. She knows too that she is able to compete successfully in the job market. It is not by accident that throughout history, human societies all over the world have denied education to women in order to ensure both their dependence on others and lack of confidence in their own abilities. As women, as human beings, we need education.

Melissa Nobles, Ph.D.
Associate Professor
Department of Political Science
Massachusetts Institute of Technology

LETTER 19

The New Cool Money Rule

Now I'm comfortable with money and money is comfortable with me.

Diana Ross

December, 10, 2007
Los Angeles

Dear Young Sistah,

I may look it, but I'm not dumb. I know when you saw the title of this letter you were like "Hmmmm, sounds boring . . . maybe I'll read it later." Stop! Don't put it down on your dresser. This letter can and will be interesting to you. I promise! Just give it a chance. For me? Please? Okay. Cool.

In your last letter, you brought up a complex issue. But I don't think you really realized it, because you kind of just mentioned it in the middle of a paragraph where you were describing your day. You said you were kind of bummed because you were gonna go see Tyler Perry's latest movie but you weren't sure if you had enough money. And you wrote, "Why is *everything* about money?" That is a deep question. People get Ph.D.'s trying to answer that. But you're not going to need a Ph.D. in finance, because I'm gonna break down my new cool money rule, right now. Here it is.

THE PURPOSE OF MONEY (contrary to what most people think) IS NOT TO SPEND IT. RATHER, THE TRUE PURPOSE OF MONEY IS TO COLLECT IT IN ORDER TO GAIN ACCESS TO CHEAPER AND CHEAPER MONEY. In some ways, this idea is complex, but in other ways, it's pretty simple. But I'm going to break it down because (as you know) I've always said that you are beautiful, brilliant, and magnificent, which means I know that you can handle complex ideas.

What do I mean by "The purpose of money is not to spend it"? Well, when most people think about money, they think about what they can buy with money. But people who truly have *wealth* view their money as part of a continuum of wealth building that they use to create more money, influence, or a legacy in the world. You know the saying "It takes money to make money"? That's what they are talking about.

Well, you may cynically look at me and say, "Yeah, that might be true for someone who's super-wealthy with all their stocks and investments and stuff. But for someone like me who's young and can barely afford to go to the movies, this doesn't apply!" Oh, but no, my Young Sistah, you are so wrong. My "new cool money rule" applies to you whether you have one dollar or a hundred million dollars. How? And why? I'll tell you.

In your last letter, you ended it by saying, "Hill, I'm frustrated with not having any money." And you asked me if I thought you were destined to repeat your family's history of being what you called "poor." And sweet pea, my answer to you is that if you choose to follow a few simple rules, I promise you can end the cycle of so-called poverty in your family. But remember, everyone has a different definition of what poverty is. There are kids in foreign countries who would consider you super-duper rich. Young people who have no electricity, no running water, no access to health care, no ability to afford school, no roof over their heads, and only a few grains of rice a day to eat. So to some, you are *already* wealthy. So remember first, so-called poverty and so-called wealth are both a matter of perspective. It's completely relative.

If you want to be wealthy, and from the frustration in your letter, it sounds like you do, then today you have to buy into this rule, my new cool money rule, and start to analyze how you *think* about money. Money is a tool. That's it. That's all it is. A lot of times, when you ask people what they want in life, it trips me out that they'll say they want money, or they'll name a thing they would buy if they had money. Rather than saying that they want happiness or health. Or even saying they want the wisdom and foresight to create the things that would manifest enduring wealth for them and

> Money is a tool.

their family. No, they go straight to m-o-n-e-y. Why? Because they have been taught to think about the purpose of money completely wrong. Why?

Because the individuals who know and understand this new cool money rule are very wealthy and they have no interest in you acquiring some of their wealth. So they don't want you to know and understand this new cool money rule. In fact, it makes them even more wealthy if you believe money is to be spent, because you will be spending your money on goods and services that they created rather than saving your money as a tool to acquire more access to less expensive money. Now, I don't want to be talking too abstractly here, so here's a story that might better explain what I'm saying.

One day, at a book signing, I was talking to this young brother. We were laughing and joking about cars. And I said to the young brother, "What kind of car do you want?" He told me, "Oh . . . I need a car like Jay-Z has." I said, "Really, that's what you want?" He said, "Yeah! That Lamborghini he has in that video, that's what I want." I said, "I thought you said you wanted a car like Jay has?" He said, "Yeah, that Lamborghini! You know, in that video, that's the one I want." I laughed and laughed.

I've met Jay-Z many times, and he knows better than to spend $325,000 on a depreciating asset like a car. He wants his money to *appreciate*, not depreciate. So the car in that video was actually rented for the video. Ninety-five percent of the cars you see in videos, the artist doesn't own. When you watch *MTV Cribs*, many of those cribs are rented by the publicist of the artist. So what happens is that a lot of young people who see the rented houses or cars start saying, "That's what I want!" Not realizing that if Jay would have spent one third of a million dollars on a Lamborghini instead of reinvesting it in his company, he never would have built the empire he has now.

Jay-Z drives a GMC Yukon! Not a Lamborghini, you understand? He's got some nice rims on it, though!

So, contrary to popular belief, all money isn't created equal. Some money is cheap and some is expensive. Here's an example of "cheap" versus "expensive" money. Say you make $6 an hour, and you work ten hours. That's $60. But that $60 cost you ten hours of your time. Think of all the things you could do in ten hours. That's some expensive money! But what if I showed you a way that you might earn $60 by using thirty minutes of your time? Or better yet, none of your time. Yeah, of course it's legal!

So, how do we gain access to this so-called cheaper money? We save, and grow the money that we bring in. We don't use credit cards, and we don't create debt. Interest rates on credit cards can range from 18 to 30 percent. Credit cards are about the most "expensive" money you could ever find. And since our goal is to seek out cheaper and cheaper money, that means we should never use credit cards. (That's the debt rule.)

But there is a way interest can work in your favor to get *real* cheap money. Imagine this. If you were to take the $100 your "show-off" uncle spent on you for your birthday and $60 you have from your Christmas money and, instead of spending it now, invest that $160 in a mutual fund for you, and only for you, the day that money goes into the fund, it starts growing and working for you. It does it while you're in class, while you're watching TV, even while you're asleep. There are a number of different, not very complicated ways to have your money, no matter how little you start with, begin to *work for* you instead of you working for it! Something as simple as opening a savings account, or buying what's called a certificate of deposit, or CD, that pays a guaranteed rate of return after a set period.

Now, I hate to use this example, and it might make you laugh, and I'm not saying this to be mean, but you know that really, really fat kid in school that you told me about, that some of the kids tease, and how you said it looked like he grew from last year to this year almost double in size? You laughed when you said it took him his whole life to get one size, and in a year it doubled. But that's what we're going to do with your money. By next year, with your money working for you in some type of investment or savings account, your money will have grown, and then the next year it will grow even more. The longer and more, the bigger and phatter it will become. Remember, it doesn't matter how small you start, as long as it's more than nothing, it will only get bigger. And you didn't even have to work for the money.

Woo! This is exciting! We're about to build wealth for you! And what's crazy about this is that anybody can do it. It's just that most of us have never been taught that this is how we create wealth and therefore create access to cheaper and cheaper money.

Okay, I hope I didn't throw too much at you at once. I sure don't want to lose you. I know that, for me, if I get confused and frustrated, sometimes I just want to shut down and give up. Like that time I was on *Jeopardy!* Not pretty. If this letter has confused you in any way, I didn't mean for it to. So don't shut down on me, 'kay?

There are some great books out there that break down how to achieve a positive relationship with money. One I really like is by Glinda Bridgforth called *Girl, Get Your Money Straight!* I'll send you my copy. (Ahem . . . well . . . ah, actually, my ex left her copy at my house and, ah . . . anyway, I'll send it to you.)

Hey, I expect to get an e-mail or letter from you soon, so hit me. Have a great night. And think about being wealthy—'cause it's your *destiny*. And so it is!!

Much love,
Hill

Date: December 12, 2007 9:21 AM
From: Young_Sistah@home.net
To: Hill@manifestyourdestiny.org
Subject: Own Business/Own Boss

Hill, I've been thinking about it a lot and I really do not want to work for anyone. I want to be my own boss. Is it possible for me to start my own company, even though I don't have a lot of money like Paris Hilton?

Date: December 16, 2007 7:56 PM
From: Hill@manifestyourdestiny.org
To: Young_Sistah@home.net
Subject: Re: Own Business/Own Boss

My publicist and good friend, Marvet Britto of the Britto Agency, is a dynamo who made a name for herself in the competitive world of celebrity publicity as well as representing major corporations. Knowing the high standards she sets for herself and seeing the affluent world she lives in, as well as the high-profile clients she attracts—it is hard to believe that she wasn't born into money.

I can't think of anyone more qualified to answer this question than a woman who started her own incredibly successful company from scratch.

HH

—————————Begin Forwarded Message—————————

Dear Sister,

It is so realistic for you to not only think you can start your own business but actually accomplish that goal with very little start-up money. What you do need is unwavering FAITH, PASSION, and DRIVE. Fourteen years ago I made the decision while waitressing that I would pursue my dream of becoming a publicist. I studied the profession and didn't see many African American women owning their own firms operating at a level from which I knew I dared to operate. I plugged in a phone and prayed that I would one day become the successful publicist I dreamed about.

I was a former flight attendant/waitress and had harbored aspirations of one day becoming an amazing publicist/brand strategist but, like you, didn't have the resources to take the first step. All my life I felt as though every job I ever had in the service industry somehow was preparing me for what I would ultimately end up being blessed to master.

Prior to starting my business I was fired from almost every job I had. I struggled until I realized God was simply moving me closer to the purpose that he ultimately had for my life, which was to start my own business, my own empire. I was determined to be successful and always had the relentless pursuit for excellence from a child. I was always a sponge soaking up knowledge from those I met along my journey. My pastor AR Bernard taught me that if you're the smartest one in your group, then get a new group.

My regimen toward accomplishing my goal started with me going to bookstores after my job waiting tables ended each night for two years, reading every book I could get my hands on about the field I wanted to enter. After two years I had finally saved enough money to rent a small office and print business cards. I worked diligently honing my skills, often for free in the beginning to prove I was worthy and capable of handling someone's career and to also show myself that I wanted to always be motivated by the love of the craft, not the pay, and I was never too good to do whatever I needed to do to excel and deliver above my client's expectations.

Today I own one of the most successful Black-owned PR firms in the world and have helped build the brands of some of the most amazing people and corporations, such as Mariah Carey, Angela Bassett, Kim Cattrall, Eve, Motorola, and Microsoft to name a few. I am also an accomplished movie producer, having produced films such as *The Woodsman, Shadowboxer,* and *Mama, I Want to Sing!* I learned that God puts things in our reach, not in our hands, and if you reach for your goal with focus and determination you will accomplish your every desire. Soar, young sister, soar!!!!!

Marvet Britto
President/CEO
The Britto Agency
"Elevating the Standards of Excellence"

LETTER 20

The Deadliest Trap: Staying Out of the Debt Pit

There's always something to suggest you'll never be who you wanted to be.
Your choice is to take it, or keep moving.

Phylicia Rashad

December 19, 2007
Los Angeles

Dear Young Sistah,

Greetings from Hollywood Boulevard. I'm at the oldest restaurant in Hollywood, sitting in a booth that may very well have been occupied by someone like Sidney Poitier, Josephine Baker, Al Pacino, or even Dorothy Parker. She was a famous writer and humorist, both straight-edged and remarkably funny. I think you'd appreciate some of her work. She once said, "I've never been a millionaire, but I know I'd be just *darling* at it."

Reading your letter, and sitting in this restaurant, made me think of Dorothy Parker's comment. Because of what you wrote to me toward the end of your letter, that I "probably wouldn't understand anything about the financial challenges" you and your mom are facing because I'm "rich." That really caught me by surprise. "Rich"? Sure, I'm pretty comfortable financially right now, but that sure wasn't the case when I was fresh out in L.A., waiting tables and paying off my student loans from law school.

You said that you and your mom have been arguing a lot about money recently. That she had to cut your allowance in half to free up some funds in the household budget to pay for other bills. You're annoyed because now when you and your friends hang out at the mall, you won't be able to spend as much. I don't want to sound unsympathetic, but it sounds like the situation you're contending with right now is one that everyone, at one point or another, has to contend with—setting financial priorities.

You said that even though you offered to get a part-time job so that you could have your own money to spend, your mother wouldn't give you permission to do that because she wants you to focus on your schoolwork. I admire your willingness to take on the task of earning your own money, but you know that I'm going to agree with your mom on this one, okay? You know I like the idea of you earning money, but I want you focused on getting into college and your eventual career, not just making a couple hundred bucks a month bagging groceries. That's an expensive way to earn money. If it costs you going to college and if you don't *have* to do it, I'd rather focus on the bigger priorities. But what's this you wrote about not being able to wait until you get to college and get a credit card? I mentioned this a little in my last letter, but you need a credit card like Eric Cartman needs a Cheesy Poof!

What your friend in college told you is true. College campuses are crawling with companies that would love for you to carry around their little plastic cards. But what does that mean for you? Credit is nothing more than somebody providing you with the ability to take merchandise or use a service with the promise to pay for it at a later date. That's a tremendous privilege, and I won't lie, it can come in handy for people who find themselves in difficult circumstances. The problem is that for many people, the temptation to use that privilege for things they should either be paying for outright or going without is too much to resist. And because the interest that credit card companies charge is so high, if you don't pay off your entire balance at the end of every month, it quickly becomes almost impossible for you to afford to *ever* pay off your debt. Why do you think there are all of those ads for credit counselors on TV, promising to help people with their credit card debt? According to bankrate.com, the average amount owed to credit card companies by people who have at least one credit card is more than $9,000! Nine. Thousand. Dollars. You think that's a coincidence? Oh no! You might be surprised to learn that each credit card company has highly paid statisticians, economists, and marketing executives whose *only* job is to figure out ways to get you to apply for their card, use their card, and then make sure that you are paying them off for the rest of your life! I'm not exaggerating. They want *you* in their debt pit. The shareholders of their company want you there! That is their business, making Mo' Money! Mo' Money! And Mo' Money off of you! And what do they give you in return? Nothing. Talk about hittin' the lotto!! When you carry a balance on your credit card, you are giving them FREE MONEY!

Take this friend of mine who had a dental emergency. She had to have a root canal, and the procedure ended up costing nearly a thousand dollars. She lived on a really tight budget, and she didn't have any savings. She did have credit cards, though, that she had gotten in case of emergency. And her dentist would have accepted that method of payment, except that when it came time to pay, she was already up to her limit on all of them. She was generally healthy and had had no reason to anticipate having an emergency. (That's the thing about emergencies; you don't see them coming.) And she'd gone ahead and used her cards on things that she wanted but couldn't immediately afford. Then when the monthly bills came, she would pay only the minimum amount that was due because that's all she could squeeze out of her budget.

You wouldn't have been able to tell from looking at her, but she was in debt. She ended up borrowing money from several of her friends to pay her dental bill, which pushed her even deeper into debt, and even worse, put her in a weird position with her friends until she'd managed to pay them back. My grandmother used to always say, "You cut your coat according to the size of your cloth." For the longest time I had no idea what she meant by that. But it means that you should only use what you have at your disposal. If my friend had done that, that root canal would have hurt her (financially) a lot less.

Credit cards have become such a part of our culture, though, we can't escape them completely. But we can think about the messages that we're being given about them. For example, check out this lyric by Bow Wow. Now, I know you like him and so do I. I met him about two years ago, and he is a very impressive young brother. He's a driven entrepreneur and a talented artist. Yet, in one of his songs, he says something that is a perfect example of thinking about money and credit in the wrong way. In the remix of "I Think They Like Me," Bow Wow says, "I'm under twenty-one with a Black Card." What's he talking about? He's talking about the black credit card from American Express called the Centurion Card. But what is he *really* talking about?

Well, he's saying that he's got this unlimited credit, so that's really cool, isn't it? He's under twenty-one years old and has unlimited credit, so therefore he's successful. And he is successful . . . but it's not because he has a Black Card. Connecting the two is False Evidence Appearing Real. Here's why.

What is an unlimited line of credit, really? It's permission for you to give unlimited money to some other company. Is that good? To me it would be much more accurate and interesting if Bow Wow bragged about Ken Chenault, a fellow Harvard Law School alum, and a bad brother. He is the CEO (which stands for chief executive officer) of American Express. The CEO is *above* the president of a company. So Ken Chenault is the man! He doesn't just carry a Black Card, he *owns* the Black Card. Which would you be more impressed by? I would much rather hear folks rappin' about owning or running the corporation that makes the card than bragging about carrying the card and trying to impress others with how much of their money they are able to give to a company that they don't own.

Young people, especially, are targeted by advertisers. Looking out of the window onto Hollywood Boulevard, I can see dozens of young people walking up and down the sidewalk. Nearly all of them are clutching a shopping bag with the name of a store printed on it. Right down the street, there's a shopping mall. It's a magnet for tourists, but it's also a regular hangout for the local teenagers. Most shopping malls are. Malls tend to be a safe place where teens can get together and sit for as long as they want in a food court or go to the movies. But it's also a place that can breed false desire. In each store window, there are glossy posters of people wearing huge smiles as they use a new electronic device or wear a new sweater or pair of shoes. They are trying to make you want something you probably don't need, and didn't even want before you saw it being advertised.

It's not my intent to trivialize the things you want to buy or to imply that you shouldn't have access to those things. I mean only to suggest that you consider a reevaluation of your relationship with money, as well as your reasons for wanting the things that you do. Is it because everybody else has that same thing? Is it because you feel owning it might send some kind of message out about you?

You know, a lot of people go into debt to buy things they can't afford because they're under the false impression that the value the world places on those items will somehow translate into the value the world will place on *them*. I've been shopping before with girlfriends who've looked longingly into store windows and said things like, "When people see me in that dress, they're gonna know I'm all that," and I know very well that they're all that no matter what they're wearing. They don't really want the dress; they want the reaction they think other people will have to the dress. And that's a misguided attempt to use money to buy attention, affection, or even admiration. Do you see what I mean? How a person spends her money can tell you volumes about her, the fears and insecurities, the ambitions and priorities. Maya Angelou once said, "Don't make money your goal. Pursue the things you love doing, and do them so well that people can't take their eyes off you."

> Pursue the things you love doing.

I said earlier that money is a tool, and it is, but it's also a metaphor. We often, unconsciously, use the word—as well as the physical tool itself—to represent something else. You've mentioned several times that you wish your mother had more money, that she never seems to have enough of it for you guys to go anywhere or to do things that are fun. Could it be possible that you were using the word *money* when what you really meant was time?

You closed your letter by telling me that you thought my understanding of your situation might be limited because of your belief that I am rich. I'll close this letter by telling you that I believe you will overcome this and any other perceived financial limitation because of your *infinite* wealth. Wealth is not a relative condition. To be wealthy is to have an abundance of something. Look for areas in your life where you already are abundant—friendships, family, knowledge—and let those things begin to help you feel abundant. There is nothing wrong with wanting more wealth out of life, wanting money, better medical care, and being able to have whatever you want when you want it. You're intelligent and creative, and I bet that if you rely on those two gifts, you will attain all of those things.

I've gotta run. The waiter just brought me my bill, but don't worry, I'm paying in *cash*. Will you write me back soon, pretty please? Have a great day!

Much Love,
Hill

Date: December 21, 2007 4:55 PM
From: Young_Sistah@home.net
To: Hill@manifestyourdestiny.org
Subject: Unhappy and Unorganized

Hill, you said that to achieve my goals I have to be an "active architect of my own life." But for some reason, I can never feel organized enough to even start working on those things you talk about. My head gets all cluttered and I get confused. What are some things I can do to be more organized and more efficient, so I'm not always feeling like I'm playing catch-up?

Date: December 26, 2007 2:53 PM
From: Hill@manifestyourdestiny.org
To: Young_Sistah@home.net
Subject: Re: Unhappy and Unorganized

One thing I recently realized is that before I could become organized and move forward, I had to "clean up" those things I had allowed to get messy in my environment. I'll explain. First of all, it's no coincidence that you e-mailed me a question about organizing your life and being more efficient on the exact day that I am moving out of my house and "downsizing" into a loft. Moving can be a very emotional experience, and I just realized that I never really knew how much stuff I had until I cleared out my entire house. We all hold on to so much stuff. Stuff we put away in back corners of closets, in cupboards, underneath beds, in the back of the freezer, in the garage—stuff tucked away everywhere. And you know what? Most of that "stuff" we tuck away isn't useful to us anymore. But for some reason, we felt we had to hold on to it. That's when I understood that it's an extension of our lives and all the "stuff" you and I have been talking about in our letters to each other. We/you/I hold on to too much stuff in our psyches, our hearts, our heads, and our spirits. There is a simplicity of being that has nothing to do with all the stuff and baggage that we collect in our journey. One of my favorite poets is a man by the name of David Whyte. He writes about how all of us have a little velvet bag that we stick things in. And as we grow older that bag gets more and more full of stuff. Eventually that bag is 200 feet long and we carry our stuff around like an albatross around our necks. It weighs us down and it stresses us out. It allows us to continue to repeat old habits.

So now that it's moving day, can we make a pact together? I want us each to promise that we'll help each other clear out our "stuff." C'mon! It's moving day! It's time to move on, move up, and clear out the clutter. So with that thought, I am going to forward your question to my friend Christina Gomes, who is an organizational expert who has an extremely successful organizational company called New Life Space. She has organized homes and offices for huge celebrities, businesspeople, and major corporations. She is an organizing guru and can help us both organize our stuff going forward. Now that we've cleared out our clutter!

P.S. As I'm moving boxes out to the truck, I've had my iPod on shuffle and you won't believe the song that just came on: "Bag Lady" by Erykah Badu. This is exactly what she sings about. Google the lyrics and you'll see what I mean! You see . . . there truly are no coincidences in life. . . . Let's see what Christina has to say to you.

HH
————————Begin Forwarded Message————————

Dear Young Sister,

My friend Hill often talks about the idea of "working hard at working smart." Working smart is exactly what the discipline of organization is. Too often we busy ourselves in chaos and disorder, valuable time wasted. To organize oneself takes discipline and practice, but once achieved, all things fall into place. A starting point to organizing is clearing the clutter in your life like unused belongings, piles of paper, etc. These things are distractions and roadblocks. Free yourself of all things unnecessary and focus on simplifying your life. Clearing out your surroundings clears your mind.

Another important "work smart" tool is to create a daily "to do" list. It's as simple as using one notebook, page by page, journaling your tasks for each day. Take pleasure in crossing off things you accomplish—it feels great to see a page of completed tasks. Discipline yourself to carry your notebook with you at all times to capture phone numbers, new tasks, and information that you may come across throughout your day. Take a moment each day to review and update your book. By taking the time each day, you are perfecting a system and exercising discipline—hence forming new patterns that you'll apply to other areas of your life, and you will be that active architect of your own life!

Christina M. Gomes
Founder & CEO
New Life Space, Inc.

The Linked S's:
Savings and Self-Empowerment

A big part of financial freedom is having your heart and mind free from worry about the what-ifs of life.

Suze Orman

December 27, 2008
Los Angeles

Dear Young Sistah,

Babysitting, eh? That's genius. Why didn't I think to suggest that? It's a great gig. I'm sure your neighbors are also thrilled to know that when they go out, their daughter is safe and in good hands. What's more, it's a win-win situation for you and your mother. You get to earn some extra money on the weekends, which, I know, makes you happy; and since it's not a regular job with set hours, it doesn't interfere with your study time, which, I'm sure, makes your mom happy. See, I knew that if you sat down and got your creative juices flowing, you'd come up with a great idea.

Most young people, after they start working and earning their own money, experience the same feelings that you expressed in your letter. There is a definite sense of pride and independence that comes from knowing you earned the cash that's in your pocket. It wasn't a gift, and you didn't have to ask anybody for it. You provided a service and were compensated. What also happens is that you start to realize the amount of effort that goes into earning money, and that makes you less inclined to spend it as quickly or as easily. Suddenly you look at a sweater and think, "That's a whole Sunday afternoon's worth of work," and you ask yourself whether you like or want it enough to fork over that much cash for it. It doesn't mean you're stingy. It just means that your relationship to money is changing. You're learning to place a different value on it than you had before.

You said that everything seems so expensive to you now and that you weren't really feelin' like spending all your babysitting money on some of the things you thought you wanted, but at the same time, it's burning a hole in your pocket. Since you asked me what I think you should do, I'll tell you. I think you should save your money. I think you should ask your mom to take you to the bank and open a savings account for you. Then you should decide what percentage of the money you earn will be saved, and stick to that plan.

The feelings you described in your letter stem from a sense of self-empowerment, from having a plethora of choices at your disposal. It's a far cry from the sense of helplessness you described in your last letter when you were telling me how bummed out you were because your mom had cut your allowance. By committing yourself to a savings plan, you'll be sustaining that feeling, that Empowerment 3.0 we talked about when we first started exchanging letters.

Saving your money is the first step in getting your money to work for you. And this is why. Think about all of the things you like. Just in your letters to me you've mentioned: Apple Bottoms and Seven jeans; Converse, Nike, Steve Madden, and Jimmy Choo; beaded jewelry and pearl and diamond earrings; iPods and iPhones and on and on. Wanting and liking all that stuff is cool. There's nothing wrong with enjoying nice things; I like having nice things, too. But how often do you buy or get those things? Maybe a couple times a year, between Christmas and birthday gifts, plus when you used to be able to scrape up enough money from your allowance? Sound about right? Now, imagine this: Just off of the money you spend on those things, and a little bit extra from money you may make at your summer job, you could turn yourself into a millionaire by forty. I'm not kidding. It's all about investing, saving, and cultivating your money. No matter how little we start with, the money begins to work for us, rather than you and I working for the money.

I'm not saying you have to save every last penny you earn. If there's something you truly want, something you feel especially moved to do or buy, then you should use a portion of the money you've earned to do that. You worked for it; you're entitled to enjoy it. But you don't have to enjoy it all at once; spread that pleasure and wonder of possibility out over weeks, months, and years. There might be something you will feel just as moved to do or buy in six months, or a year, or even ten or twenty years down the line. I know, I know, twenty years from now seems like an eternity, but it's really not. Come on, you've already started making plans to ensure your self-empowerment twenty years down the line. You're planning to go to college; you're thinking about careers. Investing in a savings plan is just another facet of that. By putting a little bit to the side each time you have money, you'll be making additional provisions for the future that you're creating.

Okay, you're probably asking, "Hill, what exactly am I saving for?" Or you could be thinking, "I'm only in high school. Even if I save all the money I earn right now, it won't mean anything in the real world. It won't even be enough to buy a car." Well, as far as what you're saving for is concerned, I can't tell you anything specific. I don't know, and you don't know either, because it's not for anything concrete, not yet. And *that* is the precise reason you should be saving, because you don't know what desires or demands the future holds, but you should position yourself in such a way that you will be able handle them, whatever they may be.

As far as the amount of the money you'll be saving not being enough, I wouldn't be too sure about that. The two things people never think they have enough of are time and money, but that's usually because they mismanage both. There are folks who are legitimately busy, just like there are folks who are living on extremely limited incomes. But even they can find ways to eke out more than they thought was possible.

Money that's being saved is, ideally, money that you don't think about. There are all different kinds of savings plans and all different reasons why people save their money. Someone might open a savings account in January because they want to put money aside to buy Christmas presents with it in December. Someone might start a savings plan when their child is born because they want to make sure that there will be enough money when the time comes to send them off to college. Others have funds stashed away so that they won't be caught unprepared in case of a medical or financial emergency. Whatever the reason, when the money has been put away, you should do your best to forget it even exists, until the time comes when you have to use it. And then, it will feel like winning the lottery.

When I was young, and I mean really young, like in elementary school, my favorite candies were Now and Laters. Each pack had about ten or so individually wrapped taffy candies in them. I especially loved the sour apple and watermelon flavors. My friends and I used to go down to the corner store in our neighborhood and buy them and we would start chewing them up right away. I took the name very literally. It even said on the wrapper, "Eat some now, save some for later." So that's exactly what I did. I'd eat about half of the candies in the package and then tuck the other half in my pocket for later or even the next day. My friends would always eat all of theirs. Watching them would sometimes make me feel tempted to pull the rest of mine out of my pocket and eat them, but I never did. I'd muster every little bit of patience I had in me and wait until later because I knew it would be worth the wait.

There were even a few times when I totally forgot I had that half pack in my pocket. My friends and I would have spent the whole afternoon together talking or playing kickball or whatever, and then on the way home, I'd stick my hand into my pocket and there it'd be, a whole half bar of Now and Laters. I'd start eating them and my friends would give me a look that told me they wished they'd saved some of their candies. Of course, I'd share, but it was a sweet feeling to know that my patience had been rewarded. Sometimes it's sweeter than the candy itself. Saving money is obviously not quite the same as eating Now and Later candies, but it's not so different either. For instance, today, since I have saved a lot of money, like my Now and Laters, I can share it with my friends and others who don't have as much as I do. And that's a good feeling!

There will be times when it might seem like a cruel exercise in discipline to keep to the savings plan you've created. Let's say you earn $75 one weekend and the commitment you've made is to save 20 percent of everything you make. But then you see a dress you really want and it costs $70. What do you do? Chances are most people will start rationalizing, finding a way to justify breaking the promise they've made to themselves. You might tell yourself that you've done a really good job saving so far, that you haven't been spending that much of the money you've made, and you've always kept to your plan. Sometimes you even deposit more than 20 percent of the money you earn into your savings account. You coax yourself and coax yourself until finally you convince yourself to just go on and buy the dress. After all, you deserve it, right?

Saving money is not about deprivation, it's about forward thinking, making an investment in your future. I want you to have a future that's purpose-driven, not one that's reactionary or impulse-driven. It might not seem like much of anything to skip making a deposit into your savings account once or twice, especially if it's to buy something you really want. It's not like the money's being used for anything, it's just sitting there. But we've already established that money is a tool, a metaphor. So the money itself is not the issue. The intention is. If it's your intention to live a purpose-driven life, then all of your actions have to conform to that intention. This doesn't mean that you can't buy the dress you want. What is does mean, though, is that you might have to find a way to buy the dress, yet still honor the commitment you've made. After you deposit 20 percent of the money you earned, you could put the rest of it to the side. The next time you babysit and earn money, you could add the amount that's left over after your savings deposit to the amount you have set aside. That should be more than enough for you to be able to buy the dress, and a few other things, too.

> Saving money is not about deprivation.

When you're saving money, consistency is important. Once you start making excuses and exceptions, you'll never stop. Something will always come up to make you start rationalizing and then, eventually, to make you start spending. And if these intrusions happen frequently enough, they might steer you so far off course that you'll stop saving altogether.

My friend Janet made a New Year's resolution that at the end of that year, she would treat herself to a vacation out of the country. She lived on a tight budget, so she wasn't sure how she was going to find room in her budget to save toward this vacation. She had also never really had a savings account before, so the whole concept was new to her. Still, she thought about what might be the best way to free up funds so she could start saving. She looked at her daily routine and found two things she did that she was willing to sacrifice. Every morning on her way to work, she stopped at Starbucks and bought herself a tall double latte with caramel (umm, good!), which cost about $4 and change. She also bought lunch every day because she didn't have the time to make her own lunch and bring it with her to work. That usually cost her between $5 and $10 each day.

She decided that if she did without the morning latte and the lunch that she bought every Monday through Friday, she would be able to save at least $50 a week, which adds up to $200 a month. Initially, it was hard for her to make the shift. It was so hard she had to find an alternate route to drive to work because she couldn't bear passing by the Starbucks every morning. But she did it. She started drinking tea. She'd take leftovers for lunch, or she'd wake up a half hour early each morning to make herself a salad. "There were lots of times I wanted to break down and go back to my old routine," Janet said, "but I was determined to go on that vacation."

By the end of the year, Janet had saved more than $2,000. She bought herself a ticket to Brazil and had the time of her life. (And drank as much fresh Brazilian coffee as she wanted!) She was so proud of herself that when she returned from her vacation, she continued with her savings plan even though she'd already met the goal that she'd set for herself. She'd grown accustomed to her new routine. She liked having tea at home in the mornings, and found that it was healthier to make her own lunch instead of eating out all the time. But more than any of those things, she loved the freedom that her savings account gave her. "I didn't realize that the little bit of money I was spending here and there could add up to something as significant as a vacation." This time, she's not saving for any particular event. She's just saving because it's become a part of her life.

THE LINKED *S*'S: SAVINGS AND SELF-EMPOWERMENT

One of the reasons Janet was so successful with her savings plan was that she stuck to it. She turned it into a habit, just like going to the coffee shop and eating out had once been a habit. Once she'd grown used to the habit of saving money, it became a permanent part of her lifestyle. If the amount she was spending on coffee and lunch seemed minor to her at first, that's because she was only thinking of it in that moment and not seeing how it could impact her future. Five dollars here and there may not feel like much when it's being spent, but it becomes a whole lot if it's being saved.

When Janet told me about her plan to save enough money to take a vacation, I had wanted to give her something that would encourage and inspire her. I went to the bookstore to see if there were any good books on financial management or starting a savings plan, but before I could even get to that part of the store I found a small box of "money cards" put together by Suze Orman, a great personal finance expert. Inside the box were dozens of colorful cards, each one about the size of a coaster, with wise, inspirational words about wealth printed on them. I bought a box for Janet, and one for myself, too.

I'll share with you the card that I keep on my desk beside my calendar. I read it every day. It says: "Do you have everything you need? Do you have everything you want? If you can distinguish between your needs and desires, and always keep tomorrow in mind today, then you will have everything you need, and more than enough of what you want." Now you know why we talked about needs versus wants before.

There was one other question you asked in your letter that I want to answer. You said that your friend Beverly borrowed some money from you and promised to pay you back in a few days, but she hasn't done that yet. You've seen her buying things, so you know she has money, but she's acting like she's forgotten about the loan. You wanted to know if you should confront her and ask for your money back or if you should just leave it alone.

That's a tough one. Money has been known to destroy friendships. It's one thing for Beverly to tell you that she doesn't have the money to pay you back yet and to ask if you could give her more time to repay the loan. It's another for her to completely ignore the fact that she didn't pay you back as she'd promised and to act like she doesn't remember. Pretending a debt doesn't exist won't make it go away.

On the other hand, maybe it's an honest mistake and she has really forgotten. It seems like an unlikely thing, but it does happen. Even important things like paying a friend back can slip your mind if you have a lot of other things going on in your life. In any case, I think you should give Beverly the benefit of the doubt. I don't think you should bring up the matter in an accusatory way, and you should avoid talking to her about it in front of other people. Find a time when the two of you are alone (or create a time for the two of you to be alone) and gently remind her that she said she'd repay you a while back and you were wondering if she had the money. If she says she doesn't have the money, but she doesn't give you any indication when she will pay you back, be direct and ask her. If she's evasive or she refuses to tell you when you'll get your money, don't push it any further.

My father believed that people often treated their money as an extension of their personalities and emotions. In other words, people who are stingy with their money tend to be stingy generally. Likewise, people who are generous with their money tend to also be generous in other ways as well. That's because our use of money, like our use of all our other resources, is guided by an internal impulse that places worth on what is being given, and importance on why it is being given. The way Beverly chooses to handle the situation will tell you a lot about her character, particularly where trust is concerned. If she values your friendship, then she will respond to you in a respectful and considerate way, even if she doesn't have the money yet to pay you back. If she (or you) allows whatever sum of money she borrowed from you to destroy your friendship, then that will also tell you what your friendship was worth.

There are some who believe that you should never loan your friends money. I agree that it's not a wise idea to make it a habit, but I also believe that it's important for us to help others who are in need. And if we can't turn to our friends for help in our times of need, then who can we turn to? That said, at this point in your life, if any of your friends were in true financial need, like an urgent medical situation, I don't think you should be the one they turn to. That's what their parents or guardians are there for.

Now I have a few questions for you. Why did Beverly ask to borrow money from you? Is it because she knows that you've started earning extra money by babysitting? I know that you and your friends are close. There are things you guys tell each other that you probably wouldn't dream of sharing with anyone else because it's private and it would be a betrayal of your relationship. But just as you're developing and nurturing relationships with them, you're developing and nurturing a relationship with your financial future, and it also demands respect and privacy. In other words, when it comes to money, you don't have to tell your girlfriends all your business. It's your money, not theirs.

As an aside, once when I was on a date with a young lady, she reached into the pocket of her coat to pull out a handkerchief and a bunch of cash came flying out. I thought she was attempting to pay the bill, which the waiter had recently placed on the table. But when I told her that she should put her money away because I was paying, she explained that the money was for something else.

"That's just the mad money my mom gave me for tonight," she said. I'd never heard of "mad money" before, so I asked her what that was. She told me that it was money a woman carried with her so she could find her own way home in case the man she was out with didn't behave properly. She told me that before cell phones, mad money almost always included a quarter in your shoe so that you could call home or a cab, even if your purse was stolen. Later, I asked my friend Anisa if she'd ever heard of mad money.

"Oh, yeah," she said. "My mom and my grandma taught me to take mad money with me whenever I go out with a guy." Apparently, mad money is an old-school phrase, one that dates back to the 1920s. In those days, women didn't have the same financial freedom and flexibility that they now have. As Anisa put it, "There's a reason why those really old evening bags are only big enough for a travel comb and a lipstick. You didn't need money because your date was paying for everything when you went out, and you didn't need a house key because your father was waiting up for you when you got back." Men were the ones who had full control of all the money. At least in theory. In practice, however, it was common for a woman to have a stash of money that she kept secret from her husband or boyfriend. I didn't know that the practice existed, and I definitely wasn't aware that women were still doing it. I wondered if all women were in on this secret of mad money, so I asked my mom. Unsurprisingly, she knew all about it.

"Hill," she told me. "A woman's got to always have her own money stashed away somewhere, money that nobody knows about. That's what guarantees her independence and gives her peace of mind."

Happily, a lot's changed for women (and everyone) since the 1920s, but there's something to be said for having the peace of mind that comes from knowing you've got yourself covered no matter what happens. From everything that you've written in your letter, I'd say that you are already starting to feel that peace of mind. Hold on to it! And don't let that money keep burning a hole in your pocket. Go on and put it in the bank and let it grow some interest! In the words of six-time Olympic medalist Jackie Joyner-Kersee, "It is better to look ahead and prepare than to look back and regret."

So whatcha think about all this? E-mail me when you can and tell me your thoughts. I hope you have a magnificent day!

I'll be looking for a letter or an e-mail!!!

Much Love,
Hill

Date: December 28, 2007 5:21 AM
From: Young_Sistah@home.net
To: Hill@manifestyourdestiny.org
Subject: Jane of All Trades, Master of None?

Hill, I have so many ideas about what I want to do and accomplish. Is it wrong to have a lot of ideas, or do I need to focus on just one? (Is it true what they say, that you can be a jack of all trades but a master of none?)

Date: January 2, 2008 9:33 PM
From: Hill@manifestyourdestiny.org
To: Young_Sistah@home.net
Subject: Re: Jane of All Trades, Master of None?

That's BS. You can be a master of all trades and succeed in any area or areas that you choose. However, to do that requires two simple things: focus and organization. And to be truly a master of many, you really need both. But if you're not organized, then you're all over the place and end up ultimately spinning your wheels.

My friends and I often joke about a guy we know. We call him "the idea man" because every time we see him, he has a different idea. But he's never focused enough to actually implement any of them. That's why he's got ideas and ideas and ideas, but not success. It's just like you've described to me in some of your letters, some of your friends who just talk, talk, talk, but they never do, do, do. That's the difference between ideas and implementation. The most successful people in the world are often successful in multiple areas of their life, because they have developed a methodology of focus and organizational skills that allow them to be successful in anything they do. Look at Condoleezza Rice, who is the U.S. secretary of state, but also a concert-level pianist and a tenured professor and provost at Stanford University.

I couldn't help but send this to my friends Angela Bassett and Nicole Loftus; they are both strong, intelligent women from two completely different careers, so I think their perspectives will be helpful. Angela is one of the greatest actors, male or female, living today. She truly is a "master" of her trade. Nicole is the founder, president, and CEO of Zorch International, Inc. Zorch is a $25 million marketing agency providing the Fortune 500s a one-of-a-kind model for sourcing branded merchandise, print, and signage. Her clients include Citigroup, BP, AT&T, Motorola, and Oprah Winfrey.

HH

——————————Begin Forwarded Message——————————

There is nothing wrong with having lots of ideas. Some may be great while others not so much. And perhaps you can accomplish some simultaneously or many in succession—very quickly.

But it seems to me that sort of thing also takes an individual who possesses the unique talent to budget her time and resources properly. Consider this: Would you like to be known as someone who has a GOOD idea and follows it through to completion or someone with a GREAT idea but lacks the drive to see it through to completion? Whatever you have the talent, drive, and ability to accomplish . . . do so . . . with the best of intention.

Angela Bassett

——————————Begin Forwarded Message——————————

Hello, friend, this is a wonderful question. I assure you it is possible to be the master of many trades. How exciting to have so many ideas about what to do with your life. Few people can identify one goal for their future. You have a gift of this happy problem of deciding which to accomplish first.

Too many people feel that life is about one script to follow. Not only is it vital that you push yourself beyond the script written for you but that you recognize your life should have many chapters that will allow you to uncover different parts of yourself. You will start to uncover your strengths and your weaknesses. Through education learn to tackle the weaknesses and focus on your strengths.

Many times when we are children our culture and our families push us gently into a path for our life. That's what I'm referring to as "the script." Sometimes the script is someone else's story. We are asked to play by rules that are for a game that we didn't choose to play. Hill Harper and many other successful people will tell you without hesitation that only you can write your own script and if that means being the jack of all trades and mastering them, too . . . then go for it.

Another saying that you may have heard is "Life is short." Well, it may be true—life does go by fast; however, it is important to remember that fifty, sixty, eighty years is a long time. Each passing day is a chance to discover a new part of ourselves that deserves to be developed and deserves to thrive.

In my family, women are raised to make babies and spaghetti, and to take care of the men. I always knew that I wanted more, and more, and more. Fortunately I've met other women and men who have proven that we all have different skill sets that are worthy of our attention. Hill Harper was a leader and successful graduate of Harvard Law School and then decided to discover a completely different world as an actor. How brave he was to take that step.

Everyone on earth is exactly the same in this regard. Yet few have the courage that you do to ask the question, "Can I do more with my life?" Everyone on the planet is multidimensional and dynamic. It's one of the things that separate us from the other mammals walking around. Do you have a nurturing side that likes to care for others? Is there a part of you that likes numbers and formulas and finding answers to number problems? Do you have a side that enjoys performing and entertaining people? It is natural to have all of these skills and unnatural to hide any of them.

Remember, all of these skills and gifts you have do not have to shine at once. Be patient. There comes a time in your life when each one is a fit, and you can "call on" those gifts as you need them.

Nicole Loftus
President and CEO
Zorch International, Inc.

LETTER 22

Careering and Steering

You have to love what you do to want to do it every day.

Aaliyah

January 3, 2008
Des Moines, Iowa

Dear Young Sistah,

WE WON!!! WE WON!!! I am in Iowa at the primary with presidential candidate Barack Obama and he won tonight. *We all* won tonight. As you know, I have been in and out of Iowa for the past two months campaigning for him. Iowa is the first state to lend a voice to selecting the next president, so it was critical that we do well here—and we did better than "well"!! Since I am on his National Finance Committee, and Iowa is where I was born, Iowa is where I have been concentrating my efforts. It is the first time I have gotten so involved with a political campaign, and the experience has been amazing! Meeting and speaking with so many people about my friend and the issues this country faces has made me very proud to be a part of this country and this campaign. There are so many good people everywhere, just like you!

A victory for one of us is always a victory for all of us since we're all connected. Being in this politically charged environment, it's been wonderful to see how calm Barack is in the face of everything. Tonight, as the votes were being counted, all the other political candidates hung out in their headquarters, undoubtedly pacing back and forth awaiting the returns to come in from each precinct. You wanna know what my former classmate chose to do in those final hours while the votes were being counted? He took his wife and two young daughters out to a family dinner. So do you see how choosing a career you love can contribute to your confidence and happiness?

It's funny that as I'm in a front-row seat, witnessing the well-deserved rise of Barack's career, you're asking me about mine. So you want a list of all the careers that I would have chosen had I *not* become an actor? Hmmm . . . Gonna have to think about that one a little bit. I saw the "new and improved" list of professions you included with your letter, though. I noticed this time you decided to rank them by their average starting salary. But . . . you know, a couple of those professions seemed to come out of left field. They weren't at all in line with any of the interests and curiosities you've expressed in your letters before. What's up with that? I hope you aren't putting those in just to impress me, or to make your mom happy, or because you think it's a "good" job that will make you a lot of money. That reminds me, you know what Barack's first job was? He was a community organizer working out of the basement of a church on the south side of Chicago. After turning down super-prestigious law firms, he took a job that paid him only $13,000 a year. Why? Because that was where his passion led him, and that was more important to him than a six-figure salary. And now he's still doing the same thing, serving his community. His community has just gotten bigger over the years. I've noticed something similar in the lives of a lot of people I know, actually, and certainly in my own: By finding a job that we're passionate about, we often wind up being way more successful than we ever thought we could be when we were considering taking jobs that we didn't love so much. But some of us thought those other jobs would be the "responsible" or "respectable" choices.

That's why I wouldn't know where to begin with this list you want me to write. Even if I hadn't followed the exact same path that's led me to be an actor on *CSI: NY*, I would still be doing something that I love as much as acting, writing, speaking, and the other things

I enjoy that I get to spend my life doing now. It's such a difficult thing to do, to imagine a future other than the one you chose and that chose you. I think anybody who is doing what they love will tell you that they didn't find their calling, it found them.

If you ask me, instead of asking young sistahs and brothas, "What do you want to do when you grow up?" I think adults should ask the question, "What do you love doing?" or "What, when you think about doing it, makes your heart beat faster?" Those questions are more in line with what folks are really trying to find out about you, and what you should be trying to find out about yourself.

When thinking about careers, some people advise, "Look to your family's careers." But the events, circumstances, and choices that led our parents and grandparents to their careers are not always the ones that will work best for us as we make our way in the world.

I come from a family of doctors and community activists. My mom's father was a pharmacist who used his education and resources to serve others at a time when the members of his community weren't able to patronize the other drugstores in town. My father's father was a doctor. Families would travel from neighboring states to go to him. Their wives, my grandmothers, worked just as hard on behalf of their communities. They sat on the boards of service organizations. They encouraged people to be more active in the political process. My parents were the same.

When I looked at myself through the lens of their accomplishments, I seemed small, completely incapable of measuring up to what I considered their greatness. But through them, I also saw things that encouraged and inspired me. I saw that community was a source of strength and support. I saw that service was vital to the survival of a community. I knew that I wanted to embrace those beliefs and make them central to my life, but I also knew I didn't want to be a doctor. I hated needles, and I can't stand the way hospitals smell (uhhgh). But even though I knew for sure what I *didn't* want to do, I had no idea what I *did* want to do. Whenever people talked about my potential, I got scared because it made me feel tiny, lost, and unsure of my abilities.

One day I had a conversation with my mom. She kept talking about "your path." After she'd mentioned it a few times, I got kind of frustrated and upset and so I asked her, "What *is* my path?" She gave me a confused look, and with one eyebrow raised, said, "How would I know that?" I shrugged and said, "Well, I don't know what it is either!" That's when she laughed, put her hand on my shoulder, and said, "Hill, you don't have to know. The best way to pave the road is by walking and being open to what you discover." A couple days later she gave me a book called *Creative Visualization*, which is the first book I read that introduced me to the idea of believing that you can visualize what you want to create in your life.

Taking my mother's words to heart ultimately freed me from my inclination to use other people's pasts to define and determine my future. What's more, I still ended up embracing those ideals and principles that mattered most to me, the ones my family instilled in me. The path I chose allows and affords me the opportunity to serve and to play an active part in strengthening my community. I'm sure you've noticed the irony in all this. I was so sure I didn't want to be a doctor, and then chose to become an actor, and now the role I play that most people recognize me from is, yeah, a doctor. Wound up following in Mom's footsteps after all!

For whatever reason, people associate being a grown-up with being serious, so when they're considering their career options, they rule out anything that they consider fun as not "serious" enough. That's what I think you might be doing with your new list. Not so much ruling it out, but forgetting that fun and joy should be a central part of any profession. Make the thing you enjoy doing the most into your life's work.

> Make the thing you enjoy most your life's work.

Now, sometimes the things that we enjoy doing don't seem to lend themselves to any sort of legitimate career choice. If you love everything about your chemistry class, it's easy to see you should consider becoming a scientist, but what if you're like my friend Joyce? All throughout high school, whenever people asked her what she wanted to do, Joyce would say she wanted to get an M.B.A. and become the CEO of a successful business. But she struggled through her high school economics class. "I knew right away it wasn't for me," she said. "It was so confusing, and I couldn't imagine being in that head space every single day." But she still insisted that she was determined to work in the world of business. Why? "I liked the way people responded when I said that," Joyce confessed. "It was such a respected profession and everybody seemed so proud of me when I said I wanted to do that."

When Joyce went to get advice from her school guidance counselor, he asked her to think about what she loved to do most and what she was good at doing. The first and only thing that came to Joyce's mind was talking on the phone. She loved to talk on the phone with her friends. She was a popular girl with a huge circle of friends and acquaintances.

"I was something of a gossip," Joyce told me, "though I never made up any lies or spread any mean information about people. I guess you could say I was like the school's minister of information. I was always in the know, and everybody, even teachers, would ask me first if they wanted to confirm a rumor or find out something."

But Joyce didn't see how that was a skill she could use to find a profession, so she kept looking. In college, Joyce studied liberal arts because she couldn't decide on a major. She hadn't yet come up with a perfect answer to that question adults always ask young people: What do you want to do when you grow up? As she was mulling it over, a few of Joyce's friends, who had a band, saw the value in her outgoing personality and knack for networking. They hired her to help them spread the word about gigs they were playing. Joyce was so effective at spreading the word, other performers on campus started hiring her, and eventually some local businesses began using her services. She was a natural at publicizing events and products. And what's more, she loved doing it. It was fun, and she couldn't believe that she was actually getting paid to do something that she loved so much.

"Never in a million years," Joyce said, "would I have thought to consider being a publicist. I'd never even met one before." But now, Joyce is one of the most sought-after publicists in the country. And what do you know? She owns her business now, too, so some of what she learned in that economics class comes in handy after all. So don't worry if you don't have a good answer to the question "What do you want to do when you grow up?" If you think of your life's work not as a single career but as a series of passions that are unfolding one after the other, then you'll spare yourself a lot of anxiety and stress. Besides, any list that you can create is, by its very definition, limiting. That's because it can only capture what already exists; it doesn't allow for the unknown. Take Madonna for instance; would the word *icon* have ever found its way onto her list of possible career choices?

Something also very important to note is that there are many people whose life's work cannot be defined by a single word. More often than not, people refer to me as an actor, but I'm also a writer, a speaker, and an activist. Those are all the places where my passions have led me. As long as we allow ourselves to be guided by our intuition (in other words, "follow your heart"), we will always end up right where we need to be, right where we're supposed to be.

Have you ever heard the saying "Do what you love and the money will follow?" It's along the same lines as "Leap and the net will appear" or "If you build it, they will come." What all of those sayings mean is that you should be true to your heart's desire because that's where you'll find life's greatest reward. And guess what? It's not money, although I'm sure you'll find some of that, too.

So, can you do me a favor? And I know this might sound strange coming from me since I am the first one to suggest you write out lists of all sorts of things in your journal. But can you do away with all those "career" lists you've researched and created? Will you just be still with yourself and think about what it is you love doing? And if you are gonna make a list, write at the top of your journal page: "I LOVE Doing:" and follow that with a list as long as you like. Okay? Don't try to think about how you can turn it into a job. Focus on your love of it and, at the risk of sounding like a commercial . . . just do it! Take that first step. I'm sure it'll lead you to places you could never have dreamed of.

OH!!! I ALMOST FORGOT!!! With all the hysteria around the election here in Iowa, I almost forgot to congratulate you! For what, you might ask? Well, that your last letter was music to my ears! My girl, my BFF, my Young Sistah opened her own savings account!! Congratulations on preparing yourself for a successful financial future. Congratulations on independently taking the steps to empower *yourself.* Opening a savings account and committing to saving 40 percent of your earnings per week and choosing to tithe 10 percent creates a healthy relationship with money.

You go!! And you know what else? I was especially struck by

your decision to tithe. A lot of people both young and old don't real-ize that giving to the universe, whether it's a charity, church, or some other donation, is an important way to keep money circulating in your world. You ever heard the phrase "conscious giving"? That means when you choose to give instead of being forced to, as in the case of paying bills, you allow the universe to mirror your relation-ship with money by creating opportunities that allow you to re-ceive.

There's a *wonderment to life* and I, YOU, WE can choose how we journey through it! So my question to you, right now, is this: Are you ready to breathe life in? Huh? Good. Me too. Okay, so let's do it. No, I'm serious. . . . Big inhale, right now . . . let's inhale life—So breathe!

Big inhale. Breathe. Big inhale—Yes—Breathe!

You are amazing and you make me smile. ☺ And I'm proud to call you a friend.

Much Love,
Hill

Date: January 5, 2008 8:11 PM
From: Young_Sistah@home.net
To: Hill@manifestyourdestiny.org
Subject: Career Choices

Hill, how can I make a good career choice?

Date: January 7, 2008 9:07 PM
From: Hill@manifestyourdestiny.org
To: Young_Sistah@home.net
Subject: Re: Career Choices

Oh! Easy answer: A few years ago I read a book called *Do What You Love, The Money Will Follow.* That's it!

But I want to forward your e-mail to someone very special, my friend Candace Bond McKeever, who seems to always make the right decisions when it comes to her career. Simply put—she's dope! From working at Essence Entertainment to de Passe Entertainment and overseeing the Essence Music Festival and Essence Awards, she understands all aspects of making the proper choice when it comes to your career journey and balancing a family!

She's worked at Motown and even abroad in Switzerland as a financial analyst. She clearly knows what she's talking about! Listen to this sister, as she is at the top of her game.

HH

----------Begin Forwarded Message----------

This is a simple yet profound question. Selecting one's vocation is a very serious matter and has a great deal to do with matching your life's passion with your gifts and talents. The selection of a career path requires a great deal of rigorous self-assessment. You must take the time to define what your dreams are, not just your career goals but your life's hopes and dreams, because ultimately your happiness will be rooted in the fulfillment of your dreams and goals that you have for yourself.

Match your experience and skill set to those dreams and explore those career choices that ultimately will assist you in achieving your life's goals. Remember that as you embark on your path, you may have to take a detour or veer in another direction because the reality is that you will grow and change as an individual and your career desires may change based on your situation in life. Be open and find the right thing for you at that time in your life. The balance between life and career is a constant dance, and I am personally still figuring out all the steps.

I suppose Hill selected me for this question because from the outside it would seem like I "have it all," a diverse and fulfilling career, two beautiful children, and a long-term marriage to my husband and soul mate. But I always remember the excellent advice that Eunice Shriver gave her daughter, Maria Shriver, "As a woman, you can have it all, just not all at one time," and I truly believe this! Life comes at you in stages, and you have to reassess and adjust for each one.

One of my favorite lessons from living abroad in Europe was "Work to live, as opposed to living to work." Your vocation is an important part of what you are but it does not define who you are. Know yourself, know what motivates you and brings you happiness, and match your career to that. That is the best advice I can give you.

Candace Bond McKeever
Partner
Impact Strategies, LLC

Date: January 10, 2008 2:46 PM
From: Young_Sistah@home.net
To: Hill@manifestyourdestiny.org
Subject: When I Grow Up, I Wanna Be . . . ?

Hill, at this point in my life, do I have to know what I want to be?

Date: January 13, 2008 6:09 PM
From: Hill@manifestyourdestiny.org
To: Young_Sistah@home.net

Subject: Re: When I Grow Up, I Wanna Be . . . ?

Of course you don't need to know what you want to be right now. Now is the time to explore all those things that you find interesting. Take the time to find out what excites you! You're at such an exciting stage in your life. Don't rush getting to know you and your interests. But don't take my word for it—try my friend Sharla Crow, who is the founder of SEED—a company that helps people realize their goals and dreams. She is an amazing woman who is a "coach" for some of the most powerful CEOs and entertainers in the world. But her client list is confidential! Ssshhh!!!

HH

----------Begin Forwarded Message----------

Dear Young Sister:

You do not have to know what you want to be, but you can begin to discover who you want to be. Focus on becoming a woman who is true to herself and cultivates her passions, and that will lead you to what you want to do in your life.

How do you do this? One of the most powerful ways is to identify for yourself three core values that you will live by. A value is something that is of importance to you, a standard of behavior or a quality of character that is authentically you and that you are committed to being. For example, let's say you are great at helping your younger sister with her schoolwork. You feel good when you can teach her something and inspire her to do her best. That might help you to discover that "sharing knowledge" is one of your core values. Maybe you are the one in your circle of friends who everyone comes to for advice. You are a good listener, and quick with ideas on how to handle tough situations: "helping others" might be another core value. This may lead you to identify that you want to be someone who (1) shares knowledge, (2) inspires, and (3) helps others. So BE that young woman in your home, at school, and in your community. Look for opportunities to share knowledge, inspire, and help others, and this will guide you toward work that is uniquely suited to who you are and what you want to contribute.

Dream big, explore your ideas, and envision yourself living your ideal life. Then pursue it with hard work, purpose, and passion.

Sharla Crow
Founder
SEED

PART FIVE

The Wonderment
of Life

Define Your Destiny

LETTER 23

Chocolate Cake and Four-Letter Words

Simplicity makes me happy.

Alicia Keys

January 15, 2008
Dallas

Dear Young Sistah,

I cried on the plane today. I know that may not seem very manly to admit. But it's real. And true. I'm not sure if the guy sitting next to me saw the tear that splashed and was quickly absorbed by the newspaper I was reading. I was heading back to Los Angeles from Iowa, where we had had a National Finance Committee meeting for the Obama presidential campaign, and I was making speeches at local churches this morning during their services. I had fully intended to write you back on the flight home, but what I didn't intend was to read an article about young women in Congo who are no older than you and are currently experiencing the horrors of rape and persecution. The article made me think of you. It made me think of how angry I would be if some man ever hurt you. But it also made me think of all those young women, thousands of miles away, that every night live in fear of mass gangs of men abusing and mutilating them.

And I felt helpless reading the article, saying to myself, "I have to do something . . . *we* have to do something." But the bad news stories didn't stop there.

Reading and hearing about these heinous crimes committed against young women about your age made me want to reach out to you. And tell you how grateful I am that we live in a place where we have freedoms that we often take for granted. Like getting a good education, going to college, practicing a religion of our choice, and owning land and creating the life we've dreamed about.

Because Thomas Jefferson inserted the term "unalienable rights" into the Declaration of Independence, we live in a country where we have the right of free speech and expression, freedom of religion and conscience, freedom of assembly, and the right to equal protection before the law. He wrote: *"We hold these truths to be self-evident, that all men are created equal, that they are endowed by their Creator with certain unalienable rights, that among these are life, liberty and the pursuit of happiness. That to secure these rights, governments are instituted among men, deriving their just powers from the consent of the governed."*

I'm not trying to give you a history lesson, especially about something you already know, since American history is part of the standard fifth-grade curriculum and you're out of elementary school. I just can't help being passionate about all the opportunities we have that so many of us fail to realize.

You and I are both so lucky to have all that we do. In this country, even the poorest people have far more access to opportunity than most of the poverty-stricken people throughout the world. None of us can control the circumstances into which we are born, but luckily we can control how we choose to live our lives. Which is why I need to come down on you a bit for something in your last letter. It had the word *try* in it again. And you know better than that! We don't use that word. Did you think I'd let you get away with it now that you are doing so well? How about a two-letter-word answer: NO!!

In fact, I don't like very many three-letter words at all. My favorite words are four-letter words. There is one three-letter word that I want you to embrace and use consistently when it comes to your life. And that is the word *YES*. Yes. Yes. Yes. Yes. I want you to get used to using that word. Will you do that for me? The answer is yes. You can build an amazing existence saying yes to life. But it just doesn't stop there. After we say yes, we have to move on to living a four-letter-word life.

As you know now, words have power, and throughout your life, I want you to be an experience monger and a word monger. By *monger* I mean that I want you to pay specific attention to the words you use and the words that are used about you. Like we talked about before, the words *ho* and *bitch* do not reflect how magnificent you are. But, this time, rather than discussing the words I don't

> Words have power.

want to hear from you, I'd rather focus on the ones I do want you to seek out and use. And, interestingly, most of them happen to be four-letter words.

Four-letter words are some of the most powerful words in the English language. They can be for good or bad. The word **fear** is a four-letter word that I can't stand, but you already knew that. So what are the four-letter words that impact our life positively? How about: **love, time, make, soul, more, know, fine, need, want, word, hope, seek, find, rich, deep, full, calm, feel, work, cure.** And there are many, many **more.** Ha-ha! See what I mean?

Your life is meant to be **full** and **rich. Have** you **ever** had a really amazing, **deep, rich** piece of chocolate **cake**? Huh? **Well, your** assignment today is to go to a store **that** makes a really **rich** chocolate fudge **cake**, and buy a piece. But don't eat it yet. Because **next** (don't laugh) I **want** you to go buy Ho Hos at the convenience store. And **when** you get **home,** put the piece of chocolate fudge **cake** on one plate and the Ho Ho on another plate. First, taste the Ho Ho. And **just** think

> Your life is meant to be full and rich.

about **what** it tastes **like** and how it feels in **your** mouth. And now, **take** a same-size piece of the chocolate fudge **cake** and taste it. They **both** are called "chocolate **cake**," but notice how one has a **deep, rich feel** and taste, and seems so strong **that** it stays with you **even** after you swallow. And notice how the other **kind** of **just** disappears. One is **deep** and **rich** . . . the other is light and vacant.

I want **your life** to be **that deep,** a chocolate-fudge-cake-like **life.**

I **want** you to be **able** to **feel your life**, taste **your life**, experience **your life**. It's almost as if a piece of **deep rich** chocolate **cake** is soulful. It's almost as if **that rich** chocolate **cake** is honest in a way. **That deep**, multifaceted, layered taste is how I **want** you to think about **your** world. **Your life** should be **bold** and **full like that**. It should **feel like that**. It should **look like that**. Author Penelope Trunk wrote a **book** called *Brazen Careerist*, and in it she **said** something very interesting. "Honest people are **more** soulful and interesting," and I guess that's why I **feel like that deep rich** chocolate **cake** is **more** honest. So, if you are really going to honestly **live your life**, you're going to **live** it in a **deep**, rich way; **with soul**. I guess **what** I'm saying is **that** I **want** you to **walk** deeper, and deeper, and deeper **into your** own **life**. But as you **walk** deeper, there are **more** unknowns, so at times you might experience **more fear**. And **that** is where living a **four**-letter-**word life** comes in. Because those **four**-letter words **will** always be **with** you. And **they** are **much** bigger, **deep**er, and **rich**er than **fear**.

Now as I close this letter, I'm gonna be real honest with you. Some of the things you wrote in your last letter scare me. I fear that after all this time exchanging letters with you, I haven't been able to *truly* convince you how magnificent you really are. To truly make you realize that the world is waiting for your genius to be spoken into it. That you are the perfect product of fifteen billion years of evolution, and that even though we sometimes make mistakes, let each other down, and worse still, let ourselves down, you and I are still doing more and have more resources at our disposal than at any time in history. You and I can change the world, right now.

You know what I also figured out? I can't make you realize your magnificence. Only you can do that. You have to believe it. You have to have faith. You have to trust me that it's true and then you must know it for yourself. Your greatness is real. Say it aloud right now: "I am magnificent and MY greatness is real." Repeat it: "I am magnificent and MY greatness is real." Again: "I am magnificent and MY greatness is real!" If saying that is difficult for you or even if a twinge of internal doubt pops up when you make that affirmation, it means *you* don't truly believe it yet. I can say it a million times, but you have to believe it.

The only person or thing that can limit you is you. We established at the top of this letter that you have the "right" to the "pursuit of happiness." So what can stop you? Nothing. You will win at your life. And remember, you don't and won't have everything in life figured out by twenty-one, twenty-five, thirty, or even eighty. *Everything,* EVERYTHING, everything happens for a reason. Good or bad, there's a reason, and you can learn from it. If you have faith in that, then you can allow yourself to follow your heart in all the decisions you make.

By following what's in your heart, you'll always be living YOUR life. Don't be afraid to make "unpopular" decisions or choices in your life. It could even be a choice you make that your parents or friends don't like. Now, am I saying here that you should go against what your parents tell you? No. What I'm saying is that if you approach whatever decisions you have with a pure heart and mind, patience, and a prayerful spirit, then God and the universe will give you all the information you need to make the right decisions for you at the right time. Does that make sense? Do you believe me?

Well, until the next time, remember, **your life** can be as **rich** and **deep** as a chocolate **cake** or it can be a Ho Ho. It can be your nana's **best** red velvet **cake** or it can be a Twinkie—unnatural, artificial, no substance. You're not a Ho Ho or a Twinkie. You are substantial, you are amazing. And you are not **just** a survivor, you are a thriver.

Much Love,
Hill

Date: January 17, 2008 1:34 PM
From: Young_Sistah@home.net
To: Hill@manifestyourdestiny.org
Subject: A Dream Deferred

Hill, can all of my dreams really come true? Or will they always just be "dreams"?

Date: February 1, 2008 11:23 AM
From: Hill@manifestyourdestiny.org
To: Young_Sistah@home.net
Subject: Re: A Dream Deferred

Come up with a plan. There's a famous quote that I use in my life, "If you fail to plan, then you are planning to fail." I really wanted to have a couple of strong Black women answer this in order for you to see what worked for them.

I hit up actress Malinda Williams, who appeared as Bird, the youngest sister on the television series *Soul Food*. Malinda is an amazing mother and actress who has been sparkling on the big screen in *First Sunday* and *Idlewild* among others. I also contacted the extraordinary congresswoman Carolyn Cheeks Kilpatrick, who is now in her *sixth* term, serving Michigan's Thirteenth Congressional District. She was the first African American woman to serve on the Michigan House Appropriations Committee. The congresswoman worked with Fannie Mae to secure $18 million in home mortgages for moderate-income families. As a member of the Homeland Security Subcommittee, she helps determine funding for the Department of Homeland Security. She is an incredible leader. Check out how similar their answers are!

HH

----------Begin Forwarded Message----------

Be the best! Be what you want to see! A good education is the equalizer for everyone. Learn, read, seek, and have a passion for knowledge and understanding. Young women must continue to DREAM and set goals. Set short-term goals → one-year → two-year, and long-term goals for yourself.

Women must build and choose a positive support system of friends, family, and mentors who will help them realize these goals. Seek out people you can look to for guidance, support, and opportunities. You must build a support system that will help you build your self-confidence and show you by example that you can do all things with God's help.

IF YOU CAN BELIEVE IT, YOU CAN ACHIEVE IT.

Congresswoman Carolyn Cheeks Kilpatrick

----------Begin Forwarded Message----------

Young Sistah,

Believe, Believe, Believe! You must first have faith in yourself that you are capable of accomplishing what it is you have set out to do. Before you get out of the bed in the morning you must first give thought to the task in your mind, believe that it is going to happen and then suddenly, your body rises. Achieving your dreams is no different.

Malinda Williams

LETTER 24

Your Heart:
Always Follow It
(Except with Boys)

To fly, we have to have resistance.
Maya Ying Lin

February 25, 2008
Los Angeles

Dear Young Sistah,

Wow, you are truly in flight. Each time I hear from you lately, it seems like you're spreading those wings wider, soaring higher and higher. Growing and changing every day. I guess what my friend India.Arie says is true: "If you want a butterfly, you've got to be a butterfly." But it takes courage to change into that butterfly and break out of the cocoon. And my girl is doin' it!

You know something, I love that word *courage*. Dictionary.com defines courage as "the quality of mind or spirit that enables a person to face difficulty, danger, pain, without fear." Now, that definition is right on point. But what is so interesting to me about the word *courage* is the root, or etymology, of the word. The word *courage* comes from the root *cour*, which means "heart." So to live your life with *cour* is where I want you to be. And it seems you are doing just that.

You sitting down and writing your dad a letter to tell him how you feel is you living your life with *cour*. What your counselor told you about the power of forgiveness is right on. Mahatma Gandhi said, "The weak can never forgive. Forgiveness is an attribute of the strong." We always have the choice to either hang on to anger or learn to forgive. You've already found out how damaging anger can be. At first it might seem like anger is a good way to shield ourselves from whatever hurt we're feeling, but in the long run, it only cements that hurt and turns us hard and cold. The most effective way to heal is to grow through the hurt, and that takes strength and commitment. But you will get to the other side, and in the process, you'll also discover the beauty of following your heart.

It's all right if you're not ready yet to send the letter. You'll know when you're ready and the time is right. The most important thing right now is that you sat down and wrote it, which means that you've started the process of healing. The thing about reaching out to people when you're ready is that they may or may not be in a place where they're ready to receive the gesture. That's why love and forgiveness can never be conditional. Neither emotion can be based on any expectation of the person on the receiving end. They have to always start and end with you, and what's inside your heart.

Now, I'm not saying this to suggest your dad won't respond positively to your letter nor to move you toward any other type of fear about how things will turn out between the two of you. But I do want to make sure you bear in mind that when it comes to an emotion like love or forgiveness, once you feel it and you express it, you also have to release it. That means you have to give those emotions freely. You can't place any restrictions on them, and that includes those of time. Just as you had to grow through your own journey to get here, to a place where you feel comfortable enough to write your dad a letter, he might need to grow through his own journey to get to a place where he is able to fully respond in the way that you've hoped for and dreamed of.

Once you mail that letter to him, he might decide to write you a letter back instead of calling or making plans to get together. And it might have more to do with him wanting to make sure that you're comfortable and that he doesn't push you too hard too fast versus him not wanting to see you and be with you right away. You get what I'm saying?

My mother and I took baby steps when we were working to make our bond as strong as it had been before my parents' divorce. For a while there, it felt like she was keeping me at arm's length and that maybe she wasn't that interested in spending more time with me. Looking back, I see now that she wanted our relationship to be natural and effortless. She didn't want me to feel like I had to force myself to be all lovey-dovey with her right away or to pretend that we were tight when things were still a little strained—and I'm really thankful for that.

Talking about being tight, you and Naomi sure seem to have gotten pretty tight over the past several weeks. I suppose meeting her the way you did, while both of you were waiting to talk with the school counselor that day after the assembly, made it a lot easier for you to open up with her. After all, it's kinda hard to have your guard up and play all hard when you're sitting in a chair obviously waiting to go and speak with a counselor. I like that both of you allowed yourselves to be vulnerable enough to exchange numbers and then start eating lunch together in the cafeteria. It sounds like you found a friend who can be a mirror for you and who you can be a mirror for as well.

You went through some painful experiences with your other group of girlfriends. I have to applaud you, on two counts. First for giving those relationships your all and doing your best to work through whatever differences and difficulties came up between you guys. You remained committed to those friendships through the best moments they had to offer, and through the worst moments you had to endure. As you become more and more the person you wish to be, that highest vision you have of yourself, you're going to find that your

> Your relationships with people will evolve.

relationships with people will evolve. Some will grow stronger and you'll become closer to those individuals. Others will fade away because you'll discover that you don't share enough values in common anymore to bind you to each other in the same way.

The next thing I want to applaud you on is your ability to gracefully move away from relationships that are as limiting as they are familiar. It's not such an easy thing to do. New situations and friendships can be refreshing, but they can also be very intimidating. There is comfort in the familiar, even if that familiar situation is not growth-inspiring. The appeal is its predictability. There are no unknowns. You may not be treated respectfully, but at least you know what to expect. And that's good enough for some people. I am proud of you for not letting it be good enough for *you*, and for taking the chance to welcome a more positive relationship into your life.

I think it's great that you and Naomi have already decided to dedicate your time together to things that are far more productive than gossiping about other girls. And talking about boys or, as you put it, "trying to impress boys." You said you can already feel the huge weight that's been lifted off your shoulders because you're not always trying to prove yourself or having to defend yourself. So now, you're just free to be you—and to make some fabulous music. And I had to laugh when I read what you wrote: "It's weird that when I am doing my own thing there are more boys coming around interested in what I'm doing than when I'm waiting around trying to get their attention." I've been telling you that for months! LOL.

That weekend songwriting workshop you and Naomi signed up to take is a great idea. It brings together two hobbies I know you really enjoy—writing and singing. Check you out! Next thing I know, you'll be burning up the Top 40 charts. You'll be saying yes to excellence, in the tradition of India.Arie, Alicia Keys, and Mariah Carey. That is, if you're not too busy solving equations at school!

Who'd have ever thought that you would be considering math as a possible major when you go to college? A year ago, you were all but screaming from the rooftops about how much you hated math, how it was so hard, blah, blah, blah. But then you got into Mr. Rodriguez's class and all that changed. Your grades are up, and so is your confidence. Then you realized that math is just like a puzzle game, and that you actually like it—enough for you to now think of it as your best subject. My Young Sistah, a math major! I can see you now in one of those college catalogues, standing next to a blackboard with things like $e = mc^2$; $\pi - \sqrt{17}$; $x = -b \pm \sqrt{(b^2 - 4ac)}/2a$ written on it. Young sistahs all over the world are gonna flip through those pages, see your picture, and go, "That is one FLY Sistah!"

And you know, the passion and creativity that move you to do your singing and songwriting are also present in the talent you're displaying in math. Albert Einstein said, "Pure mathematics is, in its own way, the poetry of logical ideas." So, you see, everything you're doing is somehow connected, whether it's working out a formula or working out a lyric or line break. That's something I want you to remember about following your heart—it's huge, and has the capacity to hold the love of more than one thing. Like how I went to law school and then became an actor. You never know, one day I might decide to start practicing law or run for a political office. There are lots of politicians who were once actors, and I bet there are a lot of mathematicians who are also passionate about the arts.

However, the one area where I'd advise you to NOT follow your heart is where boys are concerned. At least not yet. And that's because when it comes to boys, your emotions, at this stage in the game, are not always practical or based in sound judgment. Even you admitted as much in your last letter when you said that if Nasir hadn't given you that ultimatum, you probably would have ended up having sex with him sooner rather than later. Now you can look back and say how thankful you are that things didn't go in that direction. You can see what a wrong choice that would have been for your life. But back then, all you could tell me was that it was in your heart. You loved him, and he said that he loved you, and you wanted to follow your heart. See what I mean?

It's natural for you to still have feelings for him. He will probably always hold a special place in your heart. There's nothing wrong with that. Even though we were never boyfriend and girlfriend, Anisa will always hold a place in my heart as my first serious crush. (Keep that to yourself, though, cuz I never told her!) It doesn't mean I have any active romantic feelings toward her, though. She's one of my best friends, and that's that. Who knows? Maybe one day you and Nasir will be friends again. Just make sure, with him or any other guy, that you listen to what your intuition and head are telling you, not necessarily your heart.

How are your dinner and weekend dates with your mom going? Are you still having sessions with your counselor? Hit me back soon. Please!!

XXOXX
Much Love,
Hill

Date: March 1, 2008 9:08 AM
From: Young_Sistah@home.net
To: Hill@manifestyourdestiny.org
Subject: Me and My Boyfriend

Hill, do you think having a boyfriend keeps you from doing well in
school?

Date: March 15, 2008 7:56 PM
From: Hill@manifestyourdestiny.org
To: Young_Sistah@home.net
Subject: Re: Me and My Boyfriend

I never had a real girlfriend during school (I know, NOT COOL . . . I
was busy!!) so, I'm gonna give your e-mail to someone much
cooler than me, my girl Tatyana Ali, a singer and actress best
known for the role of Ashley in the hit television show *Fresh Prince
of Bel-Air*. Tatyana took a break from acting in order to attend
Harvard, where she graduated with a B.A. in anthropology, which
makes her the perfect person to answer this e-mail.

Hit me back after you get her response.

HH

----------Begin Forwarded Message----------

Hmmm . . . Let me start by saying that I think relationships are very
important in life. Loving is good for the soul. When we get discour-
aged, having someone there who believes in you is a very precious
thing. A good friend will pick you up when you feel low and spur
you on when you feel like the challenges you're facing are too
much to handle. I truly believe that our development has everything to do with learning how to handle our closest relationships.

However, oftentimes we rush into being someone's girlfriend
hoping to somehow validate ourselves, believing that we are
somehow worth more when we're in a romantic relationship. This is

true for women of all ages. Covering over what we feel is missing, a boyfriend's presence can sometimes take the place of real self-esteem, self-love, and pride.

It's easy to believe that if someone else loves you it means that you're somehow more lovable. But that's just not true. Good feelings about yourself can only come from the inside. No one can give that to you and no one should have to agree that you're beautiful to prove it to you. Love springs from within. Confidence comes from an awareness of your own potential.

When you're in school you're actually there to unlock that hidden potential. It's wonderful to be in love, and it feels good, but on the real, school is about your own personal growth and exploration. Most women are nurturers and we tend to focus our energies on our companions and the well-being of our relationships. That's not necessarily a bad trait, but there is plenty of time to be all cuddled up.

I'm not saying that having a boyfriend means you're gonna stop studying and all of a sudden flunk out, but I think it certainly can hinder your ability to find out who you really are and what you really like, and that's what school and this time of your life is all about, investing in yourself. It's important to give yourself the space you need to grow. That's real love.

Tatyana Ali

LETTER 25

Throwing Off Limitations

A bird doesn't sing because it has an answer,
it sings because it has a song.

Dr. Maya Angelou

April 2, 2008
Los Angeles

Dear Young Sistah,

You know what? You remind me of that Maya Angelou poem "Still I Rise." I know you know the one I'm talking about because you told me ages ago, after the first time I mentioned her name in a letter, that you'd gone out, bought a collection of her poems, and read them. These days especially, what comes to mind when I think of you are the lines:

> Just like moons and like suns,
> With the certainty of tides,
> Just like hopes springing high,
> Still I'll rise.

This captures the essence of what I've been witnessing with—and in—you for almost two years. You rise. You ignore limitations and let go of that which seeks to chain you down in one place or in one interpretation of who you are. When you first told me about how you were creating distance between you and your old group of girl-friends, you predicted that they might start spreading gossip about you and treating you badly, the way they treat people who aren't in their "inner circle."

I didn't want to say so, but I figured you were probably right in that prediction. When your ground starts shifting, as yours has, it causes people to examine where they're standing, and sometimes that's a little more than some folks can handle. We've discussed this before. It's easier to blame other people than to look at what's wrong with oneself. So Caroline was running around trying to get folks to believe that you and Naomi were dating each other? She assumed since you weren't having sex with any of the guys you have been hanging out with, that you must not be into guys. That's hilarious. Of course everybody has started calling her a "hater." It's because her intentions were shining through her words. Plus, she was completely contradicting herself. She was the one who initially announced that you *were* having sex with all those college boys you'd started hanging out with. I'm sure some of the kids at school were thinking, "All right, which one is it? You can't have it both ways."

Remember how torn up you were when she spread that other rumor? I hope that in the future, you'll continue to react to gossip in this new way. You weren't even fazed by this latest round of lies. "Hill, I'm not even going to dignify it with a response." That's what you wrote in your letter. I'm quoting it back to you because I want to give you props on your choice of language. I've gone on enough about how words have power and how the words you use send out a message about you to everyone who's listening.

There are so many words you could have chosen in place of *dignify* in that sentence. You could have used *justify, affirm, acknowledge, validate.* Any one of those words would have been acceptable. But you chose to use *dignify,* which means "to confer dignity and honor upon, to give distinction to." If I were a stranger on the street reading those words, what they would tell me is that you regard yourself with respect, and that you bring a natural dignity to your thoughts, comments, and interactions.

As a friend who has been exchanging letters with you for nearly two years, what those words tell me is that you're not going to let the untruths people might say sway you from being who you really are.

You have a clear vision of yourself and nothing is gonna stand in the way of you reaching that vision. You're a believer!

I was also moved by the recent observation you shared with me: "pain+perseverance=beauty." And I love how you mixed it up and wrote it out as an equation. You're right. And I know you were specifically talking about the songs you've been creating in your songwriting workshop, but it applies to other things as well. Remember how I once told you that what doesn't destroy us makes us stronger? Well, the beauty of your spirit is in that strength. And by strength, I'm not referring to anything muscular or hard. I'm not talking about stoicism or any other kind of pretend strength. I'm talking about the type of strength it takes to face each situation, and to let yourself feel the hurt, disappointment, sadness, and fear that it might bring. And to still, step by difficult step, walk through it until you reach a new season in your life, with its own set of trials, temptations, and testimonies.

Of course, the difference is that when we're younger, we're not as certain there is another side, a place where there will be less pain, where the challenges we're facing will evaporate into a memory. Janet Jackson said, "You don't have to hold on to the pain to hold on to the memory."

Now that you've gone through a thing or two and come out on the other side, I see you're becoming more confident, not only of the existence of that *other* place, but also of your ability to find your way there. I can only imagine that's why you ripped up the letter you'd written to your pops and decided to pick up the phone and call him instead.

That was huge. And I like how you pointed out that you called him when you knew he'd be home—right after he'd finished shooting hoops and left the court. You called and said pretty much everything you'd written in that letter. You even told him that he didn't have to say or do anything now if he didn't want to. He could call you or write you whenever he was ready. I wish I could have been there to see that beautiful face of yours light up when you heard him say, "Baby girl, I've always been ready."

The next time you write, tell me about how your lunch with him was. You're feeling a little nervous, that's to be expected, but don't let that stop you from having the experience. Be present through whatever nerves you feel or slight discomfort. Just take it all in stride, like you've been doing. It's making you stronger, I can already see it. You've jumped over a lot of hurdles to get to where you are right now in your relationship with your dad. Or do you need me to take you back to the time when you didn't even want to admit to yourself, let alone to him, how much you loved and missed him?

You said your biggest fear is that he might disappoint you and not show up? Now, I don't know if your pops has a history of being a no-show with his personal commitments, but even if he does, you have to give him the benefit of the doubt. People change. And I'm not just talking about him when I say that. I'm talking about you, too. You've both changed since the last time you were together. I can't speak to the changes in your dad, but I can speak to some of the changes you've made. Like how you've become more aware of your intuition, and how you've learned to trust it. If there had been any hesitation at all about seeing you, you would have heard it in your dad's voice.

I've written you many times about letting our hearts lead us in the direction of our dreams. I went to Minneapolis to visit my friend Taylor a couple of years ago. She and her husband had just gotten divorced and she'd decided to make a clean break from that part of her past. She moved to the Minneapolis area and bought a house there. At the time, she didn't know anybody there, and had never even visited the city before. I was worried for her. After all, it had been an extremely painful separation and divorce. I didn't want the isolation to be yet another hurdle she'd have to overcome in order to fully heal.

I got there and realized that Taylor wasn't in need of any type of rescue. She'd already made a bunch of friends and had even started dating again. One night while we were hanging out in front of her fireplace, she told me that she welcomed all the adversity that faced her as she was creating this new life for herself because it reminded her of a strength and beauty she'd all but forgotten she had. "I have to keep finding ways to remind myself that a broken heart is also an open heart."

> A broken heart is an open heart.

And you know what? She was right. A broken heart *is* an open heart. It's basically the same equation that you, brilliant writer, singer, and mathematician that you are, sent me in your letter: pain+perseverance=beauty. Because what could be more beautiful than a heart that's wide open to all the love there is in this world?

While I was in Minneapolis during that visit, Taylor and I went to the Mall of America, which is the largest shopping center in the country. Just thought I'd throw that in there since you and your mom have now become big shopping buddies, trolling the malls on weekends in search of a good sale. The two of you have even traded your old arguments about chores and money and time management for new arguments about shoes! Well, I guess that's an improvement, right? ☺

What happened between you and your mom that weekend crashed so many barriers, I don't even know where to begin. Okay, when you and I first started exchanging letters, one of your biggest complaints was that you and your mom never spent any time together. The two of you weren't getting along that great either, as I recall. You also said that money was always tight around your house and that stopped you from doing and having a lot of things that you wanted.

Flash forward to now, with the two of you cooking and eating dinner together at least once a week and hanging out together one afternoon each weekend. So you wanted to go shopping for your hang time, but your mom says you can't because she doesn't have any money. You could have quietly accepted that and been disappointed, but you didn't. Your priority was to spend time with your mom, not to buy stuff, so you convinced her that you guys should go anyway to walk around and window-shop. And that day, you ended up having the best time you've ever had with your mom.

A limitation is a boundary that somebody has drawn for us that tells us how far they think we can go. It's like a line in the sand. Sometimes we're the ones who draw it for ourselves. But limitations can also be used as markers of our victories. They show us that we've gone far beyond what was expected of us and what had previously been defined as our best, our greatest, our highest.

Helen Keller, the famous writer who was also both blind and deaf, wrote, "The marvelous richness of human experience would lose something of rewarding joy if there were no limitations to over-come." I celebrate and share in the joy of every victory you've achieved by throwing off your limitations.

Much Love,
Hill

Date: April 16, 2008 3:44 PM
From: Young_Sistah@home.net
To: Hill@manifestyourdestiny.org
Subject: ¡Ayúdeme!

Hill, some of my family is from the Dominican Republic, but a lot of my friends don't speak Spanish and sometimes it seems like people only hang with "their kind," either the ones that speak Spanish or the ones that don't. As if different cultures don't mix. Do I have to choose sides?

Date: April 25, 2008 9:23 PM
From: Hill@manifestyourdestiny.org
To: Young_Sistah@home.net
Subject: Re: ¡Ayúdeme!

OHHHH!!!! I have the perfect person to answer this question! She is one of the hottest young entertainers in Hollywood today. She was my costar in *Constellation,* as well as starring in such movies as *Center Stage, Drumline, Pirates of the Caribbean*, and *Avatar.* She's a beautiful Dominican sister who understands the importance of embracing multiple cultures.

HH

----------Begin Forwarded Message----------

Dear young sister,

Querida hermanita,

Not only are we all Americans—*pero somos todos hijos de Dios.* It means that whether we all look different, speak different, eat *arroz con habichuelas* or cheeseburgers and fries, we are all the same and just as special.

Rather than choosing sides, why don't we learn to admire each and every one of the virtues we have inherited from our ancestors, and teach these virtues to each other. It's wonderful that you are able to speak more than one language, and even more wonderful if you take pride in that!

Don't ever feel you have to choose who to be! Love yourself for who you are! And always remember, we have to accept ourselves first in order to accept others.

Con cariño (this is in Spanish) *y respeto,*
Tu hermana Zoe Saldana

LETTER 26

Seeing Rainbows: Wonderment of the Everyday

At some point in life, the world's beauty becomes enough. You don't need to photograph, paint, or even write about it. It is enough.

Toni Morrison

May 1, 2008
Los Angeles

Dear Young Sistah,

You know I've been staring at the calendar, counting the days while waiting for your letter. I've already told you how worried I get when you disappear on me like that—but I was elated to find out that this time your long silence was because of all the good things going on in your life, and not because you were growing through the blues again.

First off, I want you to know that your letter really brightened my day. Seriously, you had enough hope and optimism in there to pass around and share for a week. It sounds like you've really made some major strides since our last exchange.

I was happy to hear that you and your father's "lunch date" happened as planned. I had a feeling it would. We are all flawed in ways, but his love for you is pure. I'm glad that you both really enjoyed it and have already planned the next one. Small, gentle steps to repair a relationship are sometimes the most profound.

Now on the school front, I was very sorry to hear about friend Kalima's suicide attempt. Thankfully, she didn't hurt herself, and her cry for help was answered. I gotta give your principal mad props for how he handled the situation. It's obvious, from what you described, that the students needed the discussion that took place in the school assembly to help them make sense of what happened with their friend and, more critically, to know that they don't have to carry their emotional burdens alone and in silence.

It was a wise move, too, for him to encourage the students to take advantage of the school's counseling office. But since you've already been using that resource, you already knew that. For the other students, sometimes having that permission can make all the difference in the world, and by permission, I don't just mean the "no-questions-asked" excused-absence slips he allowed the counselors to give to you guys who stopped by their offices to talk. I'm talking about him making it known to everybody that talking to a counselor isn't anything to be ashamed of.

Speaking of which, I'm sending you much praise for continuing to have sessions with your counselor. I'm proud of you. No doubt, each meeting is a leap of tremendous faith. A true act of courage. I still don't understand why you'd even think I would laugh at the fact that you "like" talking to your counselor. When I was in college, I didn't have the courage to walk through the door of the counselor's *building*. So you are way, way ahead of me, Young Sistah. It's only more proof of the fact that you are a powerful individual with amazing self-compassion and sense of who you are. I know, I know, you've told me you sometimes find it hard to accept the compliments I pay you and to believe the positive things I say about you.

Kahlil Gibran wrote, "When we turn to one another for counsel, we reduce the number of our enemies." Sometimes the first "enemy" that goes away is the person in the mirror. And that's because sometimes when we are afraid and hurting, we stand in our own way. We block our own growth. When I was too frightened to walk into the counseling offices when I was growing through my own blues, when I couldn't muster the courage, I stood in my own way. Actually, I turned around and ran in the opposite direction!

The one thing that comes through so clearly in your letter is that you have finally started seeing and feeling that you are worthy of health and happiness. If your going to the counselor didn't tell me so, then your asking your mom to take you to see a doctor definitely does. The good news is that he confirmed you are not suffering from clinical depression. The better news is that he helped you establish an exercise and nutrition regimen that will give your body all the energy it needs to take you through the day without your getting tired or feeling sluggish. And you've even lost five pounds. I'm sure that makes you happy because you've mentioned a few times to me in your letters that you think you're pudgy. But I'm not as concerned with how much you weigh as I am with how good you *feel*, so if the plan you're on is getting those results as well, then it's a win-win all around.

The most admirable part of all you've been doing is that it's giving you the confidence to reclaim your power over your own life. Now, neither of us can really pinpoint what caused Kalima's breakdown, but I can only guess that those situations you shared with me probably made matters worse. It sounds like for whatever reasons, she made a series of bad choices that set off a negative chain of events in her life. I'm sure that she loved and trusted her boyfriend, and that it must have seemed like a betrayal for him to do her like he did when she told him she was pregnant. For him to tell her that he didn't believe that the baby was his is a sign of his lack of respect for her, and an indication that he wasn't the person she thought he was.

You said that he "changed up" on her. I think chances are he didn't change at all. I'm more inclined to believe that as soon as being with her stopped being easy and fun, and started demanding his responsibility and maturity, he showed his true colors. If he had cared for her, even a little bit, how could he have started openly dating somebody else? Of course she was devastated. That said, the decision to secretly have an abortion, which is a major medical procedure, was not the wisest one Kalima could have made. Anything could have happened to her. Even today, with all our advances in technology and medicine, women still die in childbirth. There is always a risk involved anytime you undergo any medical procedure.

It's not difficult at all to understand and empathize with Kalima's feelings of despair and isolation after growing through such painful events, especially back-to-back like that. It can make you lose your balance, emotionally and spiritually. And when you lose your balance, you're liable to start thinking of yourself as being powerless. My heart goes out to her during this time of recovery. But even through all this, she can survive and still fulfill every dream she ever had for herself. That's the beauty of adversity. Just like my grandmother (and now Kanye) used to say, "Whatever does not destroy us makes us stronger." I believe that's going to be the case with Kalima, particularly now that she knows she is surrounded by people who really love her and will guide her through it.

The other person my heart goes out to is the young sister who started dating Kalima's ex-boyfriend. By getting involved with somebody who has shown such disrespect to his previous girlfriend, she is essentially saying, "Hey, it's okay for you to disrespect me, too." We've written back and forth a whole lot about respect and how important it is to respect yourself. Being able to listen to yourself is an important part of respecting yourself and, by extension, requesting that others treat you with respect as well. A lot of people take it for granted that they know themselves, but we're always changing, and our conscious mind can become so cluttered with the noise of everybody else's demands and dramas that we can start to lose that knowledge. Mary J. Blige once said, "I don't want no drama in my life, even though we have a little bit, but no more letting people control you. That's drama, because then you become something that you're not."

When we take the time to listen to ourselves, we begin to feel more and more comfortable with ourselves; we learn to value ourselves; and nobody treats something or someone that they value badly. So we treat ourselves well, and we learn to avoid certain situations that might potentially cause us harm.

What you're learning—and, apparently, loving—to do in your counseling sessions is listen to yourself. The "wellness projects" that your counselor has asked you to do are pretty amazing. I might add a couple of them in my daily routine, too—like the gratitude journal.

As you know, I still keep a journal, my diary/scrapbook/mini–photo album. I also have a special box where I keep all my letters, including the ones you've sent me. It's just a fancy version of a shoebox, with all sorts of colorful designs on it, but it works.

I like the idea, though, of having a journal that's solely devoted to gratitude, and the practice of taking the time every morning to think about the things you're grateful for and commit that list to paper. It's such an empowering way to start the day. It reminds me of something my dad used to do every morning when I lived with him. He'd come into my room and say, "Hill, rise and shine." It was the first thing I heard him say every single morning, even on the days when I got up before he did. For many years after he passed away, I'd say it out loud to myself in the mornings before I got out of bed, and it helped me to still feel close to him.

After a while, I fell out of the habit of doing it. And then one day, I was sitting in the waiting area of a casting office, going over my lines one last time before they called me in for an audition. I was really nervous, and I was trying to center myself. Then I heard my dad's voice in my head telling me, "Hill, rise and shine." It seemed like such a strange place for my mind to travel. I wasn't anywhere near a bed, or my home for that matter. And it was afternoon, not morning. Nevertheless, it did the trick. It made me feel calm and centered.

Driving home after the audition, I thought about what had happened, and that's when I figured out what my dad had really meant whenever he told me to "rise and shine." Have you ever stopped to think, I mean really think, about those words, "rise and shine"? I always took it for granted that it was another way of him telling me to get my butt out of bed, or to hurry up and start my daily activities (like cleaning up my messy room). But that day in the car was the first time it occurred to me to take his words as something more than a saying, to pay attention to their true meaning. To rise means to move higher, to be lifted up. To shine means to illuminate. Together, they can be taken to mean "Lift yourself higher and show the world the light within you." That was the mandate my dad gave me every morning, and even though I didn't realize the full gist of what he was telling me on a conscious level, I must have known somewhere deep down inside of me, intuitively, because I called up his voice and those words at the times when I needed to hear them.

It's funny, you know, how we can take things for granted. One thing that illness and incapacity—any sort of adversity, really—does is allows us to open our eyes to all that we have taken for granted. You see the world with different eyes. It's as if your senses suddenly awaken and you take note of every single amazing thing the world has to offer. You know that saying "In order to see the rainbow, you have to first go through the rain"? I guess it's like that.

I sense that you're seeing the rainbow now, and I hope you will always remember how breathtaking it is, because when I compare the frustration in the earliest letters you sent me to the fascination that's in every word of this latest letter, I know that no matter what struggles come your way, you will overcome them. You've got it in you. You've always had it in you, and you always will.

Well, I should probably address that question you asked me, the one your counselor asked you: If today were your last day on earth and you wanted to make sure that the people you love knew how you felt about them, who would be on the list of people you would call?

I've been mulling it over since I read it yesterday. It's a pretty intense question. Here's what I came up with. I'm not so sure it's meant to be answered, not out loud anyway. I think the point of the question is to encourage you to think about the people in your life who you love, and to urge you to include an expression of that love in the interactions you have with them. Emotions, like anything else, are things that we can take for granted. We assume that because we know we love someone, they should automatically know as well. Even if we do things to show people that we love them, it's always good to hear it.

I'm the first to admit that I'm guilty of not doing that as often as I should. But that question sure enough made me pick up the phone today and call a few folks to tell them. How about you? Did the same thing happen with you? Who'd you call, text, IM, or Facebook? If you tell me yours, I'll tell you mine. Tell me the next time you write, okay? In the meantime, keep rising and shining!

And remember: *You are loved.*

Your Friend,
Hill

Date: May 3, 2008 10:22 PM
From: Young_Sistah@home.net
To: Hill@manifestyourdestiny.org
Subject: Dreaming Big???

Hill, what do I have to do to see my dreams realized?

Date: May 17, 2008 11:03 AM
From: Hill@manifestyourdestiny.org
To: Young_Sistah@home.net
Subject: Re: Dreaming Big???

Believe. There is nothing you can't do! And then do all of the things that we've talked about: create a blueprint for achieving those dreams, build a foundation to support those dreams, make a framework of choices that are in line with those dreams, and create doors to connect with people who will help you realize those dreams. If you take all the necessary steps, there is no possible way you can't realize anything you dream. But truly believing and knowing in the depths of your soul that that is true is the first key.

Now, someone who is an expert in realizing his own incredible dreams is Tavis Smiley. I forwarded your question to him and it's funny how you can see in his response that he reaffirms that dreaming as big as you possibly can and then dreaming bigger still is truly the way to go!

Brother Tavis, whatcha got to say to this young sister?

HH

----------Begin Forwarded Message----------

First of all, you have to dream a world that is bigger and better, kinder and gentler, more tolerant and more loving, more caring and more giving than the one we presently inhabit. If you think then that it is possible to create that better world (as I do) now you have a goal, a dream that can be realized. It's important to create an image of yourself and your world to which the future must conform.

If you've shared your dream for your life and your world with family or friends and they didn't laugh at you—then your dream isn't big enough! When people laugh, doubt, or hate on your dreams, now you know you've got something worth pursuing! So get busy dreaming and doing! Remember, dreaming is easy—doing is not so easy. So . . . try again . . . fail again . . . fail better!

Tavis Smiley

Keys to REAL Happiness:
Faith and Service

Faith is the flipside to fear.

Susan L. Taylor

May 17, 2008
New Orleans

Dear Young Sistah,

Would you believe me if I told you how happy I was when I read that your mom was the first person you thought of in your answer to the counselor's question? Of course you would, because these days your attitude is all about belief and trust. But seriously, it literally brought tears of joy to my eyes to know that even though you were nervous and afraid, when your mom got home from work, you went up to her, hugged her, looked her in the eyes, and told her how much you love her. You were true to your emotions, and look how it turned out. That is you leading with your heart—being courageous.

I'm in New Orleans to give a speech, which I have to admit I'm nervous about. Luckily your letter came as a welcome distraction. Every time I'm in New Orleans I can't help but think about the faith of the residents, especially after all that they've gone through. When I'm here, I feel a strong pull to be of service, which is what I am writing to you about. Okay. First of all, by now I know you better than you probably think I do. And I know that when you read the title of this letter you were probably like, "Oh no, boring . . . skip it . . . Can we please talk about dating again?" LOL. Well, you know what? You are wrong, because this letter is the same as all the letters I have ever written you. They're all about becoming your best self. Many people think discussions about "faith and service" are boring because they associate both of those things with stuff you are told you "have to do" as if both of those words are about sacrifice. But you know what? Just like I do about a lot of things, I come at faith and service from a completely different perspective, and maybe by the end of this letter you'll be able to see the joy in both.

When I graduated from Harvard, with my two graduate degrees with honors and all, I thought I knew so much. What I didn't realize at the time is that the saying "The more you know, the more you realize what you don't know" is true. That's why if anybody ever tries to act smarter than you, trust me, they are not. Anyway, over time I came to realize that it doesn't matter if you have advanced degrees from Harvard or if you graduated with honors from the school of hard knocks—we are all in the same life and have to find ways to help each other. One of the most powerful things I have learned in my life is that "people don't care how much you know, until they know how much you care."

Service, as in being of service and serving others, is a huge concept. It's one of those words that seem all work and no play, but that is a huge misconception. I grew up in a family that insisted on being of service in the world, so for me there has never been an option. And I can tell you that there were many times when I was the less fortunate and people helped me. Some of the ways I have been of service have been mad crazy fun. Friends and I painted murals on a school, helped build houses, taught young kids to read, and lots more things. That might not sound like fun, but I'm telling you

> Serving others is a huge concept.

it is! Doing volunteer work, I have been able to travel and meet fantastic people, some of whom have become my closest friends. One thing I particularly enjoyed was hosting a fund-raiser for my nonprofit organization. Watching everybody dancing and having a great time while donating money to a good cause was the best. It was what I would call Fun 101.

The thing I learned early about service is that it's not just about other people, it's also about you. Have you ever been in a funky mood? Something didn't go your way, or someone hurt your feelings, or the person you're crushed out on didn't like you, and now you're in a funk or angry or crabby? Let me share a secret with you. When I am mad, sad, depressed, or just generally feeling down and out, the quickest way to shift my mood is to be of service. Offering to grocery shop for a neighbor, helping someone with their homework, or reading to an elderly person are just a few of the things that can take you out of a funky mood and back into a happy, grateful place.

Years ago I used to wait tables. Ever notice that in many restaurants they refer to waiters as servers? That was one of the hardest jobs I ever had because you don't always have customers who allow you to feel good about being of service. Many times customers would be cranky and tired, but I would always remind myself that this was another opportunity to be of service. And whenever I serve, I've always wound up getting even more out of the experience than the person or people who I help do. Because by giving, you wind up being the receiver of the other person's happiness. There is nothing better than doing some act of kindness for another person, especially when it's anonymous. Like leaving flowers on someone's doorstep, or shoveling an elderly person's driveway. And there are ways you can be of service in the world everywhere you look. Donate some of your old toys to a charity or old books to the library or old clothes to Goodwill. Any of those will help make another person's life better because you chose to be of service. There's a bumper sticker that I see all the time on cars that says "Practice Random Acts of Kindness." So often, we get caught up in our own lives and forget to help others. I know from personal experience that when I spend too much time thinking about me, myself, and I, it's a miserable place to be. But as soon as I do something for another person or organization I feel good about myself. So, yeah, it's selfish, but it's a selfishness I can live with.

Now I want to talk a little bit about faith. It says in the Bible that if you have faith that is the size of one mustard seed, then all things are possible. Many of your biggest hopes and dreams can come true if you do all the things you need to do, and you have faith that it will happen. I can't tell you how many times I've gotten close to my dreams and then, because I lost faith, everything fell apart at the last moment. There were acting jobs I was so close to getting until I would start to second-guess myself or tell myself all the reasons why I wouldn't get the part . . . and then guess what happened. I didn't get the part. In high school, I met so many students who were not smarter and didn't work harder, but when it came to tests they would always get better grades than me. At first, I would get pissed off and tell myself that I just didn't test well. Not testing well became my excuse for not getting the best grades possible. Then one day I asked my buddy Paul, who was one of the students who always got straight A's on tests, how he did it. He told me that he knew he could get an A and he expected to get an A. He had faith in himself when it came to testing. He left no room in his consciousness for the possibility of getting a B+ because in his mind he had already gotten an A+, which was the grade he always got. I remember taking a test after I talked to Paul; I studied, I came to class rested and prepared just as usual, except this time I brought an extra added ingredient with me, FAITH. I chose to have faith in my ability to get an A on the test. Well, when the results came back, I didn't worry or wonder, because in my mind I had already had gotten an A, and guess what I grade I got. An A+. After you have done everything you can to make something happen, you need to always make sure you have that extra-special ingredient, faith. Mary McLeod Bethune had a great quote about it: "Without faith nothing is possible; with faith everything is possible." My pastor believes that the number one reason people do not succeed at their dreams is because most people don't have enough *faith* to even prepare for what they want. He gave this example: The other day, a young lady

> With faith everything is possible.

came up to him after the service and told him that she wanted desperately to go on a trip the church was sponsoring to Africa, but she didn't have enough to pay for it, and she didn't know where the rest of the money was going to come from. He asked her if she had done everything to prepare to go on the trip. Did she get her shots? Cancel her newspapers for those days? Pack? Break in new hiking shoes?

Research the countries where they were going? When she informed him that she hadn't done any of those things, he looked at her curiously and asked, "How do you expect to go anywhere if you haven't even packed your bags?" Too many of us don't "pack our bags" because we don't have faith that we are actually going to fly.

Faith and service are tied together, too. When you have faith and are of service, you wind up getting more in return than you ever imagined. It's like our friendship. We started out with you wanting a big brother and me wanting to be of service, but after these months I can truly say that the gifts you've given me of wisdom, support, friendship, and trust, and the lessons I have learned from you have enriched my life far more than anything I have been able to show you. That's how it works. The giver winds up getting more than the person they are giving to.

I had a friend who I knew needed some cash but I also knew would never ask for help or accept charity. So one day, I put some money in an envelope and put it in the mail slot in his front door. When I got home, a check I hadn't been expecting had arrived in my mail for more money than I had given my friend. The universe likes a giver and will reward a person who gives honorably. By giver, I mean a person who gives for no other reason than to be of service. Are there ways in your life that you can be of service today? Have you ever watched the movie *A Christmas Carol*, about Ebenezer Scrooge, a rich man who never shared anything with others or tried to help those less fortunate? Well, when he began to open his heart and to give, he discovered a joy inside of him that he didn't know existed. Giving and being of service are really about connecting to your own joy.

The reciprocity (look it up) of God and the universe is super-quick. When we do right by others, it immediately comes back to us, and when we do wrong, the same is true. We're all in this universe together, so it's important that we do what we can to help others. That is why faith and service are key elements in fulfilling our goals and dreams. The whole purpose of achieving goals and dreams is what? To be happy. I like to say "unreasonably happy" because that's how ridiculously happy I want to be and how ridiculously happy I want you to be. I wanna be that guy who knows (has faith) that I can achieve *anything* I choose to. And so can you. The people who are the *happiest* in the world are people who serve others and have faith in their lives. Faith and service are the keys to our being happy, keys to our achieving any goal or dream we have. Yes, the road to that amazing job, house, Gucci handbag, stock portfolio, Tiffany diamond ring, cure for cancer, whatever you want—is paved by faith and service. Am I making any kinda sense? I sure hope so.

One of the biggest opportunities I've ever had to be of service required a lot of work, but mostly it required faith. A number of years ago, one of my best friends from college and I invested in a hotel here in New Orleans. Yep. Your big brother Hill owns a fantastic boutique hotel down here. It's called the International House Hotel of New Orleans, and it's a few blocks outside the French Quarter. Though I'm not from here, over the past ten years, I've developed a love for New Orleans like you wouldn't believe.

But you know what I'm most proud of about this hotel? During and after Hurricane Katrina, while other companies laid off most of their employees immediately, we were one of the few businesses in the city who continued to pay our employees their salaries and health benefits, because we had faith that our hotel would reopen. For most people, losing their ability to earn a living was the main reason why they ended up having to leave New Orleans. Now they're in a variety of other cities where they've found new jobs, and they may never return to the Crescent City. (That's one of New Orleans's nicknames.) Out of our eighty employees, we lost one to the storm. That is tragic. But we didn't lose any others, all of whom made it through only to find their neighborhoods had washed away. The entire experience has left me with a very deep-rooted desire to serve the people of New Orleans and all of those I come across who experience hardship and feel they don't have any hope. It was an opportunity to give faith back to a people who had lost it, but yet again, in doing so, I wound up feeling better about myself and more connected to God. It was a win-win situation.

A few letters ago, you jokingly wrote about how you came across someone who had asked for your help, but you said, "Shoot, I can barely help myself. How am I going to help you?" Now, I know you were kind of joking, but I was still disappointed in that response. We can all serve, help, and mentor others. It doesn't matter who you are or where you life seems to be, there is always someone who needs you to be of service to them. Even if you do something as simple as helping your mother by offering to grocery shop for her, you're putting a little more of your light into the world. There are so many ways that you and I, right now, today, can serve. And you will be paid back for that service in amazing ways, I promise.

Every time I use the word *serve* or *service*, I think of Tavis Smiley, because part of the Tavis Smiley Foundation and its Leadership Institute's creed is "You can't lead the people if you don't love the people. You can't save the people if you won't serve the people." Tavis always says, "**LEAD. LOVE. SAVE. SERVE.**" I love that because it's so simple, so powerful, and so true. So as you read this letter, I want you to start thinking about new and different ways you can be of service to others. Think about new and different ways you can give to others. Identify new and different ways you can live your life. I'm so proud of you in so many ways, and that's why I feel that I can issue this type of challenge to you. You are beautiful, brilliant, and magnificently talented. I know you can come up with creative and fun ways to serve others.

Wow. It's almost time for me to give my speech. I was so honored when the amazing and brilliant Susan L. Taylor asked me to come down and give a speech at a rally protesting the government's inaction in helping New Orleans and its citizenry recover from Katrina's devastation. I immediately said yes. But I won't lie, I've been a little nervous about it. I think that's why I pulled out your letter to read. Whenever I read your letters, I am able to be myself, and my ability to speak my truth increases. And, boy, do I need that today, because many of the things I plan to say won't be very popular with some of the influential people who will be in attendance. However, if I get up there, I have to tell the truth, and I can't sugarcoat it. I shared what I planned to say with some folks who work with me, and a few of them warned me not to be so truthful. But you know what? One of the things I love about the letter exchange you and I have is that we are completely truthful. And truth and honesty are qualities that tend to replicate; if you are truthful with one person, then you tend to be truthful with all. The same holds true in reverse. If you start to hold your tongue and not speak your truth with one, then you'll start to do that with everyone. And if you always speak your truth, then you give me and others the permission and strength to do the same. Does that make sense?

I'm so happy that New Orleans is gonna come back to its "pre-Katrina" glory. Oh, and by the way, you and your mom are going to have to find time to come and meet me down here. In fact, let's do Jazz Fest next year. It's always the last weekend in April and the first weekend in May. During those weekends, some of the greatest jazz musicians in the world descend on New Orleans. It truly is magnificent, and luckily it all happens before it gets crazy hot down here. But hot or not, I'll buy you a hibiscus iced tea and we'll listen to some music and just chill. Deal?

Much Love,
Hill

Date: May 20, 2008 10:32 PM
From: Young_Sistah@home.net
To: Hill@manifestyourdestiny.org
Subject: Voting and Politics

Hill, a lot of my friends say that voting doesn't matter. What do you think, is voting important, and do you think women should be more involved in politics?

Date: May 30, 2008 4:47 PM
From: Hill@manifestyourdestiny.org
To: Young_Sistah@home.net
Subject: Re: Voting and Politics

Many people are under the illusion that one vote—one voice—cannot make a difference. For better or worse, a single voice spoken loud enough has a tremendous opportunity to create a momentum that shapes a nation and thus alters the world. Voting is essential because it changes not only the individual who votes but the community, city, state, nation, and ultimately the world in which they vote. Voting is much more than the one ballot cast on any particular day. Voting represents participation. Something happens psychologically when people participate. The voters get filled with more pride because they intrinsically understand that their vote matters, and therefore, that they matter. Additionally, a clear message is sent to those who are in so-called power, letting them know that they must be accountable to the individuals who are casting ballots. History shows us that voting is almost like dominoes. The more we participate and vote, the more the system of governance changes for the better. So, ultimately, we are in a representative democracy that only functions properly IF WE VOTE!

Obviously, I think voting and political participation are essential. But I don't want you to just take my word for it. So I asked my friend Michelle Obama for her insight. This amazing woman is obviously someone who has a lot of experience with how voting matters!

HH

----------Begin Forwarded Message----------

Dear Young Sister,

Absolutely. My feeling is everyone needs to be involved and take their seat at the table—and as a woman, as a wife, a professional, and a mother of two daughters, I think women particularly need to be involved in speaking out and taking on the issues that matter to us most.

Now, there is no doubt that we have made great strides, and because of the struggles that so many have fought, I know that my daughters can dream and see themselves as surgeons, CEOs, Supreme Court justices, and sports stars. But we have a ways to go, and we will get there if we work together.

Politics, like a school project, takes teamwork. It takes respect, and sharing ideas, and organization, and good judgment, and heart. It takes a strong team leader, but it also takes input and implementation from the entire group.

And if you don't get involved, if you don't lift your voice, then you can be certain your voice will not be heard. Don't let anyone speak for you, and don't rely on others to fight for you.

You have to be ready to get in the game. And as I've seen in my own life—and most recently, out on the campaign trail—when you stand up, when you make your voice heard, then people listen to you, people stand with you, people want to work with you and you are that much closer to taking your seat at the table. So I urge you, young sister, to stand up, get involved, and make your voice heard.

Michelle Obama

Final Letter:
Time to Make History

Well-behaved women rarely make history.
Laurel Thatcher Ulrich

June 3, 2008
Los Angeles

Dear Young Sistah,

Talk about an inspiration. You are definitely mine. It's almost ironic, me sitting in my living room, kind of choked up, reading your last letter to me. Yeah, don't protest too much. It's okay, life changes fast and relationships, like everything else, are cyclical. I know.

You graduate this week, attend a language course abroad this summer, then go off to college in the fall. You can say you'll still take the time to write me these letters, but my intuition and experience tell me otherwise. If I'm lucky, it will be the occasional texts from that new iPhone some secret admirer sent you for graduation. You so deserve it.

This letter in my hands makes me think back to when I read the very first letter that you wrote me. After I'd finished reading it, I refolded it, softly set it down, and said, "Wow."

My mother has that Laurel Thatcher Ulrich quote, which I put at the beginning of this letter, taped, in big bold colorful letters, to the edge of her kitchen counter. Every morning when she wakes and goes to make breakfast she sees those words, "Well-behaved women rarely make history." As you know, my mom already *has* made history, yet she still reads that quote every morning because she desires to make more.

> There is nothing that you cannot do.

As this new journey for you begins, I want *you* to make history. And I know that you will. For almost two years we've been exchanging letters and you have changed, grown, and matured so much. There is nothing in this world that you cannot do, and I am so excited to bear witness to the woman you are becoming and will continue to evolve into. But more so, I am so excited that *you* finally believe in *you*. That you have a deep current within you of knowing how powerful and magnificent you are. Just as you are right now today. If you did nothing else for the rest of your life, you would already be brilliant, magnificent, and beautiful. I know you understand that now.

You know what else? Your letters to me have made me feel that way about *myself*. You and I have served as each other's "doors" that we could walk through to go to another level in our lives. You have helped me become a better man. Am I perfect? Far from it. Will I continue to make mistakes? Sure. But from knowing you and exchanging stories, ideas, and encouragement, you have made me feel that I can make history, too. And I know you already know that *you will* make history!

I'd say the two of us have come full circle except that would imply we are back where we started, and we're not. Neither of us is the same person we were when we first began this exchange. We've both gone through our share of experiences and, as a result, grown a whole heck of a lot. Our friendship has also grown. Yet, even through all that growth, there is something that has remained the same: the essence of who we both are as people.

When I read what you wrote about loving the "new" you a whole lot better than the "old" you, I couldn't stop myself from smiling. There is no feeling quite as liberating and empowering as loving and accepting yourself. So many people in this world never learn to love themselves. Instead they spend their entire lives looking outside of themselves for the type of love and acceptance that can only come from within. It filled me with such happiness to know you love yourself.

At the same time, I wondered if you were aware that the differences between the "old" you and the "new" you are not as drastic as they seem. For sure, you have definitely tackled some huge obstacles in your life these past months. And each one brought with it new realizations and new resolutions. All that newness came about not because of a change in your character or the core of who you are, but because of a change in your perspective, the way you see yourself and the way you see the world.

You say that you're not afraid anymore, that you're ready now to defy all the odds, to define and claim the life that you want and deserve. I say you always have been; you just didn't see yourself in that light—until now. But I did. I saw, in that very first letter, a Young Sistah who was fearless. How else could you have picked up a pen and written to me with such honesty, certainty, and sincerity? Dropping that letter to me in the mail meant that you were already in the habit of defying odds, of naming your intentions and daring to make them come true. That's who you are, who you've always been.

I'm telling you this because I want you to keep it in mind as you journey and grow through your life and as your perspectives continue to change. When we think of something as "old," we tend to dismiss or disregard it. We feel as though we have nothing to gain from it when, in fact, we have everything to gain from it. Who you were back then is what led you to being who you are now. Just as you are your best self right now, the person you refer to as the "old" you was also her best self in that time. One state of being informs and prepares us for the next one. We are constantly evolving, growing into better and better representations and interpretations of ourselves. That's why as we celebrate who we've become, it's important to also embrace and honor who we once were.

Trust me, Young Sistah, when I tell you that the challenges will continue. Strange as it may sound, that's actually a blessing. A life without challenges is a life that's standing still. And when we stand still, we become stuck.

Have you ever heard the phrase "fabric of your life"? What that means is the substance of your life. It's all the things that make your life matter. Things like your relationships, your goals, achievements, and dreams. Those things are the fabric of your life. And much like fabric, all those things are joined by a common thread—you. Your character and your values, those are what weave all the disparate elements of your life together. Everything you touch and do, everyone you befriend and love, becomes a part of this fabric.

I like to think of this fabric as being a kind of patchwork quilt. My grandmother from South Carolina used to sew and quilt. Unfortunately, I don't know how to do either. The only needles I pick up are the ones used by the characters I play. Despite my inability to sew a button or mend a pair of socks, I did still manage to learn a lot about both arts. It was incredible to watch my grandmother as she was sewing. I got some of my most valuable life lessons that way.

This is the grandmother I told you about in an earlier letter, the one who said to me as she was pinning a pattern onto a piece of fabric, "You have to always cut your coat according to the size of your cloth." On a real practical level, it seems like common sense, doesn't it? I mean, why would you try to cut a coat that is larger than the amount of cloth you have? It wasn't until a few years later that I understood it to mean something else as well, something much less obvious: Create a life that suits your needs.

When my grandmother used to quilt, she'd lay out yards and yards of fabric. Then she'd cut blocks from them. After she was done cutting out all the blocks she needed, she'd put the fabric away. What was left was a stack of what looked to me like scraps. But she'd take each of those little squares of cloth she had cut, and she would iron them, and then she would start sewing them together. Sometimes she'd even use pieces of our old clothes, jeans and shirts that my brother and I had outgrown. She'd cut them up into squares and start sewing them onto the blocks with pieces she'd cut out from the brand-new bolts of cloth she'd bought at the store.

It would take my grandmother weeks and weeks, sometimes months, to finish a quilt, and I would never stay with her long enough to be able to witness the whole process. What I would see was the beginning, the scraps and the blocks being gathered and ironed, the first few patches being sewn together, and then I'd be gone. When I returned for my next visit, what had seemed like nothing but small, useless pieces of cloth being stitched together side by side would now be this amazing, beautiful piece of art. I would always look at that big, colorful quilt that covered my bed and recognize each piece. I'd see the square that came from the shirt that used to be my brother's favorite, and the one from those corduroy pants I got for Christmas two years before. The stitching together of those disparate pieces was the journey and using them to create something completely new, beautiful, and useful was the journey. And if any of those individual pieces hadn't been created, used, and worn for their original purpose, they would not look like they do now in this new quilt. My running and playing in those corduroy pants is what made the material soft enough to be in a quilt, but I didn't wear them anticipating that one day she might use them for a quilt—I wore them because they were great pants. And one day I outgrew them. But that didn't mean they had lost their value. No, it was actually quite the opposite. Does that make any sense?

And that wasn't all. I'd see pieces of tablecloths that had been retired years before. I'd see my grandmother's old outfits, the ones she'd wear around the house and a few I'd seen her put on for special occasions. I'd look at those quilts and what I would see were my memories, all of these different parts of my past, woven together into one fantastic piece of fabric.

What I'm telling you is that life in general is like that. It's one gigantic quilt that we start stitching at birth. And it's the pieces that create the final product, the actual fabric. Our relationships, our goals, our achievements and dreams, all of those things are the fabric of life. The "successes" as well as the so-called failures are all a part of the fabric, a part of the journey. And the journey is the destination.

> Life is like one gigantic quilt.

It's hard, as those pieces are coming together and falling into their proper place, to imagine how it will look in the end, what the grand design will ultimately be. I'm not even sure we're supposed to know. That's why I believe, in our journey, we have to go for rich. And when I say "rich" I don't mean money. I mean something much more valuable. To me, "going for rich" means attempting to add relationships and experiences that lead us deeper and deeper into a life filled with love, meaning, and purpose. The "richness" of a fabric can be determined by simply touching and feeling it. And that's how I want you to approach your life—I want you to "feel" all aspects of your life. I don't want you to fear life, I want you to feel life.

Faith Ringgold is an African American artist who incorporates her paintings into her quilts. Her work can be seen in museums all over the world. She is quoted as saying, "The great enemy of creativity is fear. When we're fearful, we freeze up. Creativity has a lot to do with a willingness to take risks." In other words, we have to go for rich and feel life.

We have to be fearless about filling our lives with all the colors and textures that our emotions provide, just as you have been in this time I've known you. Do you remember all the times that you felt powerless? All the times when you thought you couldn't do or have the one thing you most wanted? You were always present in whatever emotion you felt; I admire that. Yet you never allowed yourself to be completely swallowed up by the emotions you were feeling. Your character always came shining through. You followed your instincts and braved the unknown by walking through whatever fear, doubt, worry, anxiety, or sadness you felt. That, Young Sistah, is going for rich, allowing yourself a wealth of emotions and a wealth of experiences. They are what will ultimately make the fabric of your life a wonder to behold, a masterpiece that will take your breath away and leave you clinging to one oh-so-simple word: *Wow!*

You have already created a "Wow!" in at least one person's life—mine! I love you so much, and I am so proud of you. Can you "feel" that when I say it to you? I hope you do, because as we stop exchanging letters, I want you to feel your way through the rest of your life. If something feels wrong to you, for any reason, walk away from the situation. Don't question "why" it may feel wrong if it does. Walk away. And just the opposite is true as well. If something feels right to you, then don't allow your own or other people's fears to stop you from pursuing that. Only by acting courageously will you ultimately "make history." And that is why my mom has that quote in a place where she reads it every day. Because all of us have to be reminded constantly that to truly change the world, we have to act with courage and sometimes against all odds and advice. Sometimes we have to "behave badly" because other people will try to tell us what is "appropriate" to do or say. And those people just may be wrong. I want you to go your own way and feel your way through life. If Rosa Parks had listened to people say what was right or wrong behavior, we might still be riding in the back of the bus. And, truth be told, if we look around now and see the way many of us act, you'd think we were still "ridin' in the back of the bus" in a way. I want you to make history and elevate us! You can do it! You can have a bigger impact than Oprah and Dr. King combined! In any area of life you choose! But to do that, you truly have to have the courage to "walk deep" into your life, confront all of your fears and limiting thoughts, and make history. I know you can and I know you will. And one thing about me, when I have an intuition about something, it is always right. And I have that intuition about you!

I love you so much, and I can't wait to bear witness to the incredible woman you are already becoming. My life on this planet is better for having been in contact with you, and for that I thank God for allowing our paths to cross.

There are *no* coincidences: I was meant to *enrich* your life, and you mine. May you reach for the light and shine throughout your entire life. Your light and spirit are so incredibly bright that you can illuminate so much for so many! May you never stop shining. Shine. Shine!

I will miss reading your letters, but I will never be able to miss the light you emanate. I can feel your energy, so please keep radiating and growing. You truly are destined for greatness. And hopefully through our letter exchange you have been able to deFINE that destiny. You certainly have helped me define mine.

It's a shame that in the English language we have only one word for love, because that small word does not do justice to the magnitude of the way I feel for you. Well, maybe if I repeat it enough—I love you. I love you. I love you. Brightly shine, shine, shine—my love, shine!

Now it's time, Young Sister—*Go Make History!*

Fly. Now. Fly. Fly.

"Wow!"

Your Big Brother and Forever Friend,
Hill Harper

Date: June 3, 2008 4:54 PM
From: BigSister@manifestyourdestiny.org
To: Young_Sistah@home.net
Subject: The Secret of How to Be Happy (Growing to Be Me)

I was talking with a friend the other day and I said to her, "You know, we're so lucky." Why? she asked. "Because we're younger sisters."

We both had beautiful older sisters and we saw the traps. It's true. My sister was gorgeous. Dimples. No pimples. Talented. She was, in fact, a prodigy. She was doing Gershwin's *An American in Paris* when she was eight. Special lessons for her all the time. She could knit. Grandmother taught her how. Made beautiful sweaters. In fact, my eighth-grade photo is of me in a sweater Gary made. I should not have had it on. When she saw the photo we had a huge fight. Gary packed all her clothes and moved them up to Brenda's house just to show me. I was undaunted. We did fight but we also got over it. Gary also could tap-dance. I had a better singing voice but she could dance. Harris Rosedale gave her free lessons just so she would be in the jabberwocky things he did. It didn't matter because the Isely Brothers won all the time anyway.

They tell a story about me. Both my aunts and my mom. When people would say, "*Nikki, can you tell time?*" I would say, <u>No, but Gary can</u>. "*Nikki, can you tie your shoes?*" <u>No, but Gary can</u>. My Aunt Agnes says we were at the *Ruth Lyons Show*, a very popular radio show in Cincinnati, and Gary was singing and playing the piano. In addition to classics she could boogie woogie. Also on the show that day were Rosemary and her sister, Betty Clooney. People were throwing money on the stage to Gary. She won a great big bear. In those days folks threw coins if they liked what you were doing. I was backstage watching. I said, "<u>I don't want no money</u>." Agnes tells this story as I don't remember. I was just a little girl not even in school by then. I do know what I learned at about ten, though: I don't envy anybody anything.

I watched my sister and the toll it takes when you are beautiful. Everyone wants something from you. When you are talented everyone wants to use what you have. I remember our father waking her up some weekend nights when our parents had company over. He wanted to show Gary off. She had to play "Clair de Lune."

I didn't have any talent. Wasn't beautiful. And got left alone. I could not have said it then and didn't understand it until recently but the best thing that happened to me is my nothingness.

I could grow to be me.

I look all right. I am smart. And I have a talent in words. But what freed me to be me was the understanding of how to tuck a part of me away from me. And not let anyone define who I am.

Are you lonely sometimes? This is good. Gives you time to think. Do you feel misunderstood? Wonderful. Gives you a reason to pursue definitions. Do you feel unloved? Great. Gives you a reason to sympathize with other endangered species. Makes you know you have to reach out, reach up, reach a little further. Reach again and grab hold of yourself.

We who are forgotten are the winners in the game of life. Because we have learned the secret of how to be happy.

Nikki Giovanni

Acknowledgments

God is the creator of all things, and when it comes to expressing the gratitude in my heart, for me, that's where it forever begins.

Heartfelt thanks to all of my contributors. You are my friends and colleagues, brilliant women (and a few men) who all inspire me on a daily basis with your intelligence, spirit, creativity, and willingness to give to others. Through your thoughtful and amazing e-mails in the book, you gave generously of your time and wisdom. Thank you so much.

A special thanks to Meri Nana-Ama Danquah for all of the work that she provided for this book. Her knowledge, insight, and work can be seen throughout its pages. I cannot thank you enough.

A special thanks to Stephanie Covington for her "keep it real" cheerleading. Often it gave me the gentle nudge to tackle topics that at times made me a little uncomfortable. Also for her contributions to content and her wonderful editing and work on the foreword. You are amazing.

Thank you to my "surrogate sisters" who have offered their time, feedback, opinions, expertise, advice, encouragement, and motivation. Most of what I know as it relates to women is because of my surrogate sisters: Women whom I have the utmost respect for and who continue to uplift my life in so many ways.

The creation of this book has been divinely guided, and I would like to thank those individuals who helped shape my vision into these pages. My publisher and editors at Gotham Books: William Shinker, Lauren Marino, and Brianne Ramagosa. My exceptionally supportive book team: Meri Danquah; Stephanie Covington; Margaret Dunlap; Serene Bynum; Darrell Smith; Keith Major; Voltaire Sterling; David Vigliano; Jesse Shane; my aunt Lois Eichacker; Aunt Ercelle Pinckney; and my mother, Marilyn Hill Harper. Whether it is for poring through text, hunting for just the right picture, or offering continued encouragement to stay the course, I am indebted.

Thanks to Marvet Britto and everyone at The Britto Agency. Without championing the "Letters" book project from the beginning, the book you see today and the opportunity to touch the community in a larger capacity would not have been possible.

And thanks to my friends, family, and ancestors who, as living examples and through their words, have always encouraged me to take risks, to live a life of unreasonable happiness, and to create works that seek to uplift the human spirit.

And finally, thank you to all of the teachers and educators I have had throughout my life who have fostered in me a love of learning, including those spiritual teachers who have shown me the importance and necessity of taking God along with me on this wonderful journey, life. Thank you.

Peace and Abundant Blessings to All.